D1592688

MEASUREMENT AND
ADJUSTMENT SERIES
EDITED BY LEWIS M. TERMAN

EARLY CONCEPTIONS AND TESTS OF INTELLIGENCE

BY JOSEPH PETERSON, PH.D.

Professor of Psychology
George Peabody College
for Teachers

GREENWOOD PRESS, PUBLISHERS
WESTPORT, CONNECTICUT

Originally published in 1926
by the World Book Company

First Greenwood Reprinting 1969

SBN 8371-2836-6

PRINTED IN UNITED STATES OF AMERICA

PREFACE

THERE is at present a great popular as well as scientific interest in the subject of intelligence testing, and a considerable amount of money is being spent each year in the public schools and colleges to determine in advance of their training, by means of tests, the abilities of students who enter these institutions. The information thus obtained is regarded as useful not only in the educational guidance and training of the children and youths toward their individual careers, but also in their classification into different sections where they can be taught with groups of children of approximately their own degrees of intelligence.

The old question of repeating grades has received light from a new angle, and there are at present many well-informed individuals who contend that it is useless to ask a dull child to repeat a grade and a kind of work which have already been found to be above his limited comprehension. They hold that each child should be tested very early in his school career and should be given work of a character that will interest him and will come within the range of his abilities, so that he may make constant advance from year to year and be spared the humiliation and discouragement involved in the repetition of grades, and at the same time they are willing to give him the benefit of every bit of evidence that he can show in his work at any time for ability to do the normal child's work. They point out that there is no evidence of any very marked benefits derived from the repetition of a grade because of original failure.

Aside from the numerous uses now made of tests in the schools, important steps are being taken, by their use, toward better adjustment in the various fields of social and industrial activities, and the more progressive courts and penal institutions are adopting tests of intelligence to throw

iii

light on many problems relating to responsibility for crime. The testing by psychologists of one and three-quarters million soldiers in the recent war brought forcibly to the attention of the American public the fact that psychology may be of service in the solution of problems in the practical world. There has even been danger of late that — except for the case of psychoanalysis! — intelligence testing would be regarded by the popular mind as the whole substance of psychology.

Even on the science of psychology itself the effects of the testing movement, particularly that more successful one headed by Alfred Binet and occupying most of his attention from early in the nineties, have been considerable. There has been a noticeable shift of emphasis away from the more simple reaction and sensory discrimination activities, and the attention of psychologists has for some years now been a good deal occupied with such problems as the interrelations of different measurable traits, and the nature of "general intelligence" and methods of its quantitative measurement. Many of the old-line experiments in psychology are growing obsolete and we are becoming more and more interested in what one can do under different conditions and in different fields of activity, rather than, as formerly, in what one finds on introspecting one's "consciousness" under given experimental conditions. Indeed, the old distinction between a "psychological experiment" and a "test" has been challenged, and it has been urged that tests are not only devices used for practical purposes in rating individuals and their several capacities, but also useful instruments of scientific research. (See reference *208*.)

Questions as to the nature of intelligence, including its relations to the traditional intellectual functions and to emotions and instincts, are of great importance, and they need to be investigated thoroughly. It is obvious that individual differences in various mental traits, as distinct from intelligence in general, are so great as to leave serious doubts regarding the wisdom of adopting any single measure of one's mental capacity except for the most practical and immediate purposes; and yet it is far from clear which traits are most predictive of one's general success in the ordinary activities of life. Is there a general intelligence factor which may be measured with different degrees of completeness in the several kinds of performances, or is intelligence but a balancing of many overlapping individual processes and traits? How far can we profitably and safely go in the selection of persons for different careers according to their several traits, in view of the great plasticity of any normal human being? These are problems that still await solution, even though considerable progress has now been made, particularly as to scientific methods of studying them; and they relate to scientific research in psychology just as directly as they do to the more immediately practical problems in education.

Intelligence is vastly more complex than is usually supposed, and the problems as to its nature and the practical methods of its quantitative determination in different individuals touch vitally most of the older economic, religious, educational, penal, and even philosophical problems which have occupied great minds since the dawn of history. Many of the older problems as they were once stated are being solved by neglect; they are taking on new aspects compatible with scientific treatment. It has therefore seemed to me a matter of such importance, to the advancement both of the science of psychology and of the work of practical education, to have a rather direct, simple statement of the development of conceptions and tests of intelligence, that I have determined to undertake a presentation of this bit of interesting and useful history. The following chapters are the concrete results of this undertaking.

Some of the most difficult problems throughout this work have been what to omit. It was felt that of the omitted data some indications should be left by way of direct and indirect references, so that the interested reader could find his way intelligently beyond the limits here set for ourselves. On the other hand, it would be a mistake to burden a work of this kind — which aims fundamentally to interest the reader intelligently in a most important and inviting field and to stimulate him to build up a scientific attitude toward human conduct — with the numerous details of the studies reviewed.

For three reasons the present historical sketch of the conceptions and tests of intelligence has been limited to the period ending with the death of Binet. First, the development of tests since that time is reasonably well known by educators and by other members of the intelligent public, and is well covered by a number of books now enjoying a wide circulation. Second, an attempt to cover recent developments in a full and critical manner would require an amount of time not available at present, and it would involve the treatment of matters that are too technical for the present purpose. Recent developments are treated in various separate volumes by different authors, and many of them are yet so new and in so unsettled a state as to make a general evaluation dangerous and inadvisable. In the third place the early testing activities center so much around the life of the great French psychologist, who gave practically his entire life to researches along this line, that it seemed peculiarly fitting to stop with the end of his own contributions.

Abstract statements about various views and tests are of little interest or value to any but those already acquainted with the developments of the testing work; so I have chosen to present the contributions of each investigator from his own point of view and, as far as practicable, in his own words. The various tests have in most cases been briefly described, even at the risk of a little monotony to some readers, because they give point to the discussions and furnish suggestions for present-day experimenters who perchance do not know the tests that have formerly been used. Many of the tests that have been suggested or used doubtless have value for experimental work in college courses and for researches, which was not brought out by their authors — and, indeed, was not known to them. By different weightings and combinations several tests and measuring devices now discarded may prove to have considerable value. At any rate, to read an authority's own words and to go over with him his list of tests will give one a feeling of intimate acquaintance and a personal interest that indirect and general statements cannot yield. Readers who have the time should go to the several sources cited, and work out for themselves various details, both in point of view and in method of procedure in the tests.

It is hoped that this book will serve usefully as a textbook in college courses in the history of the testing movement, and also as a guide in certain parts of courses in present-day mental tests, in the history of psychology, and in advanced psychology. To this end exercises and suggestions for further work have been inserted at the conclusion of the several chapters. But the general reader should also find the book helpful in gaining a perspective in a subject of wide general interest and importance.

It may seem to some readers that I have given relatively too much attention to Binet's experiments and tests, and that others have been omitted which should have been included. To such criticisms I can say only that Binet's tests were in practically all cases concerned with the problem of measuring the general mental ability, or intelligence, of the subject, whereas this interest in intelligence was not present in many of the tests and experiments carried out on special functions by other investigators. In general, experiments out of which mental tests have grown have been included in our account, as well as those which have been especially devised to measure intelligence. No claim is made either to completeness or to entire freedom from errors, and constructive criticisms from readers will be gratefully received. Great pains have, however, been taken to avoid errors and to represent fairly, both in quotations and in summary statements, the views of the various authorities considered.

I wish to express here my thanks to Miss Euri Belle Bolton and Mr. Lyle H. Lanier, graduate students in psychology in George Peabody College for Teachers, for reading the entire manuscript and for making valuable suggestions. My son, Joseph Kimbark Peterson, has helped me both in the gathering of data and in the making and verifying of translations in the quotations from foreign languages. I am indebted to Professor Lewis M. Terman, editor of the Measurement and Adjustment Series, for many helpful criticisms and suggestions. My greatest indebtedness, though it is in this case indirect, is to President James R. Angell, under whose masterful direction I was once privileged to work as a student in psychology. He may find these fruits of his labors somewhat distorted in the chapters that follow!

JOSEPH PETERSON

NASHVILLE, TENNESSEE

CONTENTS

EDITOR'S INTRODUCTION

THE number of intelligence tests has increased so rapidly in recent years and the attention of workers has been so engrossed with the compelling problems arising from their practical application, that students of the subject are likely to lose sight of the psychological assumptions upon which the mental test is based and of the historical developments which gave rise to it. Thus far no really satisfactory textbook on the history, principles, technique, and results of mental measurement has been published, and the few texts that are available are in nothing more unsatisfactory than in their neglect of historical orientation. This would not be so serious if it were possible to make good the omission by required reading among convenient and suitable references. At present this is not possible, because a majority of the references which would be most useful for this purpose are in technical French and German periodicals. The result is that we are encouraging the use of psychological methods by teachers and others whose knowledge of the tools they employ is entirely inadequate.

A few years ago many believed that the only solution of the problem was to restrict the use of intelligence tests to thoroughly trained psychologists. Ten years ago the editor of the Measurement and Adjustment Series was almost alone in opposing this view. Time has emphatically vindicated his position. Experience has shown that teachers can be taught to use profitably not only the simpler forms of group tests, but even the Binet-Simon procedure. Instruction in the use of intelligence tests is now coming to be recognized as an essential part of the training of students in normal schools and teachers' colleges throughout the country. It only remains to make such instruction more thoroughgoing and substantial. Courses in mental measurement should be lengthened and more time should be devoted to underlying principles and to historical orientation.

There is no better way to introduce the student to the issues involved in the use of intelligence tests than to acquaint him with the experiments and the conceptions which led to their development. It is to serve this purpose that Professor Peterson's book has been written. The author's thorough familiarity with the pertinent historical facts, his clarity of exposition, and his freedom from bias in the treatment of unsettled questions have given us a book which is certain to prove extremely useful as a text in normal schools, colleges, and universities. It will also meet an important need among teachers in service whose formal training has not included courses in mental measurement and who want more than a superficial knowledge about the methods of testing and rating which they are expected to employ.

LEWIS M. TERMAN

EARLY CONCEPTIONS AND TESTS OF INTELLIGENCE

CHAPTER ONE

ANCIENT AND POPULAR CONCEPTIONS OF INTELLIGENCE

THE BASIS OF CONCEPTIONS OF MYSTERIOUS FORCES

FROM the very earliest times man has recognized a conflict between his own desires and purposes, on the one hand, and the forces or conditions outside himself on the other. Things do not just happen in a sort of passive way as if all events were but incidents in a flowing stream of experiences determined once for all. In general we may say that regular processes gave little trouble. Events that are regular and predictable from known circumstances are expected and can be allowed for; so they draw less attention than do happenings that seem to come somehow on their own account, arbitrarily. It is of course true that primitive thinkers attempted to account — and often accounted in extremely crude fashion — for the presence of certain regularly occurring natural objects like heavenly bodies; but the things to challenge the attention of every person were the more or less non-predictable, irregular, and infrequent happenings, such as storms, lightning, thunder, eclipses, diseases, deaths of fellows, invasions by enemies, whether man or fierce beasts, etc. These phenomena often interfered seriously with personal ends and desires, resulting in conflicts, deprivations, and struggles which were explicable only on the assumption that both within man and beast and in nature outside are arbitrary forces of some sort.

The existence of these forces, however, was not rationally inferred, any more than we rationally infer consciousness — pains, pleasures, desires, etc. — in our fellows, from their behavior; the forces were directly ascribed to phenomena

1

of the kinds mentioned, immediately on the perception of those phenomena, just as we immediately locate sounds to the right or to the left of us without any rational study, and without awareness of the intensity and phase differences of the stimuli in the two ears. As we just hear things located here and there, so primitive men simply perceived directly in various irregular and threatening phenomena about them certain arbitrary forces with consciousness, knowledge, desires, and purposes, interpreting these processes from their own directly experienced desires, hopes, disappointments, memories, etc. There were thus supposedly arbitrary forces both within and without, but naturally the attention would first be directed to outward things that tended either to frustrate their own purposes or to give aid against threatening conditions, and so the "inner life" would be neglected, or be undifferentiated from outer events.

Primitive men were not very adept at analyzing the processes of nature and at tracing each to its conditions. Frequently the calamities and great benefactions and successes would be ascribed to something that caught their attention in association with critical experiences, even though there was no necessary connection between the two events. Thus success in an encounter with enemies or in hunting would be attributed to the more striking external objects, or to acts which happened to be performed in connection with such objects, whether or not there was any real relation between the two (*102*). Any observant person will readily note that even today many individuals make similar errors in their attempts to trace the real cause of calamities and failures, or of successes and good fortune. As a result of these misinterpretations primitive men developed various means of supposed control over events; they attempted to bring about conditions which they thought were necessarily linked up somehow with the desired results. We can here only mention the ceremonies, taboos, etc., that resulted, but, for a consideration of them, must refer the reader to special treatments in other works (*162, 239*).

The conception of various mysterious and arbitrary forces in nature thus naturally arose from an inadequate analysis of causal connections; and it is not surprising that this should be true, for the causal relations of certain events are so deeply hidden and so remote that generations of work have been required to sift them out. Thus primitive man might see a storm uproot trees and bring pain and destruction to certain individuals while others were spared. He did not have an adequate conception of air, of expansion by heat, of greater weight per volume of cold than of warm air, of displacement of the latter by the former, etc., as we have today, thanks to our social inheritances enriched by the researches of thousands of individuals who have had more or less leisure for such studies. How natural, then, for primitive man to ascribe such apparently disconnected events to some arbitrary principle, such as the wrathful will of a mighty enemy. If nature always acted by *immediate and obvious contact* of one event with another, such as we see when the club in a boy's hand hits the ball and sends it flying through the air, the idea of such arbitrary forces would probably never have developed. But whenever causal relations acted indirectly or apparently irregularly, there some special power or some supernatural agency must be at work; no other account could be given.

LIFE PHENOMENA HARD TO TRACE CAUSALLY

It is chiefly in the life phenomena that these latter conditions obtained. Animals take food and expend the energy in acts which are not directly and completely aroused by external conditions. Inner metabolic processes are at work producing hunger impulses, sex impulses, and other kinds of "drives," as we now call such tendencies; and certain threatening situations, as Cannon has so well shown (*85*), stimulate internal secretions and bodily disturbances that greatly affect behavior. Thus in fear or anger the individual may seem to be beside himself, and in these states both animals and men often depart radically from their usual modes of behavior. All these hidden inner processes were to primitive men, as they still are to most persons, missing links in the chain of events, and so their results were variously interpreted. Diseases and death, which rather abruptly tore up personal relationships without any obvious and causal connections, were fearful violations of the regularity of nature and of the natural sequence of events; consequently they were objects of superstitious fear and dread, to be controlled, if at all, only by incantations, charms, ceremonies, and other acts that may by chance have been performed simultaneously with recoveries from disease and rescues from destruction. We need go back but a few decades — to periods prior to the discovery of disease germs by Pasteur — to witness civilized man using similar methods in the supposed control of diseases. Indeed, these primitive means are even today employed by the majority of mankind when sorely besieged; they are yet almost the rule among persons to whom the connections traced by science are yet unknown or unappreciated. Every newspaper carries "evidences" of the successful combating of diseases by appeals to mysterious forces, by the use of "quack medicines," and so on.

HUMAN BEHAVIOR ESPECIALLY COMPLEX AS TO CAUSAL RELATIONS

In human behavior the causal connections in the chain of events are probably of all kinds the most difficult to follow and to understand. In the first place, the germ cell from which the individual develops is an organization of substances which is determined in its nature by conditions very remote in the ancestral history (*142*); and it is yet not well understood, even by geneticists, how the organization was effected and how it is modified by environment. Within the germ cell itself, and within the growing individual resulting from it, are numerous interacting part-processes whose activities are only indirectly influenced by environmental conditions. There is thus even in the cell a strong tendency to self-determination; for example, sex, the general structure and characteristics of the race, complexion, degree of curliness of hair, degree of tendency to corpulence, to baldness, to emotional excitement; to occupation with remote conditions and abstract relationships (intelligence), and numerous other tendencies and characteristics are probably determined in the main by internal organization in the cell itself and are strongly resistant to present and immediate environmental conditions, even though general nutrition is obviously dependent upon environmental conditions. In other words, because of this inner organization and this consequent interaction, always in operation, of part-processes upon one another, the germ cell shows a strong tendency within itself to take, even against opposition, certain directions of growth and also of behavior — directions which in many respects are not understood by the unscientific and the untrained person, and which are therefore attributed to arbitrary forces of some kind within the resulting individual himself. Instinct, predisposition, interest, and intelligence are names used by all of us to designate such tendencies; voluntary attention, will, and reason designate certain expressions of these tendencies, as modified by past environmental conditions in the individual life of the person.

To the uncritical observer these various tendencies in the individual wrongly take on in higher forms of behavior the appearance of arbitrary forces, independent of antecedent conditions.   It is only on a very careful study by psychologists of the effects in behavior of heredity, of the training of the individual, and of the relations of ideas, that behavior of this kind is found to follow laws of causation in an orderly manner, and to be predictable and controllable to an increasing extent, roughly speaking, with increasing knowledge of antecedent conditions.   It is only on the possibility of such predictability and control that the science of psychology rests; and since the controlling factors of the conduct of a person are thus very largely remote, complex, and concealed, it is but natural that the science of psychology should have been relatively late in its development.   Indications are that the immediate future will bring great developments in this field, for even scientists are but now breaking away from assumptions of arbitrary faculties in the explanations and analyses of human behavior.

CONSCIOUS PHENOMENA AND VOLUNTARY ACTION PUZZLING

Another confusing thing about our own behavior is that it is conscious, and even self-conscious.   As a consequence of this the conflicts of the remote backing that we have indicated are immediately felt and interpreted, rather naturally, as arbitrary faculties overruling present obstructions and stimuli.   We feel that we *will* this or that act or thought independently of present or even past conditions.   We thus recognize even within ourselves seemingly arbitrary forces struggling with external powers in nature and with the wills and artifices of living enemies, both animal and human. How natural, then, that man should get into the habit of assuming the existence of self-directing forces, unconditioned by antecedent processes.   Does he not see all around him such forces?   Men are making nature over to their own purposes; they are cutting down trees and making out of them houses, furniture, books, etc.; they are developing agriculture, changing the form of plants and even of animals under domestication for their own ends and needs; forming unions and making laws to compel others to conform to their own purposes and principles. Is this not sufficient evidence that intelligence is a force or a power that overrules circumstances for its own ends? So must reason every one who does not take a large view of conduct and note the interaction within the organism of part-processes of very remote origin.

Careful scientists are attempting as far as possible to avoid the use of terms like "forces," "powers," "faculties," etc., in the sense of arbitrary, non-predictable or non-conditioned factors in the universe, because they find strong evidence to support the growing conviction that every such manifestation is somehow conditioned by antecedent events, if only we could ferret out their connections and accurately trace their lines of operation. It is, however, often awkward to express ourselves clearly regarding human conduct if we adhere strictly to this position. We are forced to make roundabout and even seemingly evasive statements to our inquiring fellows not so well trained; and frequently we must appear at a disadvantage to those who disregard scientific causality and who simply say that a man *wills* to do thus and so; that if he has robbed a bank he has put his will against the good of his fellows and is wholly responsible for his deliberately planned acts. Indeed he is responsible. No one would properly refuse to "hold him responsible," but the wise man would mean by this, doing something to him that would effect a change in his conduct for the better, or that would at least safeguard others from his ill-doing and his bad example; not that he should be punished retributively, merely to fulfill upon him one's grudge.

There is thus superficially much justification for the popular conceptions of mind and intelligence still current. At least from a short-sighted, ultra-practical standpoint the popular usage is the more direct and simple. "What, do you deny the freedom of the will?" is the expression one often hears from the ordinary person who first squarely confronts the scientific, more remotely orientated view; and such a person then proceeds to point out the evidences of freedom and of forces within us, already briefly indicated.

THE POPULAR VIEW OF ARBITRARY MENTAL FORCES IS INADEQUATE

Yet this popular view which seems so practical and simple, which has so thoroughly worked itself into our conceptions of morality and into our religious views as to become the orthodox view, securing the approval of many social betterment agencies, is at bottom both inhuman and unjust. Strange to say, it is only in the abstract that it is held even by the popular mind. With respect to their own relatives and intimate friends people do not accept it, and they always explain in a more thoroughly scientific manner the shortcomings and serious breaches in conduct of at least these individuals so well understood by them. They know that this or that friend or relative did not have an evil will or purpose, or at least that if he did for the time have one *it was the result* of such and such conditions, which they point out.

Since, then, the structure of nature, so to speak, is not homogeneous, since organizations exist within organizations so as greatly to conceal the sequence of events in certain compartments of our world of experience, we find men differing greatly in their interpretations and explanations of many everyday events, this being particularly true of the phenomena of human behavior;[1] and views of intelligence and will,

---

[1] The deceptive behavior of the well-known horses of Elberfeld, which made them appear to learn mathematical and other complex processes more readily than man learns them, was taken by Maeterlinck as genuine, and was ascribed in his *Unknown Guest (160)* to the "Unconscious." Scientists found after prolonged investigation that the horses had only been influenced by head movements of the trainer.

representing practically all stages of historical development, are found in the popular notions of today. There are at least two reasons for this: one is that views held by ancient thinkers become foundations of beliefs and of popular interpretations of life and have consequently become so thoroughly a part of institutions, customs, and literature as to be practically ineradicable by time; another reason is that the ordinary, untrained individual is still uncritical and credulous, largely as were our early ancestors. He has not had the training and the leisure — and in most cases also lacks the ability — for critical analysis of his experiences. So there is usually a popular as well as a scientific way of accounting for phenomena the explanation of which is not evident, phenomena which are not obviously the outcome of antecedent conditions.[1]

A SAMPLING OF THE VIEWS OF INTELLIGENCE HELD BY COLLEGE STUDENTS

The college student represents a view that is considerably in advance of the popular view; he is better trained than the average person and better endowed, having survived the elimination process in the grades and in the high school. Nevertheless, even the college student usually entertains views of mind and intelligence that are contrary to scientific principles of sequence or causality. Recently the following questions were presented to students who were beginning their work in certain courses in psychology: 1. What is intelligence? 2. Is it a force (or power) or a mechanism? 3. Is it material or immaterial (an immaterial entity)? 4. Is it a general ability or a limited function, applying par-

[1] The reader will find it profitable to contrast the popular with the scientific view of the healing of diseases as applied, not in general, but to particular cases; of the appearance of great geniuses and deliverers among certain peoples in critical periods of their history; of the interpretation of dreams and of certain abnormal experiences of neurotics; etc.

ticularly to special mental operations? 5. Is it simple and homogeneous or complex and heterogeneous? 6. What is its field of operation?

Of seventy-five students beginning work in psychology, who answered the questions, 84 per cent regarded intelligence as a force or a power, while only 40 per cent regarded it as a mechanism (some students voted for both) and 44 per cent replied that it is immaterial or an immaterial entity. Intelligence was thought to be a limited faculty or function by 61 per cent and a general ability by only 36 per cent. Seventy-six per cent replied that it is complex and heterogeneous, while 11 per cent thought that it is simple and homogeneous. In the individual statements regarding the field of operation most replies showed clearly the effect of the intellectualists' view, and held that intelligence is a higher cognitive power having to do with ideas, reasoning, and comprehending, though a considerable number of the views expressed were inclined to stress ability to adapt oneself to environment.

The same questions presented to thirteen students in an advanced course evoked answers that clearly showed the influence of psychological teaching, 77 per cent of them holding that intelligence is a mechanism, while only 54 per cent held it to be a power or a force, and these latter were all students in the course who were not doing major work in psychology. None of these students had previously been specifically indoctrinated or instructed on these points. While these data are not presented in any sense of finality, and it is recognized that in many cases the questions are ambiguous and not mutually exclusive, it is probably safe to say that the more training one gets in the study of psychology, the more is one inclined to see natural sequences in mental activities and behavior. A thorough knowledge of mental operations tends to give one a naturalistic view of behavior, one that rules out all arbitrary and (theoretically, at least) non-predictable factors.

That the term "intelligence" at the present time has no definite and common meaning to all persons, should occasion no surprise to one who has even a superficial knowledge of the historical development of the conceptions now associated with the term. Even among psychologists different views are entertained as to the nature of intelligence, but in this case the differences, with rare exceptions, relate only to the minor aspects of the general conception, not to radically different conceptions.

EARLY GREEK VIEWS OF "NOUS"

The Greeks were the first to develop scientific conceptions of intelligence and of mental operations. We find the beginnings of their concepts in the idea of *nous* as held by Anaxagoras (*cir.* 500–428 B.C.), who first used the term in a technical sense. *Nous* to him was a distinct principle of spontaneous power acting according to ends, "thus giving movement, unity, and system to what had previously been a jumble of inert elements" (*232*, pages 42 ff.). It was, however, not an immaterial something but was composed of a more attenuated, finer material than the usual inert matter on which it was supposed to act by its own spontaneity. It is thought that Anaxagoras applied this conception only to the stellar heavens, "or, at least, used it only when mechanical principles failed" (*103*); but Diogenes of Apollonia (later in the 5th century B.C.) identified this spontaneous or self-moving principle with air, which was for him the basic element, and he extended its action to organic bodies.

Plato (429–348 B.C.) generalized the *nous* of Anaxagoras as a necessary basis for his teleological explanation of natural processes and made it immaterial, the Supreme Good, the source of all conscious purposes and ends; that is, he made it an immaterial power spontaneously ordering the processes of nature, and acting upon them therefore as an outside force. Aristotle (384–322 B.C.), though departing from the dualism of Plato, assumed "souls" of various kinds and levels to account for vital processes, both vegetative and conscious. His use of the term "soul" must not, however, be confounded with the notion as developed by theological thought. To Aristotle, souls were indeed the primary movers and directive principles of both plant and animal activities or processes; but they were not separate entities, making a dualism as popular thought has it today, following more nearly after Plato; rather, they were attributes or organization of matter itself, more like our scientific notions of functions or of tendencies toward certain ends (227, pages 1 ff.). He consequently assumed different souls for different sorts of activities or processes. Plant souls, animal souls, and human souls were the chief ones; but man, for instance, also had vegetative, locomotive, sensitive, and rational souls. Aristotle's notion of the different activities and forms of behavior whose causal sequences could, as we have seen, be directly traced, was evidently not markedly different from views held by the most advanced thinkers today — that forms of organization rather than some outside or transcendental force condition the processes — and in his work psychology reached its highest development up to the modern period.

Aristotle speaks of reason, *nous*, or intelligence in a dual sense: (1) as an active, supreme principle, the unmoved mover of all things. This more general aspect, while immanent in man, is separable and imperishable, and is transcendent in the world. In this sense it is active and free in man, the source of all his insight and virtue, linking him to the divine. (2) It also has a passive aspect in man, as in the experiences which are mediated through bodily organs and stimulated from without, one that passes away with the individual in whom it appears (*232*, pages 149 ff.). The Platonic conception of a transcendental *nous* played an important part in Neo-Platonism, and its influence is easily recognizable in popular notions of mind today.

"INTELLECTUS" PUT THE EMPHASIS ON COGNITIVE FUNCTIONS

The Latin word *intellectus* was used to translate the Greek *nous* or reason, and received its meaning very largely from the Greek conception, especially the Aristotelian; but early in modern times it became limited to the cognitive functions, or the intellect, as distinguished from feeling and willing. These different functions came to be regarded as rather distinct, especially in the faculty psychology, which assumed a variety of mental powers resembling arbitrary forces, as we have characterized them.

THE INFLUENCE OF LOCKE'S RESEARCH

Under the influence of authorities like John Locke (1632–1704) — whose great *Essay Concerning Human Understanding* (1690) aimed essentially to solve a special problem relating to knowledge — reason and understanding, as the intellectual functions were called, came to be regarded as the higher, more abstract aspects of our cognitive life as opposed to the perceptual and sensory processes. Locke maintained that all knowledge comes through the senses; that there are no innate ideas, but that all ideas are derived from simple sense data. Later associationists, especially Hartley (*127*) and James Mill (*164*), developed this idea, and attempted to show that our mental life is made up of trains of ideas connected by laws of association, derived from early conceptions of molecular vibrations developed by Isaac Newton (1642–1727) and others. Thus they attempted to show that order reigns in our mental life as in the physical world, and in this sense they contributed much toward the science of psychology, but they also developed a very unsatisfactory view of ideas as discrete unities and neglected innate action tendencies, emotion, and general motivation factors.

In thus building up logical abstractions which are really untrue of our behavior, as we shall see in subsequent pages, they merely developed an academic discipline which bears only a rather remote resemblance to the actual human behavior that psychology seeks to understand and to control. One of the chief defects of associationism and of the intellectual philosophy connected with it was its failure to see that the individual, because of inherited organization and general metabolic changes, has at birth, without any immediate external stimulus, a very strong tendency to certain types of activity — that he is really born an *acting* individual. It was the development of biology through the work of Charles Darwin (1809–1882) and the evolutionary school generally, and the experimentation on animal behavior, that did much to bring psychology to the current conception of intelligence and behavior.

INNATE DIFFERENCES IN INDIVIDUALS NEGLECTED

It was characteristic of the primitive views of intelligence as an arbitrary, spontaneous force that they overlooked entirely or to a large extent the individual differences among men, and this same neglect of so patent a fact is seen in faculty psychology and even in associationism. Self-moved forces and faculties might of course choose to do anything, and so individual maladjustments and crimes were ascribed to an arbitrary will and were punished accordingly. Our inhuman doctrines of retributive punishment, now fortunately fading gradually from penology and religion, were logical results of these early views. Even associationism, based upon ideas derived from sense experience, ideas which but reflect

objects in the external world, naturally gave small consideration to individual differences — except in cases of deafness
or blindness or other obvious sensory defects. With the
same experiences why should the train of ideas in different
minds not be identical? Differences were thus accounted
for chiefly in terms of opportunity during the individual's
life; that is, they were differences in education. Only the
later associationists found it worth while to take explicit
note of innate individual differences.[1]

The popular mind today likewise neglects innate individual
differences. Many of the weaknesses of our present educational system are directly due to the view, now disappearing,
that we are born "free and equal" in the sense that all alike
can learn what the schools teach. Failures, according to
this view, are attributed to stubbornness, laziness, etc., rather
than to inability or to innate differences in the structure and
organization of individuals. It is curious how popular
thought has separated so-called mind from physical organization; for it was obvious to every one that persons differed
materially in size, weight, complexion, and so on. But mind,
supposed to be immaterial and more or less arbitrary in its
operation, was not thought to be handicapped by innate defi-
ciencies. How could the laws of heredity, which in our day
have become recognized by all, especially as applied to plants
and domestic animals, be applied to such an immaterial
thing as mind or intelligence?

It should be noted here, too, that in our schools the content of the curriculum was at first made up largely of classifications and abstractions about language and numbers, and of
other abstract relationships, materials organized by superior

[1] It is significant that Francis Bacon's inductive method was supposed
to work well in almost any one's hands once it was developed, whereas Bain
and James pointed out that scientific discovery really demands in the individual a certain "sagacity" or ability to see relationships and similarities
in nature.

minds who conceived all individuals to be like themselves. Thus grammar was largely the application to a live language of the logical forms of analysis developed in the study of dead languages, and arithmetic dealt principally with abstract relationships. It is only in our own day that the schools are beginning to put the emphasis on studies suitable to the several abilities of the children and on practical as opposed to so-called disciplinary subjects. The modern idea of testing the *intelligence* of a child who is beginning his education, to see what he is capable of doing, is yet foreign to many persons, even to many educators, but it has steadily made progress against resistance that is known only to those who have worked to give it wider application in our education and in the problems of our social and economic life.

EXERCISES

1. After reading the chapter write out the best definition of intelligence that you can formulate, one that is free from any assumptions of a spontaneous power and at the same time not influenced too much by the objectionable aspects of associationism. A good way to proceed is to write down first the main conceptions you wish to include in your definition, and then to organize them into a good statement of probably a single sentence. Do not do this carelessly or hastily, but let your definition be the best you can formulate now. You may desire to change it in certain particulars before we get through the book. Any change you may desire to make later will be a mark of your progress, if you now do the best you can. [The instructor will find it very useful to secure from each student a carefully constructed definition *before* this chapter is read, to compare in later discussions with the one called for here. At the end of the course he may ask for a third definition.]

2. Gather for class discussions all the illustrations of different conceptions that you have encountered, and endeavor to make a classification of them.

3. Is there any objection to our thinking of intelligence as a mechanism? If so, what is the objection? See McDougall, *Outline of Psychology* (1923), and also *Psychological Review* (1924), *31*,

281–287, for different views. Consider the possibilities of the conception expressed by James in the quotation at the end of the article cited here. What is "freedom" on such a conception? Does it contradict the law of the conservation of energy? On the basis of this view, how does good intelligence differ from poor intelligence? Is it true that if one's behavior can be predicted it is not free?

4. Illustrate what is meant by holding a person "responsible" for his conduct. On which view — mind as an arbitrary force, or mind as the potential operation of a very delicately adjustable and complex mechanism — is the holding of a person responsible for his acts most justifiable? Why? Consider the relation of this problem to the rapid learning of an individual under the application of regular and immediate reward for "right" acts and punishment for "wrong" ones.

CHAPTER TWO

Early Conceptions and Treatment of Exceptional Individuals

INDIVIDUAL DIFFERENCES WERE NOT UNKNOWN TO THE ANCIENTS

THERE is no question at all that man has recognized individual differences in a practical sense from the very first. Even cattle and horses recognize some of their members as stronger and superior to others in a fight, and so certain individuals become leaders in a rather real sense. In the legends and early history of different peoples we find a similar recognition of individual differences. Thus Achilles is described in the *Iliad* of Homer as lion-hearted, swift-footed, and godlike; Ulysses as fertile in resources; and so on. So, too, the Greeks recognized extremely inferior individuals and exposed them to the beasts or otherwise destroyed them in infancy. Different racial traits of peoples with whom they came into contact were early recognized both by the Greeks and by the Romans. Even though some of these differences were not explicitly attributed to what we call nature as opposed to nurture, there is ample evidence that such innate individual differences were rather commonly recognized among early peoples. Thus Esau is described as being born "red all over like a hairy garment," and so different from his twin brother, Jacob, that when the latter was to present himself to their blind father to secure Esau's blessing it was necessary for Rebecca to put "skins of the kids of the goats upon his hands, and upon the smooth of his neck," for, in Jacob's own words, "Esau my brother is a hairy man, and I am a smooth man." It is not clear to what extent the different mental qualities of the twin brothers were recognized as innate. The innate qualities must have been important in their minds, for Jacob was more "smooth" than his brother

18

in a figurative sense as well as literally, and seems to have been selected for first place because of his greater fitness by nature. Wherever individuals came into close proximity it was inevitable that certain differences among them would be recognized, and in so far as this is true the limitations of personal wills and of other abilities would of necessity be implied. One would not voluntarily be stupid or inept. Hereditary conditions as well as environment were thus recognized as having some weight, as imposing some limitations on the arbitrary mental powers. This position finds support in the study of the behavior of children. Unsophisticated as their view of mind is, they early recognize innate differences among themselves, and in coöperative play the leaders assign rôles to different individuals according to abilities that have become rather well known through habitual failure or success in certain kinds of performances; and they are more outspoken than adults in the use of names to designate the characteristic abilities or lack of abilities detected in one another.

EXTREME DIFFERENCES UNUSUAL AND THEREFORE PUZZLING

Yet extreme individual variations presented their puzzling aspects. Idiots and great geniuses were comparatively seldom met, and their conscious lives could not be so easily entered into by the masses. Between the idiot and the common man there was a barrier, due to the failure of the former to learn language and the common meanings of the group, and so the unfortunate one was looked upon as possessing some sort of foreign spirit. Inability of the feeble-minded and the insane to explain themselves and to enter into the thought of the group life was easily regarded as unwillingness to do so, and the natural consequence was too often punishment and maltreatment. Even loathsome physical diseases were rather naturally attributed to some sort of divine punishment, since their causes were unknown. Job's misfortunes and physical distress were thus accounted for by his friends. The popular mind easily found justification for its attitude of neglect and torture of the mentally incompetent, for in these cases causal connections were far more difficult to trace than in the case of diseases. However, even when the latter were highly contagious, easily traced in their sequences, and therefore almost universal, they were looked upon as some sort of scourge or divine punishment sent upon the whole community because of unknown offense to the gods.

THE FEEBLE-MINDED AND THE DERANGED COULD NOT ENTER THE SOCIAL LIFE

Feeble-mindedness and mental derangement were strictly individualistic, never coming upon entire communities and never having been experienced by the normal person, so that belief in a supernatural cause of these ailments was bound to survive longer. It is much easier for all of us to see faults meriting punishment in others than in ourselves. Furthermore, the mentally incompetent and deranged were not able to initiate and carry on investigations into the causes of their own troubles. Indeed, their defects were usually not known to or recognized by themselves — as a few hours' visit to a mental hospital will soon demonstrate to a doubter — and so the very perverseness of the mentally deranged only gave additional grounds for their exclusion and maltreatment. Since many of the insane [1] — especially those

---

[1] The insane are persons whose minds have been normal or practically normal, but who have become either demented or deranged in such a manner that they seriously misinterpret their relations to other individuals, while the feeble-minded (including three grades — idiocy, the most serious defect, imbecility, and moronity) are persons whose minds have never developed very far. These latter have remained seriously limited in ability from birth. The former are known as "dements" and the latter as "aments."

with such functional diseases as paranoia and some forms of
dementia præcox — were generally more capable of justify-
ing their behavior and views than were the feeble-minded,
it is but natural that they would receive the more serious opposition and mistreatment at the hands of normal
persons. It was easier to understand that the feeble-
minded were limited in their abilities and incapable, this
being true to a considerable degree because their condition
persisted from birth. The insane had once been more capable
and more able to enter into the life of the normal community,
but had withdrawn from this social life of common meanings.

It was, therefore, perhaps natural that under such conditions the madness of the unfortunate, deranged minds was
attributed to possession by some alien spirit. Thus Saul's
periods of depression were attributed to "the evil spirit
of the Lord." This interpretation of insanity is known as
demonological. "The phenomena were regarded as the manifestations of some spiritual being, god or demon, who either
actually inhabited the body of his victim, or who merely
played upon him from without. If the phenomena manifested were in harmony with the religious views of the time,
it was concluded that the controlling spirit was benign in
character, and the individual 'possessed' was revered as
an exceptionally holy person. If, on the other hand, the
individual's conduct conflicted with the dominating ethical
code, he was thought to be the victim of a malignant devil.
As long as this view was generally accepted, it was natural
that the only curative treatment in force was the employment
of religious ceremonials and incantations" (*126,* pages *2* f.).
It was most unfortunate for the victim of these mental disorders to be regarded as possessed of an evil spirit, for he
would then in all probability become an outcast or be made
to undergo certain tortures to make it so unpleasant for the
devil possessing him that it might be induced to leave. The

demonological view is clearly expressed in the New Testament, where we are told that the people brought to Jesus "many that were possessed with devils: and he cast out the spirits with his word, and healed all that were sick" (Matt. 8 : 16).

Hippocrates, however, in the fifth century B.C. conceived a physiological view of insanity. Regarding the brain as the organ of the mind, he maintained that insanity was merely the result of some disturbance of this organ. This view was of comparatively short duration, however, and gave way through the Dark Ages to the demonological conception. It was not reëstablished until the nineteenth century, when it was definitely placed on a permanent footing by the advancement of science.

Even from those who did not hold the "possession" view, the insane received very little sympathy or understanding. These unfortunates were crowded into asylums in a way that we should not today treat our worst criminals. "Men covered with filth cowered in cells of stone, cold, damp, without air or light, and furnished with a straw bed that was rarely renewed, and which soon became infectious — frightful dens where we should scruple to lodge the vilest animals. The insane thrown into these receptacles were at the mercy of their attendants, and these attendants were convicts from prison. The unhappy patients were loaded with chains and bound like galley slaves." [1] It is beyond the scope of this book to trace out the changing conceptions of insanity and the humane treatment that finally resulted to the insane from regarding their behavior as the result of certain diseased conditions in the organism. To the insane, as well as to the normal person, the advancement of science has indeed been a blessing and a protection.

[1] From a quotation in *126*, page 7.

THE FEEBLE-MINDED DID NOT DRAW THE ATTENTION OF
MANY PERSONS

We go back to a consideration of the feeble-minded, or
aments, those who from birth have not grown normally in
intelligence and who are therefore unable to make the
required practical adjustments in life. On this class of "exceptional persons" we have very little authentic information
dating back beyond the nineteenth century. Casual references to incompetent individuals may be found, but as these
individuals are generally less dangerous and less inclined
to oppose management and care by others, they have come
down through the ages of human development and have
fitted severally into the existing order of things as best they
could, and have passed away each in his turn — little
lamented, no doubt, by those on whom they have been bur-
dens, and soon forgotten by the world. The higher grades —
by far the most numerous — have easily become adapted to
the performance of certain menial tasks, and so, in ages when
education was not a common privilege of children, these
individuals attracted little public notice. Unquestionably
wise men in all ages have regarded the lowest grades of aments
as innately defective in some way. The fact of their innate
defectiveness is too patent to escape the notice of thinking
men, since these individuals cannot learn to use language
and thereby enter into the common life of their fellows.

Facts now available through numerous studies of the mentality of criminal persons make it clear that a large per cent
of such persons are so seriously lacking in mentality as to be
classed as feeble-minded. There are, of course, and have been
in all ages, many normal persons, who fall into crime either
because of neglect in childhood or through group conflicts and
consequent oppositions to society, or to public officers in
whose actions they find or imagine they see imperfections of

various sorts; but it is nevertheless true that in the main most criminal acts are short-sighted and stupid, and would be avoided by intelligent individuals. In many cases, of course, persons of very limited mental capacity become the henchmen or tools of able leaders who selfishly work for personal gain against the general social welfare, and so these unfortunate feeble-minded individuals become agents of crime. Recent investigations, however, have shown that they do not usually, if indeed ever, have innate tendencies toward specific types of crime. Even their cruelties are largely accounted for merely on the basis of lack of sensibility and insight.

THE ABILITIES OF MORONS USUALLY OVERESTIMATED

Despite the present-day recognition of a physiological and even a hereditary basis of feeble-mindedness, there is a strong tendency, on becoming closely acquainted with them, always to act toward the unfortunate individuals suffering from this defect in its lighter forms as if they could themselves voluntarily better their condition. Mothers who come to clinics with such children will explain that they have constantly talked with them and have tried to get them to do so and so — often something that is wholly beyond the capacity of the unfortunate child in question. Only recently I was told of a feeble-minded boy whose mother had talked to him and labored with him to get him to see that he was not taking hold of his studies as he should do. Since the upper-grade feeble-minded and the simply dull persons are able to grasp our meanings in ordinary conversations and to enter into the common everyday social life of the group, we are likely to feel, when we come to abstractions into which we can ourselves pass without any felt difficulty, that it is pure arbitrariness on their part not to go on with us. This is especially noticeable when a bright, rather impatient person is attempting to teach or to assist a dull one in school subjects. Demonstration and explanation, often in abstract terms, go on for a short time; then the learner is confronted with a question or with an exercise or problem to be worked. When he hesitates unduly or makes a ridiculous blunder, he is scolded, belittled, or ridiculed, according to the relationship between the individuals. That is, the mentally inferior person is regarded more or less as rather arbitrarily or willfully failing to take advantage of the situation and to grasp the abstract principles involved, or as refusing to act in accordance with them, so prone are we to suppose that persons with whom we converse in normal social life apprehend all our meanings as we ourselves appreciate them. The simplest sort of experiments of the mental-test type will readily show the fallacy of this attitude, but it will take long practice to rid ourselves of it.[1]

It is not surprising, then, to find men in earlier times ready to inflict punishments upon those who apparently refused to participate in the common social life, nor to find that menta"y disorganized persons were looked upon as possessed by some alien spirit and that they were reacted to accordingly. It is not a coincidence that in our own day persons who treat such unfortunates are called "alienists."

THE ABILITIES OF THE GENIUS UNDERESTIMATED BY THE COMMON MAN

On the other hand, persons of unusual ability have always been able to accomplish things that are so far beyond those done by the usual individual as to draw the attention of their fellows. It is an interesting fact that as a rule we overestimate what we are *capable of doing* and therefore usually give, for the fact that others accomplish more than we do,

[1] It is a question whether a dull, slow, conscientious, and well-trained teacher is not far better for dull and feeble-minded students than a bright, mentally quick teacher.

some other explanation than that they have more ability. The reason for this overestimation of our own ability is probably this : when a thing is done it is easier to understand how it was accomplished than it was to project it and carry it through originally, and so we underestimate in comparison with ourselves the person who first accomplished it.

Some illustrations will readily make this fact clear. Children will often deny that once they could not talk and walk. Ask a small child how he learned to walk, and you will probably get the reply : "I didn't learn. I could always walk." Unless we reflect carefully and invoke aid from the older members of our household, we probably all feel thus about our present views and many of our abilities which have been rather gradually and incidentally acquired. The things we have learned to do have either been acquired by a trial and error process or by an adaptation of something thus learned. Take learning to talk, for instance. This was accomplished so gradually and so naturally by a process of trial and error that little memory remains of the process. That is, we learned our vernacular by a process of struggling by varied reactions to acquire certain objects and to control certain individuals and situations, with attention so much on these ends of action that the *methods* by which success was obtained and the useless acts that were eliminated almost wholly escaped our notice. We feel, then, that talking is really part of ourselves and that it is not an acquirement. And so for other abilities.

And just as we tend to overestimate inferiors by failing to see their limitations, and, knowing that we ourselves can easily "will" to do this or that, we feel that they can do likewise, so we underestimate the powers of geniuses or greatly superior persons. Not having lived through their struggles and not having had the opportunity of measuring skill with them and of seeing how here and there in almost everything they undertook they accomplished more than we could have done, we naturally "perceive" their abilities as like our own.

It is also to be remarked that most performances of genius are based on a persistence that is not characteristic of the common man. The genius seems to have an unusual ability to occupy himself, against various distractions, with remote ends and conditions and to feel a satisfaction in these things. This is probably what Galton meant when he said, as we shall presently see, that genius is characterized by exceptional energy. It is probably well, however, to distinguish between this persistence in activity of remote bearing and mere energy; for many persons of ordinary ability seem to have great energy, but they waste it in acts of little moment because of a failure to be motivated by remote and significant relationships.

GREAT ACCOMPLISHMENTS ATTRIBUTED TO SUPERNATURAL AID

The performances of the genius, therefore, which count in the long run and finally put him conspicuously before his fellows, must somehow be accounted for or explained by the latter. Not recognizing his superior abilities as due to innate conditions, they are likely to ascribe his success — not rationally, perhaps, but perceptually — to some external agency such as inspiration from supernatural sources or "possession" by some benign spirit. Similar success therefore would be sought through propitiation and favor obtained by means of various sorts of religious appeals and ceremonials. There is no question, moreover, that opportunity of the kind and at the time suitable to one's genius is a further factor necessary for success (*93; 3*, Chapter 18; *139; 90*).

GENIUSES OFTEN MISUNDERSTAND THEMSELVES

But probably the most interesting and instructive point is that even the genius himself may be misled, just as the untrained observer is misled, with respect to causal factors in his own will. Our best thoughts often do not come to us when we are actively struggling to solve some problem, but are likely to come in a moment of relaxation. It is well known that after we have been embarrassed by failure to recall names of friends just when we needed them, the names will come to our minds when the occasion demanding them is past. Thus the genius, who for long periods of time has been working at certain problems from all angles, getting numerous data bearing on the subject, may in rather passive moments chance to get the proper elements together by association, when presto! the problem is solved. It has solved itself! Often ideas that thus come to mind (as well as certain automatisms) seem actually to be forced on one as if by some outside agency, so that a person thus assisted may, if unaccustomed to thinking in naturalistic terms, be deceived into the thought that the causal factor is some supernatural agency. Thus the genius becomes to others, and often also to himself, an example of the operation in a mind of mysterious outside forces, and the natural sequence of events is lost sight of either completely or to a considerable extent. Here again the interactions upon one another of various part-processes in the organism are of such a nature as to modify the effects of immediate objective stimuli, thus concealing the sequence of natural events to the extent that the effects of present stimuli, which fail to evoke direct and immediate responses, are overlooked. The cumulative effects in the organism of various experiences thus become lost to human observation, and the behavior, though a function of the complex external situation, both present and past, comes to be regarded as disconnected from natural antecedent conditions as if it were some manifestation of forces without the system of nature. The alleged messages of "mediums" are good illustrations of extreme forms of this, and they are not always mere deception of others, but are often unintended self-deception.[1]

From the foregoing considerations, as well as from those in the previous chapter dealing with causal relations in mental processes, we see that it is but natural that the genius who meets successfully great emergencies in the social life, like the mentally deranged person who seems to be dominated by opposing arbitrary forces, should be looked upon as under the influence of extraneous forces or minds. They are therefore examples, the one class as well as the other, of individuals whose behavior is somehow outside the pale of the normal, and so have been classed together. Prophets as well as deranged individuals have been regarded as inspired by evil powers, and both likewise have been considered spokesmen of the divine will, their classification depending on whether or not their contributions were acceptable to the group. Paranoiacs have now and then become for a time successful leaders of groups, whereas long-visioned leaders have been put to death or cast out of the groups.

RELATIONS OF GENIUS TO MENTAL DEFICIENCY

A modern school headed by Lombroso has held, on a somewhat more scientific basis, that both the genius and the idiot, being unusual variations from the norm, have much in common and are both unstable types; that in every genius there are marks of degeneracy and in every degenerate or feeble-minded person there are certain marks of genius. While it is undeniable that some feeble-minded persons have special gifts (221), and also that certain geniuses have shown signs

---

[1] This statement is made in a sort of dogmatic fashion, simply because the writer feels sure that it is a true account of numerous cases known to any reader. He does not, however, wish to close the reader's mind to other possible explanations or to make him unsympathetic with experimental work in the rather forbidden field called (or miscalled) "psychic research." We must have open minds as long as the evidence is not convincing to all scientific investigators.

of degenerate tendencies, it is now known that these extreme types of mentalities, instead of being much alike, are really each more like the normal individual than like the other extreme. They are both of them "variations from the normal," it is true, but opposite variations. Superior ability has been shown to be closely associated in heredity through successive generations (*123, 236*), and feeble-mindedness likewise, though being in some cases closely related to certain forms of dementia, is highly hereditary (*122, 123*).

As a result of these various studies and extensive testing, and also of the general development of psychology, the behavior of all individuals, normal, subnormal, and supernormal, is regarded by psychologists as following natural laws just as other events in nature do, even though the causal relations, for reasons already given, are in many cases so concealed that only careful scientific research can trace the different results of stimulations back to their proper sources. The general fact that definite causal relations obtain in all our behavior is yet far from demonstrated, and many persons, even including some scientifically trained individuals, still believe in supernatural interferences in human behavior. The evidence in a large sense is now so strongly in favor of the naturalistic interpretation of all behavior that in many minds there is not even any alternative hypothesis entertained. Extensive studies of the destinies of certain families or groups, as well as detailed investigations of alleged mediumship, of genius, of conversion phenomena, and of alleged inspiration all point in the same direction and strengthen the view that "mental processes," or behavior in general, follow laws just as truly as physical processes do. The mind of the defective is simply not equal to the task of adjustment to the complexities of his environment, and so maladjustments arise. These maladjustments are not usually sudden and immediately obvious, though on occasions marked incompetency to deal with a situation may be seen. Usually the single maladjustments are so small as to escape notice. The general effect of them is more obvious to everybody, and the unfortunate defective is frequently regarded as not willing to put forth the effort to succeed.

INSANITY COMMONLY MISUNDERSTOOD

In certain extreme types of mental disorganization it is so obvious that the person is acting contrary to his usual conduct and that he is irrational, — that is to say, fails to take into consideration the more remote bearings of his acts, — that we call him insane. Insane persons are confined in mental hospitals where they are seen by only a small part of the people. This isolation, as well as the rash acts committed by certain persons before they are confined, leads many persons to think of the insane as a different species of humanity, whose mental life is wholly discontinuous and whose acts are therefore so disjointed that it is impossible to say what will be the next act. This is a grossly exaggerated view of the discontinuity of the behavior of insane persons. Indeed, those attendants and physicians who care for the insane soon learn the repertory of each inmate so well that they can anticipate most of his acts just as regularly as we can predict what one of our fellows, with whom we associate closely, will do under certain conditions. Each insane person has his cycle of activities and of emotional ups and downs which soon come to be well known, because, indeed, they are so simple. If they seem to the stranger to be impulsive and wholly discontinuous, this is only because they are conditioned to a larger extent than is true of normal persons by various internal and unnatural stimuli, such as infections, excessive secretions of ductless glands, and so on. The individual thus affected is consequently unable to respond in the manner that we ourselves would do to the various objective circumstances so obvious to us and so influential in behavior. Any person who has seen a relative or a friend in a delirium knows how much the poison in his blood outweighs the effects of external conditions and makes him respond in ways that seem wholly irrational. While all cases of insanity are not so directly and obviously caused by inner organic disturbances as these statements may seem to imply, there is little doubt that every case is conditioned by an organic or physiological disorder of some sort, often too delicate and functional in its nature to be susceptible of definite location.

The popular, and to a large extent even the legal, idea of insanity reflects the older notion that the normal mind is a sort of mysteriously arbitrary force in itself and that when deranged it entirely loses its direction and its means of control. The ordinary layman supposes that to find a person "insane" is to understand his case, and unfortunately the courts are not far in advance of this notion. Insanity is not sufficiently recognized as a purely relative term, one that may mean one thing in one case and almost a totally different thing in another, a degree of irresponsibility being possibly the only thing common to all. But what is irresponsibility and why is the person irresponsible? A perfectly normal young child is also irresponsible. If we seek to know *why* an insane person is irresponsible, we shall find almost as many answers as there are insane individuals. No two cases are quite alike, just as no two adult normal persons are alike. Even the names for special types of disorders — such as dementia præcox, paranoia, hysteria, manic-depressive psychosis — are not free from this lack of definiteness as to what they imply.

All these classifications of disordered minds are made for certain practical purposes. If a disorganized person is found to show certain symptoms common to a class of other cases, it is but natural to suppose that the causes of his mental derangement are somewhat like those common to this class of cases, and to attempt a prognostication on the basis of the developments that were observed in the other cases. But the human organism is vastly too complex for any marked similarities to be found between two such persons without the occurrence at the same time of striking differences. Qualifying terms or hyphenated names — such as paranoid-dementia præcox — thus are invented to cover new classes of cases, and finally we have a complex classification the names of which often satisfy the popular or the formal mind, and stand for it as designations of rather distinct and well-marked types of insanity.

When a person with such views visits a mental hospital, he finds no good or perfect representatives of the functional types of classes of mental derangement that he has learned, but, instead of this, a number of individuals differing markedly among one another, and shading off gradually in the symptoms they show into other types classed under different names. Confusion therefore results, and if he comes to have close and varied experiences with these several individuals and to know their different "histories," individualities, and possibilities, he in time really becomes able to study their behavior in a causal manner, just as he is able to do with his intimate normal associates. It is only then that he can take a really rational attitude toward them and see the practical value of certain groupings. Until this stage is reached any person is likely to regard the insane of different classifications as somehow ruled by the dominance of certain mystical, arbitrary faculties, instead of considering each one as responding in the manner that his inherited and acquired organization permits, and indeed determines, in the circumstances or conditions under which he is placed.

In the case of the insane, as in that of normal persons, both

habits and innate structure or organization have much influence on behavior, and mind when studied at close range
and scientifically loses its arbitrariness and mystical qualities.
This statement does not imply that any one now knows all
the intricacies of our numerous mental operations. The
human organism is so extremely complex as to lead us to
expect that it will never be understood in all details. At
present we have made but a fair beginning toward the scientific understanding and control of human behavior. But
the things we have found out are so useful and important as
amply to reward all the efforts that have been put forth.
We are coming to see mind and personality as aspects of the
processes of nature. How this happy result has been attained
we shall see in subsequent chapters.

EXERCISES

1. On the basis of the view expressed in this chapter, why are
some people afraid of being alone with a corpse? Some persons are
genuinely afraid of the brains of a human being. How do you
account for this fear? Why are "spiritualistic" phenomena often
feared?

2. Select various examples of the assumption of supernatural or
arbitrary forces in behavior or in nature, and test the statements
made in the text by a study of them. It would be well to embody
the results of your study in a short, critical paper. Be as impartial
as you can, even if this is difficult; remember that we are looking
for facts, not for ultimate explanations of nature.

3. How does the assumption of demonology differ from the view
that "gravitation" makes objects fall?

4. Select examples of reactions to the work of morons and of
geniuses by the unsophisticated person, and test the assertions in
the text about the overestimation of morons and the underestima-
tion of geniuses. Do people usually overestimate or underestimate
their own abilities? Give evidence.

CHAPTER THREE

Intelligence Conceived as a Complex of Intellectual Faculties

THE ELEVATION OF THE COGNITIVE FUNCTIONS BY THE GREEKS

The early Greeks, to whom we look for the beginnings of philosophical speculations that later developed into various of our fundamental sciences, did not overlook man himself as an object of study. The conflict of different inner impulses, the purposive nature of human actions, and the spontaneity that every person feels in his own mental operations were recognized by them, and were explained by assumptions of vital, spontaneous principles, or souls, which were conceived as regulating and directing in a measure the individual's thoughts and activities. Modern views of intelligence are still influenced to a very considerable extent by conceptions of this kind, and it is important to trace the development of these views of spontaneous faculties and to see how the supposed powers constituting intelligence became limited to the cognitive powers, as opposed to feeling and will.

Plato recognized an important division in man, which, by him, was characterized as desire, on the one hand, and reason on the other. These were attributed to the "irrational soul" and to the "rational soul," respectively. The rational soul was located in the head and the irrational soul, which was divided into a better and a worse part, was placed in the body. The better part was ascribed to the heart and was supposed to function in manifestations of energy, courage, and ambition, while the worse part was placed below the diaphragm and was thought to manifest itself in desire and in the nutritive functions (74, page 68). It has been a characteristic of thought ever since Plato's time to elevate

35

reason more or less as an exalted desire-free faculty, while the nutritive functions have been considered of slight importance, little worthy of study, and often needing suppression for the sake of the higher souls or faculties, to which these lower ones were seemingly in opposition.

For Plato the higher, or rational, soul gradually establishes greater independence of external movements affecting the body. "In the beginning there is a chaos of movement, all possible forms of external movement taking effect on the body which aimlessly yields to every force. This state can never be quite superseded in the life of a human being, because he is always in intimate connection with the outer world" (74, page 72). Sensation is impossible to the soul in the early chaotic condition of the whole organism, for it implies an inner discriminative reaction, or "motion," of the soul. Sensation emerges only when a certain degree of order is established. But the life of mortal man can never quite free itself from the outer world, a desirable accomplishment for Plato.

In sleep the soul is cut off from external influences, but often a certain amount of agitation remains; and thus dreams were explained. "'If the quiet is profound, sleep with few dreams falls on us; but if some of the stronger motions are left, according to their nature and the places where they remain they engender visions corresponding in number and kind.' On the meaning of dreams Plato speaks a little uncertainly. He regards them sometimes as an activity of the desiring part of the soul, and in the *Republic* a remarkable passage on the moral character of dreams shows that he considered them the expression of desires which are usually suppressed" (74, page 70). One is reminded here of the Freudian theory of dreams, which, however, restricts the field of the desires, thus being less true to life than was Plato. The good man, in whom the rational soul prevails, is to suppress these rebellious activities of the desires, for in him desires and ambition must give place to the rational life. Brett points out that in the *Timæus* Plato seems to regard dreams, inspiration, and possession alike as mere abnormal conditions, "or at best a dim expression of desires that might indicate some reaching out after the final objects of desire and so be, as it were, intimations of things eternal," reminding one somewhat of James's view (*140*, pages 151 ff. and 189 ff.) ; while in the *Republic* "he seems to favor the idea that in sleep the rational soul, if it is not troubled by the irrational parts, can attain truths not otherwise revealed" (*74*, page 71).

For Plato, knowledge is the result of an inner activity of the rational soul, but, as we have seen, it is by no means always "pure." Certain activities were thought to be intermediate between rational knowledge and the more passive "affections," or sensory impressions, though these received scant attention. These activities are memory, association, imagination, and emotion. In his later writings "the lower parts of the soul are conceived as acquisitions of the earthly life, so that the original nature of the soul appears as a purely cognitive power" (*101*, page 12). Thus the perceptual and particular is subordinated to the conceptual and universal. It is because the human soul carries within itself conceptual images that it is able to apprehend the universal.

Thus we find in Plato a strong emphasis on the higher rational functions, an emphasis that doubtless has had much weight in the history of psychology. This tendency is continued in the work of Aristotle, for whom reason gives form and movement to nature. Aristotle divided mental functions into the "cognitive powers" — knowledge and reason — on the one hand, and the "motive powers" — feeling, desire, and action — on the other. "This division," says Baldwin, "survived until the threefold Kantian classification of intellect, feeling, and will came in" (*9*, page 77). For Aristotle all perceptions were accompanied by pleasure and displeasure, and these feelings themselves were regarded as indications of free or of obstructed activity of the cognitive and motive powers, pleasure indicating unhindered and displeasure hindered activity. Emotions, which were likely to disturb the judgment and therefore were not in high favor, resulted from a mixture of these feelings.

For Aristotle as for Plato, sensation is not a mere passive impression, and nothing is transmitted thereby to the soul, contrary to the contentions of the Greek atomists of the fifth century B.C. The object stimulating the sense is not like the sensation, but the latter must nevertheless correspond in some way to that object. What they have in common is "form" (nearly our figure, or shape, or organization) as distinct from matter. "Form" is a term that was made much of by Aristotle, but that fell into disfavor with the waning of his influence. Kant used "form" in only a slightly different meaning, as a category of perception. For Aristotle objects in the world could therefore be perceived only in as far as they admit of assimilation by some one or more of the various sense forms. But the true sense organ is not the "flesh" in any particular case; it is rather a "common sense" located in the heart. It is only by means of this common sense that perceptions and images of the various sense organs obtain unity and consistency. In this common sense, too, is where the judgment of true and false takes place. The effects of outer stimulation of the senses were supposed to be transmitted to the common sense by a substance or organism of a sensitive nature spread through the body and acting as a universal medium of sensation — the forerunner of the later term "animal spirits," and of our modern term "nerve impulse."

After the stimulating object is removed inner motions persist, and these motions, by restimulating the central sense, reproduce in consciousness the same effect, as far as form is concerned, that the sensible object produced. It is thus that images or presentations come about, and their reproduction in the absence of the original stimulus was by Aristotle called "imagination." "By virtue of these inner movements, which are psychic, man is able to store up and reproduce many images, and one image may be the cause of another, or more correctly one movement may set up another movement which previously occurred in some relation with it. The possibility of storing up the movement is the condition of memory" (*74*, page 124). Without the relation of such movements memory is not possible, for such retention is the condition of memory, though it is not memory itself. "Memory is a condition in which an image present to mind is known to be the copy of an object which had been present itself on some former occasion" (page 125). Thus memory always involves more time than the immediate movement, an important point to which we shall return when we come to later conceptions of intelligence. Recollection is the voluntary effort or activity which, by exciting an idea, creates a stimulus for a chain of ideas on the basis of the laws of association, as we should now say; but for Aristotle this does not preclude a sort of self-initiation manifested in the voluntary effort which takes us at once to the essence of reason. It is by the common sense that images, through contiguity, similarity, and contrast, become memories, dreams, and fancies; that judgments of things as true or false are made; that "sensible qualities" — motion, number, shape, size, etc. — are attributed to things; and that unity is given to our experiences. But the constructive imagination is necessary to thought just as sensation is to imagination; it supplies the schemata to reason (*9*, pages 72 ff.). Aristotle's emphasis on thought proper is indicated by the fact that he contributed what is known as the "Aristotelian logic."

"The theory of syllogistic inference sprang full-formed from the brain of Aristotle," says Baldwin (page 79).

THE INFLUENCE OF PLATO AND ARISTOTLE

These were the high marks of psychological development in the ancient world. For centuries men quoted these masters. The views of Plato were made suitable for religious purposes and so through Neo-Platonism exercised a great influence on Christianity. Saint Augustine (354–430), however, was greatly influenced by Aristotle. "He held that the soul was to be approached and known directly through consciousness; that it was immaterial in character and immortal; that inner observation was possible and necessary. From such observation, he found that the mental life was one of continual movement in the one spiritual principle, and [that it] showed itself in three fundamental functions: intellect (*intellectus*), will (*voluntas*), and 'self-conscious memory' (perhaps the best rendering of *memoria*, as Saint Augustine used the term). The fundamental moving principle of the entire mental life is will. The other functions manifest will" (*9*, pages 96 f.). The dualism of mind (the active controlling principle) and matter (the inert substance upon which it acted) left its stamp deeply on the thought and entire life of the Middle Ages, as is well known, and it is still the dominant view of popular thought, as we have already shown.

The confusions and breakdowns of older systems of thought resulting in the Renaissance and in the inventions, discoveries, and renewed interest in life in the world, threw new demands on reconstructive thinking and empirical methods; but dualism and pure rationalistic methods were too thoroughly impressed on the culture of the times not to show themselves strongly. Empirical methods were much more easily applied to objective, physical phenomena than to the mind of man, and so the scientific development of psychology was still to be retarded a long period of time.

THE ORIGIN OF MODERN DUALISM AND OF CONCEPTIONS OF INNATE IDEAS

René Descartes (1596–1650), a man of a strong mathematical and rationalistic turn of mind, steeped so thoroughly in the learning of his time and yet so able to see its weaknesses and errors, "stands," as Baldwin has so well said, "at the portals of modern philosophy and psychology" (9, page 131). If an empiricist had led out in modern psychology with an objective study of the behavior of animals and children, we might have had a radically different science today from that which was so greatly influenced by superior minds steeped in rationalism, looking in upon themselves for the facts of psychology. Descartes opened up the way for an independent consideration of the mental processes, but he was an extreme dualist, holding to a sharp distinction between mind and matter, and he opened up explicitly the philosophical difficulties involved in views of their interaction. His empirical tendencies show themselves in his treatment of perception and of the passions, tendencies influenced by Kepler, an early contemporary, who died when Descartes was thirty-four years old.

Descartes found it necessary to discard as "untrustworthy" the writings of the ancients. "I cannot have any hope of reaching the truth, except by abandoning the paths which they have followed," he said. "All that which we experience in ourselves which we can also see take place in bodies entirely inanimate is to be attributed only to our body; and, on the contrary, all that which is in us and which we cannot conceive in any manner possible to pertain to a body is to be attributed to our soul" (*181*, pages 168 f.). Heat and movements of limbs are of the body and come from the physical world, but thoughts come from the soul, which, for him, has spontaneous powers that it can exert on matter. The soul departs at death because heat fails and the organs decay — not the reverse, as has been held.   The life processes are therefore not due to the soul, but to all automatic bodily movements which "run down" as a clock may do.   He gives an interesting account of these processes, including circulation of the blood, which recently had been discovered by Harvey (in 1628), and which was understood by those "whom the authority of the ancients had not entirely blinded" (*181*, page 171).   The force of the blood and of the "animal spirits" — a term which has given way to the more modern term "nerve impulse" — being sent with varying strength and in different directions by "outside motions" (external stimuli) and by bodily changes themselves, may explain, he holds, how the bodily movements are *automatically performed* "without the aid of the soul."   All lower animals are automata; they have no souls.   In man the soul operates from a point of the pineal gland, which seems to be centrally located at the confluence of the blood vessels and nerves, and where structures are not double or bilateral as are most structures of the brain, and it controls voluntary action by diverting the blood flow and the animal spirits as is necessary for the desired actions.   This view contradicts his principle of the conservation of energy, but he thought that "only the total amount of motion in space, not however the direction thereof, is unchangeable" (*101*, page 91).   Thus Descartes dispensed with all the souls of the ancients but the *rational* soul.   This soul gets its perceptions from the various motions of the animal spirits coming against the pineal gland.   It also, "by the simple fact of its willing anything," modifies the course of these animal spirits from this point and thus regulates action. Thus the higher intellectual operations, in so far as they are not automatic, are manifestations of its activity.

These extracts give the reader an idea of Descartes' independence and originality and of his general point of view. It is clear that, while he lays open a most interesting field in the study of these automatic processes, including most of the emotional disturbances, he points the way to the higher intellectual faculties as the most fruitful and dignified study of man. The intellectual, self-conscious part of man belonged for him to the soul, which does not have spatial or temporal attributes but to which are attributed such activities as perceiving, knowing, and willing. The soul's main characteristic is self-consciousness, but besides this immediate knowledge of itself the soul also has certain *innate ideas* — ideas of extension, number, duration, existence, cause and effect, etc. — as principles which are basic to its thinking. Here his mathematical training shows itself. When he comes to certainty of knowledge, he finds that all knowledge rests on self-existence as introspectively manifested: "I think, therefore I am" (*cogito, ergo sum*). The real self is not a developing thing: it is that which an adult philosopher can find by looking in upon himself, as it were. But we must not enter into Descartes' interesting philosophy except simply to indicate that he opened up certain problems of knowledge which under the conditions of his time were bound to usurp much of the attention of the scholars *and to direct it particularly to the higher thought processes.*

Geulincx (1625–1669) and Malebranche (1638–1715) considered the difficulties which Descartes' dualism had so explicitly disclosed and attempted to distinguish between the cause of an event and the circumstances under which it acts. This was a superficial distinction showing ulterior purposes or theological and free-will interests which, by seeking merely to support certain views already held rather than to discover truth unaffected by bias and current social concepts, operate against a purely scientific procedure. But

Malebranche made several contributions to the development of psychology. He was the first one to apprehend, says Dessoir (*101*, page 99), that because of this two-sided correspondence between mind and body, a sort of parallelistic hypothesis might be useful to psychology. Such an hypothesis is stated, for instance, by Titchener (*219*, pages 13 ff.) and by Stratton (*205*, Chapter 14). Contrary to Descartes, Malebranche did not suppose that the "inner sense," or awareness of one's own mental states, gives any knowledge or proof of the soul, but only of the phenomena of consciousness. He thus contributed toward freeing psychology from philosophical speculations and methods, and he became distinguished for useful investigations of perceptual processes, in the line that had received a great impetus through the work of the Arabian physiological psychologists more than six centuries earlier, particularly that of Alhacen.

The dualistic theory was developed by the great Jewish philosopher Spinoza (1632–1677) into a form which many psychologists have found satisfactory as a hypothesis, given the "mind and matter" dualism which has been bequeathed to them from philosophy. Accepting Descartes' distinction between mind and matter and also his principle of the conservation of energy — that the total amount of "motion" in the universe is fixed — he perceived clearly the impossibility of interaction between mind and matter, and formulated another principle regarded as equally indisputable, the strict correlation between changes taking place in these two "attributes" of the one infinite substance, God: "the order and connection of ideas is the same as the order and connection of things " (*9*, page 143). In short, mind and matter are but two aspects, or attributes, of the ultimate reality.

Although Spinoza recognized the empirical origin of our knowledge of external objects in the world, he nevertheless laid solidly the foundation for *innate* conceptions, or innate ideas, which, arising from pure reason, have the advantage of being clear and distinct. *They are apprehended immediately as being true.* He, of course, refers to such things as mathematical axioms, another of our intellectual inheritances of the past.

The great philosopher Leibnitz (1646–1716), who shares with Newton (1642–1727) the distinction of having invented (in 1675) the differential calculus, gave strong support to the doctrine of innate ideas, and therefore he was an important factor in stimulating the British empiricism, as we shall presently see.

THE BRITISH EMPIRICAL MOVEMENT

To this movement we now turn. Hobbes (1588–1679) begins an extremely empirical reaction by attempting to bring under the dominance of natural or mechanical processes the entire behavior of man (*130, 131*). He was himself a mild and timid man, though an energetic thinker and controversialist. While traveling in continental Europe, he became personally acquainted in Italy with Galileo (1564–1642), and in France with Gassendi (1592–1655), the mathematician and atomist, from whose writings Newton derived the atomic theory and adapted it to chemistry. Hobbes, however, seems to have arrived independently at the theory that all change is motion, and in a discussion with friends he came to the conclusion that if there were no motion there would be no sensation. "A change of motion is therefore the condition of sensation. For sensing unceasingly one and the same thing and sensing nothing at all amounts to the same thing" (*133,* page *59*). This principle, accepted early in his life, makes the basis of his psychology. He rejects the view of Descartes, that mind is a separate substance different from body. Thinking does imply a thinking thing just as walking does, but that thing is the body. Mind is a function of the body and reason is a product of sensation. "Man's nature is the *sum of his natural faculties and powers, as the faculties of nutrition, motion, generation, sense, reason, etc.*," said Hobbes, clearly using the term "faculties" as we might use "functions." "These powers we do unanimously call *natural*, and are contained in the definition of man, under these words, *animal* and *rational*" (*131*, Chapter 1; *181*, page 147). He proceeds to divide man's faculties, according to these two principal parts, into (1) those of the body — nutritive, motive, and generative — and (2) those of the mind — cognitive and motive. The cognitive, or conceptive, power of man is that "*faculty* or power by which we are capable of" such knowledge and imagination as we have of the things in the outer world, things whose images or conceptions would remain even if they themselves were destroyed. All these conceptions come originally from the action of the things themselves on our organs, producing sensations on which all knowledge of the outer world is based. So all our sense experiences are but "apparitions" of the motion which works on "the *brain*, or spirits, or some internal substance of the head." But he also recognizes that inward bodily disturbances as well as outward stimulations serve to recall images (association). Thus "the *causes* of dreams, if they be natural, are the *actions* or violence of the *inward* parts of man upon his *brain*, by which the *passages* of sense by sleep *benumbed*, are *restored* to their motion" (*181*, page 153). These sense data, and the images which result from them, when the action on the senses has ceased, are not inherited. It is only the sentient power that is inherited. The outer stimulations set up motions about the heart some of which either help or hinder the vital processes, thus conditioning either pleasure or pain, as the case may be, and bringing about various complex experiences and also tendencies "to draw near to the thing that pleaseth, or to retire from the thing that displeaseth." Beliefs, passions, and will are built upon these foundations by various associations and inner motions, and thus is laid, though not very consistently by Hobbes, a foundation for a strong emphasis by empiricism on the intellectual or cognitive functions.

This tendency was greatly strengthened by Locke (1632–1704), by whom modern psychology texts are more influenced than most readers of them suspect. Locke's problem and its origin are thus briefly put by himself in his "Epistle to the Reader and Introduction" of his *Essay (158)*: "Were it fit to trouble thee with the history of this Essay I should tell thee, that five or six friends, meeting at my chamber, and discoursing on a subject very remote from this, found themselves quickly at a stand by the difficulties that arose on every side. After we had awhile puzzled ourselves without coming any nearer a resolution of those doubts which perplexed us, it came to my thoughts, that we took a wrong course; and that, before we set ourselves upon inquiries of that nature, it was necessary to examine our own abilities, and see what objects our understandings were or were not fitted to deal with. This I proposed to the company, who all readily assented; and therefore it was agreed, that this should be our first inquiry." "This, therefore, being my purpose, to inquire into the original, certainty, and extent of human knowledge, together with the grounds and degrees of belief, opinion, and assent, I shall not at present meddle with the physical consideration of the mind, or trouble myself to examine wherein its essence consists, or by what motions of our spirits, or alterations of our bodies, we came to have any sensations by our organs, or any ideas in our understandings; and whether those ideas do, in their formation, any or all of them, depend on matter or no; these are speculations which, however curious or entertaining, I shall decline, as lying out of my way in the design I now am upon." His problem, then, deals with knowledge primarily; but as the *Essay* became very influential, it not only became a text for study but it became the chief authority upon which were based numerous texts and courses of study in both Europe and America; and it is largely through the empirical movement into which Locke threw the weight of his influence, that sensations have been so heavily stressed in psychology.

LOCKE REACTS AGAINST THE DOCTRINE OF INNATE IDEAS

Locke, on empirical grounds, took the position first of all that we have no innate ideas, but that the mind begins a *tabula rasa* and must gain all its knowledge through the senses and through "the perception of the operations of our own minds within us, as it [the understanding] is employed about the ideas it has got" (*181*, page 235). This perception of one's own mental operations Locke called "reflection." The argument for certain "innate ideas," that they are universal among mankind, he meets upon purely empirical grounds by asserting that if they are innate they should appear "fairest and clearest in the minds of children, idiots, savages, and illiterate people who are of all the least corrupted by custom or borrowed opinions." But just here he does not find these alleged innate ideas.

He then proceeds to show in great detail just how our ideas, knowledge, beliefs, etc., actually originate. Into these details we cannot enter. The feelings receive but little attention, and it is obvious that they play a secondary rôle for Locke. He rejects the idea of faculties, but calls the understanding and the will "powers or abilities of the mind."

He, however, pointed out the futility of attempting to explain the supposed freedom of the will by the assumption of a faculty of volition. For him this would be similar to explaining singing by ascribing it to a vocal faculty. Will for Locke was not a spontaneous force. He tried to substitute the term "power" (in the sense of ability) for "faculty," but with poor success, and some of his writings have even given encouragement to the idea that training of a mental power or function in a certain way would give it general efficiency — the doctrine of formal discipline (*147*, pages 58 ff., and *159*).

THE ELEVATION OF THE UNDERSTANDING

"Since it is the *understanding* that sets man above the rest of sensible beings, and gives him all the advantages and dominion which he has over them, it is certainly a subject, even for its nobleness, worth our labor to inquire into" (Book 1, Chapter 1). We cannot follow up the various developments of Locke's psychology, but must merely emphasize the well-known fact, that down to the time of the biological movement represented in Darwin great stress was laid on "intellectual faculties," with but scant recognition of individual differences. In these developments the "association of ideas," a term that originated with Locke, came to play a leading rôle.

FACULTY PSYCHOLOGY AND ITS DISSOLUTION

In the meantime there had developed in continental Europe after Leibnitz a movement headed by Christian von Wolff (1679–1754) which has been called faculty psychology, because it was concerned chiefly with classifying the "faculties of the soul." For Wolff "soul is not body nor an attribute communicated to the body." It is a simple substance endowed with certain faculties or "potencies of action." "The essence of the soul consists in its power of re-presenting the universe, which power is materially limited by its location in an organic body in the universe, and formally limited by the constitution of the sensory organs" (*181*, page 231), for its knowledge of the world is dependent upon the excitation of the senses.

The faculty psychology was an attempt to analyze conscious experiences and then to find the elementary powers of which they were manifestations. To ascribe any mental activity to a faculty was, for Wolff and his followers, to explain it.

We need not enumerate the various faculties of this school, but must point out that any ascription of a mental process to a faculty or power is itself an obstacle to its analysis and further understanding, for the mere giving of a name to it usually satisfies our curiosity and saves us from further effort. The tendency thus to avoid explanation of mental processes is even yet very noticeable in current psychology textbooks. Beneke (1798–1854) tended to counteract faculty psychology by reducing the faculties to a practically infinite number of elementary processes, operating in all conceivable relationships and degrees (*11*, Chapter 2). "Observation teaches us that every degree of any one of these fundamental conditions can occur together with any degree of the others" (*181*, page 424).

Phrenology was an empirical attempt, based on faculty psychology, to locate in the different parts of the brain the various mental faculties and powers; but it was found to have very little scientific basis in its finer details, and is now wholly discredited by reliable scientists.

These early views of our intellectual functions, ascribing to them as a rule an other-worldness and a spontaneity or power not accounted for by ordinary life processes as affected by external stimulation, have had a great influence on modern conceptions of intelligence. Many persons today regard mind as some sort of arbitrary force which is not only not measurable, but which is so variable in any given individual that mental measurement at any one moment would throw either no light at all or only very little light at best on the behavior possibilities of that individual at subsequent periods.

Such people, in other words, do not see how human behavior can be predictable, since it depends on the "will." With a thing that is arbitrary and self-moved in the sense that it is not conditioned by anything else in the universe, science can of course do nothing. In this view, still strongly represented in the popular mind, man is not really a part of the natural world, but an outsider; he comes endowed with a free will, with which he can at his own choice do good or evil. In times when such views prevailed among leaders man was cruel to the unfortunate victims of his passions and his selfish impulses. He regarded those who departed from the paths of rectitude as voluntarily choosing evil, and so he was ready to see them condemned to endless retributive punishment.

In such an age scientific methods of studying human behavior could obviously be little appreciated. Any tendencies to depart from such views of arbitrariness in mental functions would doubtless be significant of scientific progress, even though it would take a long time for the appreciation of experimental studies and for the development of reliable tests of intelligence. We shall in the next chapter turn our attention to a tendency that early developed in psychology and counteracted the views which would make man's mental life a play of arbitrary forces.

EXERCISES

1. Examine a number of texts in psychology and education for evidences of dualism. Organize your results carefully in the form of a paper. Is dualism necessary or even helpful to religion? to science? to education? Specify.

2. Make a list of all the faculties you can find assumed or implied in current psychologies and educational books. Is faculty psychology necessarily dualistic? Why?

3. What is right and what is wrong apparently in the doctrine of innate ideas criticized by Locke? What criticisms have you to offer against Locke's view?

CHAPTER FOUR

The Effects of Associationism on Primitive Conceptions of Intelligence

WE have seen that our conceptions of intelligence have come down from early views of the soul as a spontaneous and unconditioned force; that the recognition of certain higher and lower mental processes led to assumptions of different souls and faculties; and that in modern times some of these processes were explained on purely mechanical principles while others continued, though not uninterruptedly, to be thought of as more or less distinct from material or physiological operations and as somehow possessing powers of their own. Examples of such mental powers or faculties are "the understanding," reason, consciousness, attention, constructive imagination, and will, several of which may still be found treated as powers in certain of our modern texts.

THE LIMITATION OF "FREE" FACULTIES WAS EARLY RECOGNIZED

Difficulties early arose with the conception of arbitrary powers ascribed to the soul and with certain faculties. Probably every careful observer has noticed that what we feel, think, and do at any time has a tendency to influence our later feelings, thoughts, and actions, and that our lives are affected materially by our associations and physical surroundings. We have already noted that Plato recognized in dreams not only the impulsions of desires but also of the effects of "strong motions" surviving from the stimuli of the previous day. He also points out in *Phædo*, though somewhat casually, the effects of past experiences on our thoughts. The knowledge of a lyre is not the same as that of a man, "and yet what is the feeling of lovers when they recognize a lyre, or a garment, or anything else that the beloved has been in the habit of using? Do not they, from knowing the lyre, form in the mind's eye an image of the youth to whom the lyre belongs? And this is recollection. In like manner any one who sees Simmias may remember Cebes; and there are endless examples of the same thing . . . and from the picture of Simmias, you may be led to remember Cebes. . . . Or you may be led to a recollection of Simmias himself. . . . And in all these cases the recollection may be derived from things either like or unlike. . . . When we perceive something, either by the help of sight, or hearing, or some other sense, from that perception we are able to obtain a notion of some other thing like or unlike which is associated with it but has been forgotten" (*175*, pages 73–76). It is clear that these association processes would, if carried very far, limit considerably the freedom of the soul.

This natural sequence of our thoughts did not escape the attention of Aristotle, who recognized that we recall past experiences on the basis of association. He said that because of the fact that one experience naturally succeeds another, when we try to recollect something "we keep stimulating certain earlier experiences until we have stimulated the one which the one in question is wont to succeed" (*228*, pages 25 f.). In this way both with and without effort we call up past experiences. In this sequence of thought he recognizes both a necessary and a habitual connection, the latter greatly predominating. The principles of contiguity, similarity, and contrast, as stated in present-day texts, were clearly recognized by him.

Various other writers before Descartes also recognized association either theoretically or practically, as in the preparation of speeches. Klemm says that when we remember that

up to the time of Augustus (63 B.C.–14 A.D.) "no public
speaker would dare to appear in public with even the scantiest
notes, the interest in mnemotechnical devices is easily intel-
ligible." Mental pictures were recommended in the time
of Cicero as aids to memory. In order to have at one's
command large masses of ideas, one must localize them,
say in a given city, and within the city in different buildings,
chambers, etc. (*147*, page 91). Thus the soul is forced to
use mechanism to accomplish its objects, but this use of
mechanical means was not always a hindrance to the soul,
for, as James has pointed out, habits may be made our serv-
ants instead of our masters. Thus to Maximus of Tyre
(2d century A.D.), who enumerated the different types of association, the following sentence is ascribed: "As a motion
imparted to one end of a cord traverses the whole length of
the cord, so the reason requires only a slight impulse in
order to recall whole trains of ideas" (*147*, page 90; *186*,
page 310).

LIMITATIONS IMPOSED BY THE "PASSIONS"

For the Stoics, as for Aristotle, reason was a controlling
influence in the world and soul was the active principle in
all animate creatures. Soul is the subtlest form of substance,
and "pervades the whole organism of the creature just as
reason pervades the universe. . . . Mental activity as it is
found in men is a developed and specialized form of the universal reason" (*74*, page 164). The passions or emotions
gave some degree of trouble. For Zeno (cir. 490–430) emotions seem to have been regarded as an irrational or at least
unnatural movement of the soul, an excess impulse; but as
the individual attains a higher degree of reason these obscure
inclinations or subconscious workings of reason become more
explicit, and conscious ends of action are adopted. For later
Stoics, however, the passions are diseases of reason (*74*,

pages 175 f.). They also seem to have recognized the limiting effects of past experiences on the influence of the soul.

EARLY MECHANISTIC VIEWS OF BEHAVIOR

Jean Buridan (1297–1358), the French rationalist who studied under William of Occam, recognized the mechanistic factors in behavior to the extent that he has been called the Herbartian among the Scholastics. He denied the freedom of the will as a special power in addition to the intellect; the two are but activities of the soul. After a judgment as to an object or situation there follows pleasure or displeasure, which stimulates the will. The only "freedom" that he admits is a certain power of the intellect, or of the will, to keep motives before the intellect long enough for it to get a view of the circumstances — to apprehend the situation. The will is entirely dependent on this view. The comparison of the will, tied between two equally balanced motives, to a donkey dying of hunger between two equidistant bundles of hay of equal size, ascribed to him, is probably an invention of his opponents in ridicule of his determinism. It is not found in his works (*81*, and *147*, page 365).

DESCARTES FORCED TO A DUALISTIC EXPLANATION
OF BEHAVIOR

Descartes, though emphasizing the freedom and spontaneity of the soul, resorted to a very mechanical illustration of how it probably affects and controls action in man. "It is, also, necessary to know that, although the soul is joined to the entire body, there is, nevertheless, a certain part of the body in which it exercises its functions more particularly than in all the rest; and it is commonly thought that this part is the brain, or, perhaps, the heart: the brain, because to it the organs of sense are related; and the heart, because it is as if there the passions are felt. But, after careful ex-

amination, it seems to me quite evident that the part of the
body in which the soul immediately exercises its functions
is neither the heart, nor even the brain as a whole, but solely
the most interior part of it, which is a certain very small
gland [the pineal gland], situated in the middle of its substance, and so suspended above the passage by which the
spirits of its anterior cavities communicate with those of
the posterior, that the slightest motions in it may greatly
affect the course of these spirits, and, reciprocally, that the
slightest change which takes place in the course of the spirits
may greatly affect the motions of this gland" (*181*, pages 173
f.).   This seat of operation of the soul was chosen by him
because "other parts of the brain are all double," and there
must necessarily be some place where the two images from
the eyes or the two impressions from the ears "may unite
in one before they reach the mind, in order that they may
not present to it two objects in place of one"; also because
only at this point is there, he supposed, a confluence "of the
spirits which fill the cavities of the brain."

The will has the actions "absolutely in its power" and to
effect any action needs only incline the gland so as to bring
this about.   But motions of the spirits coming from the body
or from strong external excitations may affect the gland and
thus bring about the disturbances known to Descartes
as passions, nearly the same as is implied in our word
"emotions."

BEGINNINGS OF ASSOCIATIONISM

Descartes also noted that the mind may be aided by habits.
Thus when it wills to recall anything, "this volition causes
the gland, by inclining successively to different sides, to im-
pel the spirits toward different parts of the brain until they
come upon that where the traces are left of the thing it wills
to remember; for these traces are due to nothing else than

the circumstance that the pores of the brain, through which the spirits have already taken their course, on presentation of that object, have thereby acquired a greater facility than the rest to be opened again in the same way by the spirits which come to them; so that these spirits coming upon these pores, enter therein more readily than into the others, by which means they excite a particular motion in the gland, which represents to the mind the same object, and causes it to recognize that it is that which it willed to remember" (*181*, pages 177 f.). In the *Traité de l'homme* he makes a similar statement, and then continues: "And also it must be noticed that if we open only certain ones . . . this of itself may be the cause of others . . . reopening also at the same time, especially if they had all been opened together several times and had not been used to being so one without the others. This shows how the recollection of one thing may be excited by that of another which was formerly impressed upon the memory at the same time as it" (*228*, page 32). Warren points out that Descartes held also that an experience will call up another that partly resembles it, and that he compares the effect of past experience on the brain with that seen on paper or cloth which has once been folded and is therefore more fit to be folded in the same place again. Descartes thus clearly recognizes associative connections between brain processes themselves rather than merely between mental experiences.

For Hobbes, as we have seen, all knowledge comes from sensory experiences. "There is no conception in a man's mind which hath not first, totally or by parts, been begotten upon the organs of sense" (*130*, Chapter 1). Thus all imaginations and even dreams are limited. "Whatever we imagine is *finite*," the infinite being incomprehensible (Chapter 3). Moreover, past experiences can give us no absolute guarantee of future happenings; "for though a man has always

seen the day and night to follow one another hitherto; yet
can he not thence conclude they shall do so, or that they have
done so eternally: *experience concludeth nothing universally*"
(*131*, Chapter 4, and *181*, page 159).

Though thus thoroughly empirical, he did not come upon
the full significance of association as a principle in the control
of our experiences, directive "cognitive powers" being still
a good deal in evidence, even though based, as to content,
on sensations. In his dealing with trains of imagination we
find, however, clear recognition of both contiguity and similarity association, the first being "*unguided, without design,*
and inconstant; wherein there is no passionate thought to
govern and direct" the thoughts or ideas that follow. So
"the thoughts are said to wander, and seem impertinent one
to another, as in a dream. . . . And yet in this wild ranging of the mind, a man may oftimes perceive the way of it,
and the dependence of one thought upon another." . . .
"The second is more constant, as being *regulated* by some
desire and design. . . . From desire, ariseth the thought
of some means we have seen produce the like of that which we
aim at; and from the thought of that, the thought of means
to that means; and so continually till we come to some beginning within our own power." But such trains of thought
have their physical basis, and one's "next thought after [any
one] is not altogether so casual as it seems to be. . . .
All fancies are motions within us, relics of those made in the
sense; and those motions that immediately succeeded one
another in the sense continue also together after sense;
insomuch that the former coming again to take place and be
predominant, the latter followeth, by coherence of the matter
moved, in such a manner as water upon a plane table is
drawn which way any one part of it is guided by the finger"
(*130*, Chapter 3). If he had been entirely consistent he
would not have stopped, after such a beginning, until he had

involved all the mental processes; but this was too great a step to be taken at once.

Locke did not recognize association as an important principle in the succession of ideas, even though we owe to him the expression, "the association of ideas." This is probably due to his use of reflection, reason, etc., as though they were arbitrary forces which act upon the ideas, once the latter have been acquired. He recognized "a natural correspondence and connection" among ideas, which "it is the office and excellency of our reason to trace," and also "another connection of ideas wholly owing to chance or custom; ideas that in themselves are not at all of kin, come to be so united in some men's minds that it is very hard to separate them; they always keep in company, and the one no sooner at any time comes into the understanding but its associate appears with it." These connections of ideas which are not of kin, may originally be due either to will or to chance, so that individuals in time become very different. He then makes a statement, now classic, as to the cause of such connections: "Custom settles habits of thinking in the understanding, as well as of determining in the will, and of motions in the body; all which seem to be but trains of motion in the animal spirits, which, once set a-going, continue in the same steps they have been used to, which, by often treading, are worn into a smooth path, and the motion in it becomes easy, and as it were natural" (*158*, Chapter 33). Unfortunately he does not carry out far the implications of this view. This was left for his successors, Hume and Hartley, especially the latter.

Berkeley (1685–1753), Bishop of Cloyne, whom we must mention before passing to Hume, used the term "suggestion" instead of "association." In his well-known *Essay towards a New Theory of Vision* (*12*) he held that the distance of objects cannot be and is not directly perceived, but "is suggested to the mind by the mediation of some other idea, which is itself perceived in the act of seeing." An example of what he means may clarify his conception. Suppose you see a tree in the distance. Now what you really see is not directly *distance* but a "visible appearance" or an object of a certain magnitude, a certain "confusion or distinctness," a certain intensity of colors, of brightness differences, etc., and you notice that some other objects intervening cover part of the tree or obstruct your vision of it while farther objects are covered in part by the tree; moreover, you have certain strains in the muscles of accommodation and of convergence (of which you may easily become conscious by attention to them). So there are various intervening "ideas" (sensations and images) which vary in a number of respects with the distance of the object seen. These "suggest" to you immediately how far the tree is away; that is, they suggest that after having walked, say, so many steps and moved around certain intervening objects you can receive *touch experiences* of, or contact with, the tree. Distance for Berkeley is really only the amount of such intervening experiences that will take place before you can touch or handle the object perceived. "I believe," he says, "whoever will look narrowly into his own thoughts [i.e., carefully analyze his own experiences], and examine what he means by saying he sees this or that thing at a distance, will agree with me, that what he sees only *suggests* to his understanding that, after having passed a certain distance, *to be measured by the motion of his body, which is perceivable by touch*, he shall come to perceive such and such tangible ideas, which have been usually connected with such and such visible ideas" (*181*, page 265).

Berkeley (*13*) denies the existence of external objects as things other than what we experience them to be, and he attributes these experiences directly to Deity; but for him suggestion, or habit connections among experiences, plays a large rôle. There is no *necessary connection* between these "ideas" and the visible objects they suggest. "All which visible objects are only in the mind; nor do they suggest aught external, whether distance or magnitude, otherwise than by habitual connection, as words do things" (*181*, page 271).

EXPLANATIONS OF BEHAVIOR BY THE ASSUMPTION OF
FACULTIES IS CHALLENGED BY HUME

Berkeley's position had its effect on Hume (1711–1776), who carried it out further and greatly influenced the thought of his time. For Hume (*136*) all causality becomes only a succession of contiguous events, that which we call the cause always going before the effect. "Having thus discovered or supposed the two relations of *contiguity* and *succession* to be essential to causes and effects, I find I am stopt short, and can proceed no farther in considering any single instance of cause and effect" (*181*, page 301). It is obvious that this doctrine if applied rigorously to mental operations would do away with spontaneous faculties and original powers of the soul, as well as raise serious problems in philosophy which lie outside our present interest. As to mental powers, Hume says in another connection (*137*): "It may be said that we are every moment conscious of internal power; while we feel that, by the simple command of our will, we can move the organs of our body, or direct the faculties of our mind. An act of volition produces motion in our limbs, or raises a new idea in our imagination. This influence of the will we know by consciousness. Hence we acquire the idea of power or energy; and are certain, that we ourselves and all other intelligent beings are possessed of power. . . . We shall proceed to examine this pretension. . . . The motion of our body follows upon the command of our will. Of this we are every moment conscious," and in the preceding sentence, here omitted, he admits this command of the will to be a fact. "But the means by which it is effected; the energy by which the will performs so extraordinary an operation; of this we are so far from being immediately conscious, that it must forever escape our most diligent enquiry" (*180*, page 330).

He points out that we cannot move all the organs of the body in this way; e.g., the tongue and fingers are thus controlled but not the heart and liver. Moreover, anatomy shows "that the immediate object of power in voluntary motion, is not the member itself which is moved, but certain muscles, and nerves, and animal spirits, and, perhaps, something still more minute and more unknown" (*180*, page 331). Thus we are ignorant both of the means of control and of any controlling agency. And if the soul is supposed to produce this power of will we are reminded that this "is a real creation; a production of something out of nothing; which implies a power so great, that it may be seen, at first sight, beyond the reach of any being less than the infinite. At least it must be owned, that such a power is not felt, nor known, nor even conceivable by the mind." Moreover, Hume points out that this "self-command is very different at different times. A man in health possesses more of it than one languishing with sickness. We are more masters of our thought in the morning than in the evening; fasting, than after a full meal. Can we give any reason for these variations, except experience? Where then is the power, of which we pretend to be conscious? Is there not here, either in a spiritual or material substance, or both, some secret mechanism or structure of parts, upon which the effect depends?" (*180*, page 333). Here is a remarkable passage in which Hume suggests rather clearly a mechanistic basis even of acts of will.

In the *Treatise* where he is discussing "the connection or association of ideas" he comes definitely to some controlling principle even in as free a thing as the imagination. "As all simple ideas may be separated by the imagination, and may be united again in what form it pleases, nothing would be more unaccountable than the operations of that faculty, were it not guided by some universal principles, which render it, in some measure, uniform with itself in all times and places. Were ideas entirely loose and unconnected, chance alone would join them; and 'tis impossible the same simple ideas should fall regularly into complex ones (as they commonly do) without some bond of union among them, some associating quality, by which one idea naturally introduces another. This uniting principle among ideas is not to be considered as an inseparable connection; for that has been already excluded from the imagination: nor yet are we to conclude, that without it the mind cannot join two ideas; for nothing is more free than that faculty: [1] but we are only to regard it as a gentle force which commonly prevails. . . . The qualities, from which this association arises, and by which the mind is after this manner conveyed from one idea to another, are three; viz., *Resemblance, Contiguity* in time or place, and *Cause* and *Effect*" [2] (*181*, pages 287 f.).

Though usually concerned only with connections among ideas, Hume says also in the *Treatise*, "there is an attraction or association among impressions as well as among ideas; though with this remarkable difference, that ideas are associated by resemblance, contiguity, and causation, and impressions only by resemblance" (*228*, page 45).

[1] The passage quoted above from *The Enquiry*, which was published some years after this sentence appeared, is probably not considered a contradiction to this statement, for there he wrote also: "Nothing is more free than the imagination of man; and though it cannot exceed that original stock of ideas furnished by the internal and external senses, it has unlimited power of mixing, compounding, separating, and dividing these ideas." Quoted by Warren, *op. cit.*, page 45.

[2] Hume seems to have been ignorant of Aristotle's classification of the laws of association.

ASSOCIATION SUGGESTED AS A UNIVERSAL PRINCIPLE SIMILAR
TO ATTRACTION

After some paragraphs of elaboration on these laws he makes this general statement as to the importance of association in the mental life : "These are therefore the principles of union or cohesion among our simple ideas, and in the imagination [they] supply the place of that inseparable connection, by which they [the ideas] are united in our memory. Here is a kind of *attraction*, which in the mental world will be found to have as extraordinary effects as in the natural, and to show itself in as many and as various forms. Its effects are everywhere conspicuous ; but as to its causes, they are mostly unknown, and must be resolved into *original* qualities of human nåture, which I pretend not to explain" (*181*, pages 289 f.).

Thus Hume put up squarely the proposition of explaining mental processes in terms of certain laws of connection between their different units, rather than in terms of souls or faculties or mental powers, which as explanatory means he rejects. His service in thus putting psychology into the same position in this respect as the physical sciences is doubtless very great, even though he did not introduce the experimental method. If this view is carried out to its logical implications, the spontaneity of the soul and of mental faculties as arbitrary, indeterminate powers, affecting behavior and thought, comes to an end, so far as empirical science is concerned, and the way is open to observation and experiment. It was the work of Hartley to carry out this position further, but the day of experimental psychology was yet not so near.

HARTLEY A THOROUGHGOING ASSOCIATIONIST

In the preface of *Observations on Man*, published in 1749, we find that Hume was not the one who suggested the problem of the importance of association in psychology to Hartley, but that the same empirical tendency influenced both these writers. In the preface of this work Hartley says: "About eighteen years ago [1731, or eight years before the *Treatise* appeared] I was informed that the Reverend Mr. Gay, then living, asserted the possibility of deducing all our intellectual pleasures and pains from association. This put me upon considering the power of association."[1] Gay in turn acknowledges his indebtedness to Newton and to Locke for the doctrines of vibration and association, respectively.

BEHAVIOR EXPLAINED ON GROSSLY MECHANICAL PRINCIPLES

Hartley is the first writer to attempt an explanation of all forms of mental activity on the basis of association — that is, on a mechanistic basis (*127*). He accepts the Newtonian principle of molecular vibration, and applies it to the physiological processes, which he believed are subject to investigation "in the same manner as the other parts of the external material world." Thus the external vibrations set in motion the "white medullary substance of the brain," with which sensations and ideas, the elements of the mental life, are immediately associated, "in other words, whatever changes are made, corresponding changes are made in our ideas; and vice versa."[2] The sensations, resulting from vibrations of the medullary substance of the brain, remain in the mind a short time after the sensible objects exciting the nerves are removed; moreover, sensations which have been often re-

[1] Hartley, David, *Observations on Man*, etc., 1749, preface. Quoted from Rand, *The Classical Psychologists*, page 313, who asserts that the internal evidence also shows that the anonymous tract, *An Inquiry into the Origin of Human Appetites and Affections, Showing How Each Arises from Association*, 1747, was written by Gay.

[2] *Observations on Man*, Chapter 1, Section 1, Prop. 2. His method is to state propositions, as did Spinoza, and then to give evidence for each one immediately after the statement. All the propositions were printed in italics.

peated leave certain vestiges, types, or images of themselves, which he calls simple ideas of sensations (Props. 3 and 8). Of these ideas the most vivid are those whose corresponding sensations were most vividly or perfectly impressed.

Sensations, he held, may be associated together either when their impressions are made in the same instant of time (synchronous association) or in immediately successive instants (successive association). Now, any *sensations* may, by occurring together a sufficient number of times, become so closely associated that the impression of any one sensation alone is able to excite in the mind the *ideas* which have habitually followed or accompanied it; likewise grosser external *vibrations* may revive the *miniature vibrations* which immediately condition sensations. Thus an external object may arouse any succession of ideas which have been previously associated with it, the succession aroused depending on such factors as vividness, or intensity, and frequency of association. The influence of association therefore becomes very great, and "all that has been delivered by the ancients and moderns, concerning the power of habit, custom, example, education, authority, party-prejudice, the manner of learning the manual and liberal arts, etc., goes upon this doctrine as its foundation, and may be considered as the detail of it, in various circumstances."[1] But associations can go only forward, not in the reverse order of their original occurrence.

On these principles Hartley proceeds to show in detail how simple ideas run into higher complex mental processes.

THE QUESTION OF MORAL FREEDOM

"One of the principal objections to the opinion of mechanism," says Hartley, "is that deduced from the existence of the moral sense." He also recognizes the difficulty regarding freedom. "But it appears [from his own account given

[1] From discussion of Prop. 10.

previous to this statement] . . . that God has so formed the world, and perhaps (with reverence be it spoken) was obliged by his moral perfections so to form it, as that virtue must have amiable and pleasing ideas affixed to it; vice, odious ones. The moral sense is therefore generated necessarily and mechanically" (*127*, page 504). Pleasure and pain are thus innately provided for as motives to action, and the foundation for will, based on association, is laid. Hartley believed that man's conduct is little affected by this mechanistic view; "that the affections of gratitude and resentment, which are intimately connected with the moral sense, remain notwithstanding the doctrine of mechanism." "When a person first changes his opinion from free-will to mechanism, or more properly first sees part of the mechanism of the mind, and believes the rest from analogy, he is just as much affected by his wonted pleasures and pains, hopes and fears, as before, by the moral and religious ones, as by others" (page 505). Indeed, Hartley's own life is an example of his doctrine; he was active in his profession as a physician and has been described as "a noble and philanthropic man." Part II of his *Observations on Man* is concerned with ethics and theology.

FACULTIES AS ARBITRARY POWERS RULED OUT

Thus Hartley builds up an extremely mechanical view of the individual as a passive agent whose conduct is determined by the order and intensity of stimulation of external objects. He does not recognize the law of association by similarity, but bases all on contiguity. It is but a natural consequence of this that he should so completely neglect the treatment of the reconstructive process called "reasoning." This seriously limits his psychology, and may be said to be a characteristic limitation of associationism. Milder associationists have usually introduced, explicitly or otherwise, certain faculties, such as reason or intelligence or a "spiritual force" to supplement the principles of association. Hartley, though a self-acknowledged disciple of Locke, consistently rejected Locke's "reflection" as a source of ideas, this being in his own words "an unknown quantity" with which nothing can be done.[1] While he recognizes in his Introduction the "faculties" of memory, imagination or fancy, understanding, affectation, and will, these are really only conscious aspects of processes driven by stimuli and association, not forces. Hartley distinguishes between automatic acts, so called "from their resemblance to the motions of *automata*, or machines, whose principle of motion is within themselves," and voluntary acts, "which arise from ideas and affectations, and which therefore are referred to the mind." It is the state of mind immediately preceding these voluntary actions that he calls will, and this state is for him determined from sense impressions by the laws of association.

TWO CONDITIONS DETERMINING BEHAVIOR ACCORDING
TO HARTLEY

Our actions are thus determined by two general conditions : (1) heredity or innate structure, conditioning more directly the automatic acts, and, as we have seen, tendencies to feel actions leading to favorable results as pleasant, and those leading to harmful results as unpleasant or painful, and (2) impressions by, or stimulations of, things in the external world, their intensity and their frequency of stimulation being most important. Will and our deliberately chosen acts are but natural outcomes of these conditions, and the faculties mentioned above seem to be only the subjective aspects of the various "motions" thus brought about. This

---

[1] Peter Browne, taking literally the simile of the *tabula rasa*, had already rejected Locke's reflection as a source of ideas, and Condillac, soon after Hartley, also rejected it. See Dessoir, *op. cit.*, page 117.

view resembles closely the conceptions of certain modern authorities, and it is obviously favorable to intelligence testing if hereditary differences are stressed.

Hartley did not work out causal relationships between body and mind but rested his views on the simple assumption that vibrations of the "white medullary substance of the brain" is immediately and directly accompanied by corresponding states of consciousness. He asserted explicitly at the end of the first volume that his mechanistic view did not prejudice one way or the other the question of the survival of personal consciousness after death.

LATER DEVELOPMENTS IN ASSOCIATIONISM

The lack of space forbids us to follow out further the various lines of later development in associationism as a mechanistic interpretation of our mental processes and our behavior. We can only refer the reader to this interesting development in psychology,[1] and say that in James Mill (1773–1836) associationism reached its most extreme statement. He attempted to analyze the complex forms of mental life into their ultimate constituents (ideas derived at first from sensations) and then to show how by the laws of synchronous and successive association by contiguity all the complex forms might result. Once he is beyond the sensations, he derives very little aid from physiology but gives his psychology chiefly a logical basis. He accepted, as did Hartley, pleasurable and painful sensations, and he emphasized frequency or repetition, vividness, and recency as the important

---

[1] See especially the writings of Joseph Priestley (1733–1804), Thomas Brown (1778–1820), James and J. S. Mill (1806–1873), Étienne Bonnet de Condillac (1715–1780), Julien Offray de La Mattrie (1709–1751), Charles Bonnet (1720–1793), Pierre Jean Georges Cabanis (1757–1808), Johan Friedrich Herbart (1776–1841), Alexander Bain (1818–1903), William James (1842–1910). Warren's *A History of the Association Psychology* gives an account of the development and limitations of associationism.

factors in association. Thus for him the order and intensity of stimulation, rather than the general consistency of the external and the internal or bodily conditions, determine conduct. The result was that associationism gave a too passive, receptive, and mechanical view of the individual to secure the general assent of psychologists, a view that has consequently undergone numerous modifications. The general conception of association is, however, still utilized extensively in current psychological literature, and attempts to revive this doctrine in a thoroughly physiological setting have been made.

BIOLOGICAL FACTORS AND INDIVIDUAL DIFFERENCES
NEGLECTED

Mill's work was more influential than Hartley's. His famous *Analysis of the Phenomena of the Human Mind* (1829) occupies a place of very great importance in the history of psychology, and was edited and annotated by his son, John Stuart Mill, together with Alexander Bain and others, in 1869. The older Mill's views were subjected to important modifications by these later writers and they were given broad applications to social and economic problems, particularly in the utilitarian doctrine of John Stuart Mill and his followers.

The associationism of James Mill was, however, inclined to neglect innate factors and therefore individual differences, and it was essentially a logical and not an empirical study of the intelligence of man. From such an approach little could be expected in the way of tests of the larger human traits and abilities. From associationism little more could be looked for in the way of tests than attempts to measure the senses of different individuals — the supposed avenues of their knowledge and motives to action — and possibly the speed of various associative processes, even though this philosophy contributed very much to the understanding of certain aspects of the operations of our minds. Associationism is closely connected with the sensory experimental psychology that was early developed in Germany under the influence of men like Weber (1795–1878), Fechner (1801–1887), Helmholtz (1821–1894), and Wundt (1832–1921), whose works have contributed very little to intelligence testing as now understood. Galton was also much influenced by the associationist philosophy, but he at the same time represents a marked biological interest then taking hold of the leaders of scientific thought in England. It was this combination of intellectual influences, as we shall see in the chapter that follows, which was to bring about the beginnings of intelligence testing.

EXERCISES

1. What are some defects in the associationist's view of intelligence?

2. What inconsistencies do you find in James's chapter on Association? Compare his view of freedom expressed here with that implied by him in the quotation referred to in Question 3, Chapter 1.

3. Make in writing a brief summary of James Mill's association doctrine, and see what evidence you can find of his recognition of individual differences. Is his point of view chiefly logical or biological? Give evidence.

4. Try to arrange experimentally a situation to test the view of the associationists that frequency, recency, and vividness determine the course of our thoughts. Consider also the effects of hunger, fatigue, and other bodily conditions and emotions.

CHAPTER FIVE

EARLY TESTS OF INTELLIGENCE

THE INFLUENCE OF BIOLOGY ON ASSOCIATIONISM

ONE of the defects of the association movement in early psychology was its emphasis on ideas as units of the complex mental operations. While it displaced souls and faculties, in the form of original forces, it became so much occupied with ideas, which came to be considered somewhat as discrete entities, that the individual tended to sink into the background. It also — more in Mill's than in Hartley's work — tended to emphasize sensations to the exclusion of innate reaction tendencies; so while in one sense psychology was forced from the useless enumeration of faculties, it nevertheless did not become emancipated from merely logical analysis, as distinct from observation and experiment.

Bain, who was really the last of the so-called pure associationists, grounded his psychology on a physiology that was a great advance over that of the early associationists, and he emphasized individual differences in general retentiveness "specific to each person," in bodily strength, in "spontaneity or the active temperament," in muscular delicacy, and in the sort of constructiveness that employs similarity association. But he was little influenced by the evolutionary movement and gave scant attention to empirical methods of investigation, although numerous expressions of this sort might well have given encouragement to experimentation and testing: "We find a great inequality in the progress of learners placed almost exactly in the same circumstances. Sometimes the difference refers only to single departments, as mechanical art, music, or language; it is then referable to special and local endowments, as muscular sensibility, the musical ear, and so forth. Often, however, the superiority of individuals is seen in acquirement as a whole, in which

form it is better regarded as a general power of retentiveness "
(*8*, Chapter 1, III). But these suggestions as to the measurable differences in individuals were not yet put to the test
of experimental methods, and Bain's important books, the
one from which we have quoted and the second volume, *The
Emotions and the Will*, published four years later, in 1859, soon
became overshadowed by the evolutionary hypothesis of
Darwin, published in the same year as the second volume.
While later revisions show the effect of the biological movement, Bain clearly belongs to the preëvolutionary period.

The general effect of the subsequent developments in the
biological sciences has undoubtedly been to operate against
the association conception of ideas and to place the emphasis
on the individual as a unit. One of the chief influences
toward this fortunate change of emphasis was doubtless the
studies of animal behavior, studies beginning to take a
definitely experimental turn just shortly before the close of
the last century. In these studies it early became evident
that the principles of the associationists were inadequate to
account for the elimination of erroneous movements in
learning processes, and that the entire animal was the real
unit, whatever differentiations in particular kinds of responses
it manifested. But while these were mainly studies in learning, investigations along another line had for some time been
in progress.

GALTON'S STUDIES OF INDIVIDUAL DIFFERENCES

The genius of Francis Galton (1822–1911) was occupied
largely with investigations of individual differences. In
1869 he published his well-known *Hereditary Genius;* and
his *Inquiries into Human Faculty*, which brought together
in a condensed and reorganized form numerous memoirs
published before that date, appeared in 1883. In the Introduction of this latter book he says : "My general object has

been to take note of the varied hereditary faculties of different men, and of the great differences in different families and races, to learn how far history may have shown the practicability of supplanting inefficient human stock by better strains, and to consider whether it might not be our duty to do so by such efforts as may be reasonable, thus exerting ourselves to further the ends of evolution more rapidly and with less distress than if events were left to their own course." This general plan of his work as outlined by himself shows how thoroughly the new developments in biological evolution had gripped him. But the influence of the older pre-evolutionary psychology of sensations and ideas continued to be very great for some decades, and even Galton, with so thoroughly biological interests, shows unmistakably the effect of it. But his originality in the attack on the larger human nature problems is nevertheless refreshing. "The instincts and faculties of different men and races," he continues, "differ in a variety of ways almost as profoundly as those of animals in different cages of the zoölogical gardens; and however diverse and antagonistic they are each may be good of its kind."

His broad interest in animals and in the development of human races gave him, fortunately, an objective point of view which was favorable to the measurement of their differences, and while his studies of the physical features of man were but a means to his main purpose, they nevertheless served to compel objective, scientific methods. He says: "It is with the innate moral and intellectual faculties that this book is chiefly concerned, but they are so closely bound up with the physical ones that these must be considered as well" (*ibid.*). He was influential through an anthropometric committee of the British Association for the Advancement of Science, established in 1878, in inducing "several institutions, such as Marlborough College, to undertake a regular system of anthropometric record," and in 1882 he established his famous laboratory in South Kensington Museum, London. "There, by the payment of a small fee, individuals could go and have certain physical measurements made and undergo tests of keenness of vision and hearing, dynamometer pressure, reaction time, etc." (*86*, page 1).

Galton regarded energy, "the capacity for labor," as the most important quality to favor in any scheme of eugenics, since it "is eminently transmissible by descent," and since his previous studies had shown "that leaders of scientific thought were generally gifted with remarkable energy" (*115*, pages 25, 27); but the influence of the Lockian school of psychology is evident when Galton says: "The only information that reaches us concerning outward events appears to pass through the avenue of our senses; and the more perceptive the senses are of difference, the larger is the field upon which our judgment and intelligence can act" (*ibid.*).

GALTON'S SENSORY TESTS OF INTELLIGENCE

From observations to the effect that the discriminative capacity of idiots for heat, cold, and pain is very obtuse, and from the tests that he had thus far made on the sensitivity of different persons, he supposed that this sensory discriminative capacity "would on the whole be highest among the intellectually ablest" (page 29). He therefore devised a system of weights, even yet in use in psychological laboratories, arranged in a geometrical series, for testing the delicacy of weight discrimination in different individuals. These weights were based on Weber's law "that when stimuli of all kinds increase by geometric grades the sensations they give rise to will increase by arithmetic grades" (page 34).

He also suggested devices for similar tests of other senses. Thus he very definitely assumed at this early date the essentials of the theory of mental tests, and he worked out actual quantitative tests of intelligence, based on this view. The theory that certain measurable abilities correlate with intelligence and can be used to predict in a measure one's degree of intelligence, is clearly implied; and Galton also recognized that the validity of a test of this kind is determined by its degree of correlation with a reliable criterion, for he chose persons of extreme differences in general mental ability to see whether they also differed correspondingly in sensory discrimination. It is, of course, true that the particular sort of test chosen has since been found to have little validity for persons who are within the limits of normality, but the essential procedure for the discovery of more valuable tests was clearly in mind. Unfortunately, Galton did not continue to follow up this good beginning in mental testing, but was diverted by other problems.

TESTS OF SENSITIVITY TO HIGH TONES

Galton also devised the well-known Galton whistle for testing the upper range of sensibility to high tones, and he carried out interesting experiments both on various animals at zoölogical gardens — with the small whistle concealed in the end of his walking stick — and on persons of various ages. Among animals, cats were found most sensitive to high tones, and, as to humans, it was discovered that elderly persons were very greatly limited in their upper range of hearing as compared with younger ones, the former commonly betraying "much dislike to the discovery" (page 39).

VARIOUS OTHER TRAITS INVESTIGATED

There seems to be no evidence that he regarded this auditory pitch test as having value for intelligence measurement; neither is it made very clear in his writing just what qualities, aside from great energy, are supposed to contribute directly to superior intelligence. He, however, used thoroughly empirical methods in the study of various character traits, a subject to which we are now in psychology beginning to pay attention as supplementary to intelligence determinations. He noted certain sex differences, such as coyness in the female. "The willy-nilly disposition of the female in matters of love is as apparent in the butterfly as in the man, and must have been continuously favored from the earliest stages of animal evolution" (page 57). Since natural character and temperament traits are difficult to estimate in adults, owing to their tendency to conceal undesirable traits, he resorted for the evaluation of different traits to the opinion of teachers who have opportunities of observing young school children. "The replies have differed, but those on which most stress was laid [by the teachers] were connected with energy, sociability, desire to attract notice, truthfulness, thoroughness, and refinement" (page 58). It is impossible now to say how much these replies of the teachers were influenced by the manner in which the questions were put to them. Galton himself also noted, both in persons and in animals, wide and striking differences in emotional constitution and in likings and antipathies.

Galton also made interesting studies of various mental differences in imagery, devising a mental imagery test that was formerly much used in experimental psychology; but his greatest service to intelligence testing is doubtless the work of developing various mathematical methods of handling data statistically. Among these methods, which we cannot here consider, are the use of standard measures and the correlation method, the former being a means of representing all scores in similar and directly comparable units — units of the standard deviation of the distribution.[1] The method

---

[1] For example, any score, x, by this method is stated as a deviation from the mean score of the group, in terms of standard deviation, σ, units, as

$$\text{score} = \frac{x - \text{mean}}{\sigma}.$$

of correlation, which in its fundamental properties was discovered and presented graphically by Galton from 1877 to 1888 (*145*, page 152), is now so well known and so extensively used as to need no comment here.

The now familiar term "mental tests" seems to have been first used by Cattell, who as early as 1890 published an article entitled "Mental Tests and Measurements" (*87*), describing tests then actually in use in his own laboratory in the University of Pennsylvania. To this article Galton appended a remark suggesting the desirability of comparing such laboratory measures, to use his own words, with "an independent estimate of the man's powers. . . . The sort I would suggest is something of this kind, — 'mobile, eager, energetic; well shaped; successful at games requiring good eye and hand; sensitive; good at music and drawing'" (*198*, page 206). Cattell in the tests he was using had followed Galton in combining physical with mental tests, but he went farther in regard to method than Galton had done and emphasized the necessity of standardization of the procedure in the administration of the tests in order to secure strictly comparable results. Cattell's tests, some of which seem to have been published as early as 1885, and which even then had probably been delayed because Wundt was not favorable to "individual psychology" (*91*, note, page 618), as the testing was then called, comprised ten records and twenty-six measurements, aside from physical measurements, and certain personal data supplied by the students. They were given individually and required from forty minutes to one hour for each person. Results of these tests applied to one hundred freshmen students were published in 1896, in the article cited.

The tests were on keenness of eyesight and of hearing, reaction time, after-images, color vision, perception of pitch and of weights, sensitivity to pain, color preferences, perception of time, accuracy of movement, rate of perception and of movement, memory, and imagery. Blanks for numerous additional data on physical features, personal traits, diseases, dreams, habits, artistic tastes, preferences for games and recreations, and future plans are presented in this report, some of these data to be taken by the tester himself and some to be supplied later by the subject. Students were asked to have the tests repeated at the end of their sophomore and senior years. These authors, Cattell and Farrand, say that they fully appreciate certain arguments put forth by Münsterberg and by Binet and Henri in favor of tests of a strictly psychological nature, but they add that their present concern is with anthropometric work, "and measurements of the body and of the senses come as completely within our scope as the higher mental processes." They state a preference for these more definite and simple tests. "If we undertake to study attention or suggestibility, we find it difficult to measure definitely a definite thing. We have a complex problem still requiring much research in the laboratory and careful analyses before the results can be interpreted, and, indeed, before suitable tests can be devised" (*91*, page 623). Thus they justify their emphasis of the sensory processes and of the simple reactions.

TESTS OF PRECONCEIVED MENTAL FUNCTIONS
BY KRAEPELIN AND OEHRN

In the meantime several other test series had been proposed. As early as 1889 Oehrn (*170*), working under the direction of Kraepelin, had pursued a different method, and had published results of tests which are probably the "earliest

actual experiments in mental correlation" (*198*, page 207).
Tests were devised to measure certain mental capacities,
selected by Kraepelin somewhat subjectively and arbitrarily,
and were applied intensively to ten subjects. These tests
and their classifications were as follows: 1. Perception,
(*a*) the counting of letters from the printed page, (*b*) the
search for particular letters, or the cancellation test, and
(*c*) the noting of errors in proof reading. 2. Memory, the
learning of series of twelve digits and series of twelve nonsense syllables. 3. Association, the adding of single-digit
numbers. 4. Motor functions, (*a*) writing from dictation
and (*b*) reading, in both cases as fast as possible. Oehrn
found a positive relationship between numbers 1, 2, and 4,
but "association" held rather an inverse relation to the other
capacities thus tested. In a review of this work, Henri
emphasizes the fact that individual differences increase
directly with the complexity of the psychical processes
studied. To the possible significance of this fact we shall
give attention later.

Kraepelin, who was professor of psychiatry at Heidelberg,
proposed a little later, in 1895 (*148*, and *53*, page 431), a
series of fundamental traits, or mental capacities, which he
regarded as basic factors in the characterization of an individual, whether normal or mentally unstable, and which
were to be guides in the construction of tests. These so-
called fundamental traits or dispositions include (1) the
ability to be influenced by practice, (2) the persistence of
practice effects, or general memory, (4) special memory
abilities, (5) fatigability, (6) capacity to recover from fatigue,
(7) the depth of sleep, (8) the capacity for concentration of
attention against distraction, and (9) ability to adapt oneself to effective work under distracting conditions. This
list is not complete, we are told, and may be extended.

For each of these traits Kraepelin devised a certain test

and assumed, rather arbitrarily, that the degree of the trait present in any given individual would be indicated by his relative performance in the test. The tests proposed dealt chiefly with simple arithmetical processes, and some of them were to be extended over long periods of time, requiring for their administration one hour daily for five successive days. The defects in such a system of tests for most purposes are obvious today, though the tests undoubtedly have merits for special studies of certain abnormal cases.

In 1891 Münsterberg (*166*) described various tests which he had made on school children, but he did not give results. The tests consisted of (1) reading aloud as rapidly as possible; (2) stating as quickly as possible the colors of ten objects whose names were written on a sheet, as "white" for "snow"; (3) reading ten given names of animals, plants, or minerals, and giving as quickly as possible the classification of each; (4) doing the same for names of cloth, of food, and of parts of the body; (5) giving as quickly as possible, when the objects were seen, the names of ten simple designs and of ten squares of colors; (6) adding ten given single-digit numbers; (7) giving as quickly as possible the number of angles in ten different irregular polygons; (8) naming three different perfumes or odors. Then came tests of another kind: (9) finding the number of digits and of letters retained by the subject after a single presentation; (10) bisecting a distance of eighty centimeters; (11) judging how many times one length is contained in another; (12) reproducing a perceived length after five seconds; (13) locating a sound; and, finally, (14) constructing a square and an equilateral triangle of which only the base in each case is given. Time records were kept in the speed tests. The whole series of tests occupied about one hour for each subject.

These tests, while regarded by Binet and Henri as better from the psychological point of view than those of Cattell, were nevertheless criticized by them as also being too special as regards the simple processes involved, and as devoting too much time relatively to speed. They contended that there are other mental processes of more importance than those tested by Münsterberg; that while they could not be measured with as much precision as these simpler processes, they are nevertheless more significant as to individual differences (*53*, page 429).

JASTROW'S TESTS

"During the fall of 1890," says Jastrow, "it was decided to ask the students in the general class in psychology to lend themselves to a series of physical and psychological tests with a view of interesting the students in such tests as well as acquiring a body of statistical material which when sufficiently extended and properly compared with other statistics might prove of considerable value" (*141*, page 420). This was in the University of Wisconsin. The tests used were applied individually and required about fifty minutes per subject. The psychological tests were mainly sensory and bilateral movement tests. They were supplemented by answers to various questions regarding personal and family characteristics.

In the Columbian Exposition in Chicago, Jastrow had, in 1893, a collection of psychological apparatus and tests, as well as norms of physical growth and of mental development. The tests comprised five touch and cutaneous sensibility tests, (1) estimation of distance of unseen movement of the finger, (2) estimation of a surface by touch, (3) weight discrimination, (4) sensibility to pain, and (5) judgment of distances by attempting with eyes closed to make five equidistant marks; five tests involving both touch and vision,

(1) making bilaterally equal movements, (2) reproducing from memory lines that one has just drawn, (3) tracing lines for exactness of movement, (4) hitting with a blunt point the center of a cross, for accuracy of perception, and (5) spiking a moving object, for rapidity and accuracy of localization; and five purely visual tests, (1) arranging lines in order of length, (2) marking off certain fractions of a given length, (3) marking off a distance on each of the three arms of a cross to equal that given by a mark on the fourth arm, (4) selecting certain required forms from a heterogeneity of forms, (5) reproducing letters, words, or colors after momentary exposure by means of a tachistoscope. To these last were added tests of visual acuity, tests of color zones, and tests of color blindness. There were also memory tests, the reproduction after a given time of letters, lines, colors, and forms previously exposed; and, finally, tests of reaction time, — rapidity in opening and closing the key of an interrupter, and quickness in the simple reaction experiment (*173*).

Persons who were interested were invited to submit themselves to these tests. The tests are obviously all of a quantitative nature and some are both ingenious and original, but comparatively little space is given to tests that involve the more complex and general mental functions. Results of these tests have not been published, so far as the writer is aware.

TESTS OF CHILDREN BY BOAS AND BOLTON

In 1891 Boas, then of Clark University, made certain anthropological measurements of about 1500 school children, and he tested them as to vision, hearing and "memory." He also secured from their teachers estimates of their "intellectual acuteness." Results of the memory tests, only, seem to have been published, these being the now well-known digit span test first used by Jacobs. This is probably the first attempt to make a comparison of test scores with independent estimates of the subjects by other persons, as first suggested by Galton. T. L. Bolton, who reported the results of an analysis of these data, found that "intellectual acuteness, while more often accompanied by a good memory-span and great power of concentrated and prolonged attention, is not necessarily accompanied by them" (*71*, page 317).

GILBERT'S TESTS OF CHILDREN AND ADULTS

Gilbert (*116*), at New Haven, in 1893, applied several mental tests to about 1200 children, and then compared the results with their "general ability" as estimated by their teachers. He used eight tests besides measures of weight, height, and lung capacity — two on sensations; one on rapidity of tapping; two on reaction time, simple and choice reaction; one on memory of the duration of tones; and one on suggestibility. Results show constant improvement with age up to the point of puberty, where advancement is retarded.[1]

Gilbert found what he supposes to be a correspondence of intelligence with sensory discrimination both of weights and of shades. There was also a slight positive relationship between intelligence, as estimated by teachers, and memory, tested by having the subject indicate when a tone had continued as long as a previously given standard tone. The most marked relationship, however, was found between intelligence

---

[1] This may have influenced Binet in the making of his well-known scale later, for in a review of this work he and Henri commented on this fact and this sort of criterion. These reviewers say also that while the same scheme serves to represent all kinds of results in a quantitative estimate, it is certain that Gilbert's researches do not give all the differences between children and adults. The child has not just simply less memory, less motor ability, less attention, etc., but he has also a manner of thinking, of reasoning, of willing, and of remembering peculiar to himself, as a child; that is, they feel that qualitative differences also exist (*53*, page 433).

and simple reaction time; but with discrimination and choice reactions this relationship was lowered.

In a second report (*117*), which appeared three years later than his first one, Gilbert describes further tests. For each age from six to nineteen years about one hundred children were used. The object was (1) to study physical and intellectual sex differences, (2) to ascertain the comparative development of physical and intellectual growth and to determine whether it is different in the two sexes, and (3) to study the interrelations of physical and intellectual growth — i.e., to find whether the more intelligent children have also the advantage in physical strength and development. The tests used were pulse before and after fatigue, height, weight, vital capacity, force of raising the wrist and of the arm, threshold of pain, estimation of a distance by movement of the arm, judgment of distance seen, rate of tapping, fatigue effects of tapping. The intelligence of the subjects was estimated by their teachers, who classed them into three groups, bright, median, and dull. Binet, who reviews these tests, comments critically on the length, the probable different fatigue effects on subjects of different ages, the inability of the younger subjects to indicate uniformly just when pain appears, etc., and he says of the experimenter: "It seems that he set his goal and then proceeded to it with eyes closed, looking neither to the right nor to the left." He deplores the lack of "psychological insight" of the author, but expresses a deep interest in his experiments (*26*, page 654).

Among the important results, for our present purpose, we may note that tapping rate regularly increased with age, and that boys were slightly more rapid than girls; that fatigue effects decreased with age; that in the judgment tests (estimating the length of a line) accuracy increased with age and no sex difference appeared. Porter's (*177*) findings in St. Louis, then recently published, to the effect that the larger and heavier the children are the more intelligent they are, were not supported by Gilbert's correlations of size with estimated intelligence. Moreover, on only two tests did children rated as superior intellectually surpass other children, — in rate of tapping and in the judgment of length of distances.

BINET AND HENRI ON TESTS IN "INDIVIDUAL PSYCHOLOGY"

Binet and Henri (*53*) published, in 1895, an article on "individual psychology," a term that had already been used by other writers. They reviewed most of the studies mentioned in the foregoing paragraphs, and criticized them as being on the whole too sensory and too much given to the study of special and limited abilities of minor significance for the determination of important individual differences. Even the memory studies that had been made are subject to this criticism. They point out that memory is not a simple function. One may have a good memory for figures and only a medium memory for letters, for example, or for colors. Partial memories, as Ribot, Charcot, and others had shown, may be impaired or lost in abnormal cases without influence on the other memories. "One cannot say, then, of an individual simply that he has a good memory; it is always necessary to state precisely of which memory one speaks. Therefore, in order to have an idea of an individual one must not simply be content with studies of a particular partial memory, such as that of letters or of figures, but must include as many partial memories as possible" (page 419).

They also raise the question of the interrelation of the different mental functions of any individual. Some persons are found to be slow in certain reactions, such as walking; they prefer slow music, probably are slow in reaction experiments, etc., but are we justified in concluding that such persons are in general slower than others whose reactions in these respects are different? Certainly not; we can only say that *probably* one is slower than another whose reactions of this sort are quicker. It is necessary, then, they hold, to be very cautious regarding conclusions on these different methods and on the data they yield.

These authors believe it possible to select certain tests that will suffice for given practical purposes, and they emphasize the need of having different tests for different purposes and different endowments. One should not employ the same tests "to compare two masons as would be used to compare two students or two children of a school" (page 434). While it is not necessary, of course, to test all functions in which individuals differ, it is important to select for our testing those functions that are most characteristic or most significant in distinguishing between any two persons. They chose for their purpose not the simplest and the most elementary functions, but the "superior psychic faculties" or the higher complex functions. They contend that in the measurement of these functions great precision is not necessary because individual differences are more marked here than in the simple functions that have been most studied.

They propose to study the following ten mental processes or functions: "memory, the nature of mental images, imagination, attention, the faculty of comprehension, suggestibility, æsthetic appreciation, moral sentiments, muscular force and force of will, motor skill, and judgment of visual space (*coup d'œil*)" (page 435). The methods, they hold, should be simple and should not take too much time, and they should be objective so that results of different experimenters may be comparable. Let us examine these tests.

1. The *memory tests* proposed comprise (*a*) visual memory of a geometrical design, (*b*) memory of a sentence, (*c*) memory of some musical notes played by the tester, (*d*) memory of colors, and (*e*) memory of digits. The authors hold that the

memory tests should give information regarding the subject's
general power of acquisition; his power of voluntary concentration of attention; his tastes and tendencies, inasmuch
as these will influence certain special or particular memories;
his general mental dispositions as shown in the sort of errors,
substitutions, omissions, etc., that he makes; and finally,
and most important of all, his power of comprehension, by
which his memories will be greatly affected.

2. The *test of images* suggested is that of letting the
subject reproduce by writing what he can recall of twelve
randomly selected letters in three rows of four in each row,
previously shown him long enough for two readings at a
natural rate.

3. The *tests of imagination* were to begin with a few questions regarding the subject's tastes, the nature of his preferred readings, the kind of pleasure which he seeks, his
tastes as to music, theaters, etc. The authors then propose
for involuntary imagination such tests as the ink-blot tests,
and for voluntary or creative imagination, the linguistic
invention test. Of the latter class are given (*a*) the construction of a sentence which must embody three given
nouns or verbs and no other words of the same part of speech;
and (*b*) the development in writing of some given theme, as
"A child lost in a forest." For the latter a specified amount
of time, six minutes for example, should be allowed and
announced in advance.

4. *Attention tests* are divided into measurements of the
duration and the scope of attention. The authors express
embarrassment at having to describe tests of "attention,"
which, despite the many attempts to study it, is still little
understood as to its essential aspects. They suggest for
duration of attention tests like reproduction by memory,
in several successive trials, of a line of a given length previously seen, the subject to see the original model but once.

The successive lengths are to be noted, as to whether they vary regularly or irregularly, and a curve plotted. They also cite an *a*-cancellation test (now well known) by Bourdon. For the scope-of-attention test they suggest the counting of the total number of strokes of two metronomes of but slightly different speeds. Speeds are to be increased gradually in successive trials up to the subject's limit. Normal persons, they find, can count the strokes at a rate up to fifty or sixty a minute. The execution of several acts simultaneously is also given as a test for scope of attention. For example, the subject's natural time for reading ten lines is noted, and then the time is again taken for reading ten similar lines while he also writes the letters of the alphabet or while he writes numbers.

5. *Tests of comprehension* — which they admit is a complex function, including "talent of observation," "spirit of ingenuity" (*l'esprit de finesse*), and others — must be somewhat complex. Tests tentatively proposed are (*a*) the description of the movements made by a sewing machine in a given period of time, or those of a crawling insect; (*b*) the giving of the similarities and the differences between two or among several synonyms, as *goodness, tenderness,* and *amiability;* and (*c*) the criticizing of certain statements each of which contains some impropriety of terms, some sophism, or some error of reasoning.

6. *Suggestibility tests,* which must not be mere illusion tests, fall under several heads :

(*a*) Sensations and Perceptions. These are tests published by the authors themselves in 1894. The subject selects from a group of lines on separate cards one line each time to match another shown just previously or simultaneously by the tester, so that the test may be performed either by memory or by direct perception. The tester presents successively lines of increasing length and returns each to the tray, from which the subject selects lines to match. But finally he presents a line which, unknown to the subject, was not selected from this group and which is longer than any line in the tray. Of children about ten years of age the majority choose lines from the tray, which they suppose are equal to it. Also a series of bottles containing faint odors is presented to the subject, who smells each and records its odor. All actually have odors except one or two bottles, in which there is only pure water.

(*b*) Imagination or Expectant Attention. A tube is adjusted to a wheel which revolves and gives for each revolution a sharp click. The subject is told to put his finger into this tube, that he will feel with each click an extremely weak sensation (the nature of which is not indicated to him), and that the sensation will increase in intensity with every turn of the wheel. He is required to describe what he experiences. The quality of sensation imagined, as well as the intensity, is to be noted in the subject's report.

(*c*) Emotivity, Apprehension, Fear. Many tests may be made with the algesiometer. Two examples given are: (1) The subject is told that successively increased pressure is to be applied and he is to say when pain appears. The experiment is repeated. According to Jastrow's observations, in the first test the subject stops the pressure earlier than in the second. The difference is the measure of apprehension. (2) The subject is himself allowed to choose the degree of pain to which he is willing to submit.

(*d*) Involuntary Conscious and Unconscious Movements. (1) Conscious Movements. The subject is asked to copy in capitals as quickly as possible a given list of words, both nouns and adjectives. The list is printed in small letters. There is thus a conflict between the text seen and the instructions of the experimenter. A much larger per cent of errors (omission of capitals) is made on the adjectives than on the nouns.

(2) Unconscious Movements. The noting or recording of automatic movements (behind a screen) of one's hand while one reads or converses attentively or while one thinks attentively of some name.

7. *Æsthetic appreciation.* The subject is to arrange in order of preference a number of objects or experiences of varying degree of beauty, such as a number of rectangles of different proportions, a number of cards of different colors, and a graduated series of musical phrases. The correct order of the members in these series is to be determined, as a criterion, by getting the judgments of a number of competent persons.

8. *Moral sentiments.* Objects capable of exciting the subject, and various important pictures, are shown him in a natural way so that he does not know it is an experiment but will think it is done just for his interest in the object and the views themselves. His behavior is then carefully noted, special attention being given to what he looks at and how long, apparent effects produced, and so on.

9. *Muscular force and force of will.* For this they suggest the lifting and sustaining of certain weights and the noting of the subject's duration of effort, the trembling in sustained effort, the degree of lowering of the hand, respiratory and other changes; also, pulling with one finger against a certain known weight, so that the amount of work done can be calculated, the subject being required to make a series of movements as rapidly as possible and to continue as long as possible despite fatigue. The duration of voluntary muscular effort of this kind affords a "true measure of will." The authors do not regard the dynamometer and the Mosso ergograph as suitable for these tests, but prefer simpler tests not necessitating complex apparatus and not requiring particular methods of pressure or flexion movements.

10. *Motor skill and judgment of visual space.* For

motor skill the well-known tapping test, early used by W. L. Bryan (79), and the steadiness test are recommended. As visual judgment tests they suggest such things as having the subject estimate how many times a given line is contained in another longer line, having him divide a line into seven equal parts, and having him indicate on a circumference the third part of its entire length.

Their suggestions are put forth as tentative and the tests are recognized by them as needing additions and modifications; but they hold that changes should be made only by means of practical tests and experimentation. "We believe all the same," they say, "that having obtained responses to all the preceding questions and having afterwards interrogated the subject on his principal occupations, one will be able to form an idea of the ensemble of the faculties of the individual" (pages 463, 464).

The tests as outlined were so chosen that a subject could be taken through the entire series in an hour, or in an hour and a half at most, and the authors suggest that they be added to or modified as conditions demand. They doubt the sufficiency of the tests to characterize well the differences between two persons of the same occupation and living in similar social environment, but believe them suitable to give useful information concerning such differences when the subjects differ more widely than this. They indicate various practical fields in which the tests may be used to advantage by educators, doctors, justices, and others. Mental tests, they conclude, ought to be as varied as possible so as to include a large number of functions, especially of the higher complex ones; they should be so varied that in the sixty to ninety minutes of their administration they will neither fatigue nor bore the individual subjected to them; they should be adapted to the conditions of social environment under which the subject lives; and, finally, they should not require complicated apparatus.

No results, other than those indicated incidentally in our discussion of the several tests, were given in this early test series by Binet and his collaborator, and no suggestions regarding standardization into a scale are made.

EARLY AMERICAN COMMITTEES ON TESTS

The test developments and systems of tests which we have considered give, probably, a fair idea of the movement in the early nineties toward intelligence testing. There were also used at that comparatively early date numerous single tests, such as tests of memory, imagery, and other special functions, these being employed for various psychological purposes. The tests that we have considered, however, were suggested or used with more or less explicit reference to use as intelligence tests or tests of one's general abilities, as distinct from special abilities.

At the Philadelphia meeting of the American Psychological Association in December, 1895, a committee, consisting of Professors Cattell, J. M. Baldwin, Jastrow, Sanford, and Witmer, "was appointed to consider the feasibility of co- operation among the various psychological laboratories in the collection of mental and physical statistics" (*91*, page 619). It should also be noted that at the Buffalo meeting of the American Association for the Advancement of Science, in August, 1896, "a standing committee, consisting of Messrs. Brinton, Cattell, McGee, Newell, and Boas, was appointed to organize an ethnographic survey of the white race in the United States." "It is important," says Cattell in this same year, in referring to this committee, "that psychological tests be included in this survey, and that the work be co- ordinated with that proposed by the Psychological Association" (*ibid.*, pages 619, 620).

It is not difficult to discover the moving spirit behind the appointment of these committees, especially when one knows that Cattell had described his early experiments in testing before the New York Academy of Sciences in May, 1895, and also before the American Association for the Advancement of Science in August, 1896, and that his student, Dr. L. Farrand, had presented a paper on this subject before the American Psychological Association in the Philadelphia meeting, in 1895, already mentioned.

The testing movement in the nineties seems to have become so important in the minds of some live educational administrators who themselves were not psychologists, that in 1899 President W. R. Harper of the University of Chicago, then a very young institution, "recommended that a special study be made of the college student's character, intellectual capacity, and tastes, by the questionnaire method" (*86*, page 4). It will be recalled that both Galton and Cattell had made use of this method in connection with tests. Individual tests were, of course, too detailed and time-consuming to be employed for such practical purposes and on so large a scale.

WHY DID THIS TESTING MOVEMENT ABATE?

Why did this whole movement, then, come to so little immediate practical effect, as we know it did, that actual testing of students on a large scale in educational institutions was delayed for about twenty years? Why, moreover, did not the psychological laboratories, with rare exceptions to be noted, and the American Psychological Association keep up the large interest that had been aroused in this early testing movement? The answer to this question is probably not difficult when we follow for a few years further, as we shall do in the next chapter, the work in the laboratory directed by the principal supporter in America of this testing movement, and when we also consider the effects of an experimental study on the evaluation of certain tests, carried out in the Cornell University laboratory. There were, of course, also several other factors operating toward this general minimizing of the importance of tests in America.

EXERCISES

1. Select from the tests described in this chapter those which you think would be best to measure one's general ability. Give reasons for each choice. Try some of the tests on persons whom you know well and on schoolmates. Rank your tests, by the results, in the order of their diagnostic value for this purpose.

2. Study several currently used tests and see which of them are modifications of, or are derived from, tests described in this chapter.

3. Which of the tests described in this chapter were constructed to test some preconceived view of intelligence? Which ones have a somewhat empirical basis?

CHAPTER SIX

Sensory and Particular Tests versus Tests of Complex and Higher Functions

"individual psychology" and its problems

Binet seems to have been the first French psychologist to employ the term "individual psychology" (27, note, page 113). The term was also used by Oehrn in the study cited in the last chapter, and his and Kraepelin's work certainly dealt with aspects of the subject even though Kraepelin worked mainly with abnormal cases. The significance given to the term by Binet is practically that implied by our "mental measurement" today and refers to the differentiation of one individual from another in general ability on the basis of tests of characteristic traits. In their article on *La Psychologie Individuelle*, Binet and Henri make clear their conception of individual psychology and of the methods to be employed by it, and they bring clearly to the foreground the question as to differences between the conventional experimental psychology and this newer field of study. We have already seen that the various studies by American writers, considered in the foregoing chapter, as well as some of the studies by Galton, were aiming rather directly at the question of evaluating and distinguishing the general mentalities of different individuals.

The idea of developing a system of mental tests for practical purposes in the scientific study of man and in his education and betterment had, indeed, become rather explicit in the early nineties, but the article by the two French psychologists attempted not only to outline definitely the problems of this newer field of psychological research, but to evaluate the different methods which had been proposed or actually used by various investigators. The English and American studies had included a large proportion of anthropometric measurements as well as of the conventional tests of sensory discrimination and reaction time, and there were appearing a number of studies of memory as influenced by different sorts of factors and measured in various ways, and of tests of other more or less special mental functions, with little relation to general mental ability; so this important article by the great pioneer in mental testing and his collaborator was timely.

While Binet and Henri classified the main problems of individual psychology as (1) the study of the extent and the nature of the variations of the psychic processes from one individual to another, and (2) the determination of the interrelations of these various processes in any single individual as to whether they are mutually dependent or whether some are fundamental processes upon which all others depend, it is clear that their interest was really more in the individual than in the processes themselves. What they were after was a series of tests which would bring out most clearly the large differences in ability among different persons.

ARE COMPLEX MENTAL FUNCTIONS THE MOST IMPORTANT TO MEASURE?

It will be recalled that most of the other experimenters whom we have considered put the emphasis on the sensory discriminative functions, reaction times, and certain other particular functions. Galton had suggested that there may be a relation between sensory discrimination and general intellectual ability and had devised for weight discrimination, association, and memory span certain tests that could be carried out quantitatively. His influence on early tests in America is obvious from the tests enumerated in the preceding chapter. Such tests, like his own, attempted to take some simple function and to study it with great accuracy. The simple functions, as opposed to the complex ones, were held, rightly in the main, to yield the more constant or reliable results; and so they seemed to many investigators the more suitable for scientific testing. This was in line with the objectivity of the anthropometric measurements which were usually closely associated with mental tests. Thus Cattell and Farrand had expressed their preference for the more definite and simple tests over the more complex ones which needed much research and careful analysis before their results could be interpreted.

Gilbert's tests were all subject to exact numerical measurements. The "voluntary motor ability" was determined by measuring the number of taps the subject could make on a suitable piece of apparatus in five minutes, and fatigue was measured by the proportion of loss of speed after forty-five seconds. Reaction times, both simple and discriminative, were measured with a chronoscope in hundredths of a second. The "force of suggestion" was determined by the difference in weights picked out by the child to match respectively a large and a small object of equal weight. Memory of time intervals was measured by letting the chronoscope run for a certain period of time and then, in a second trial, having the subject stop it when it had, in his estimation, run an equal period of time. There could be no question as to the objectivity of such tests. Similar definiteness and precision characterized the tests by Jastrow and those by Münsterberg. All these tests in America reflect clearly, besides the influence of Galton, that of the German experimental psychology, which had taken hold of so many of the early American psychologists who had been students of Wundt.

In the work of Kraepelin and Oehrn exactness of measurement is also emphasized. Strict time records were kept in the various measurements, and their mean variations in different individuals were investigated; however, these tests demanded little apparatus and no highly refined technique. They approached more closely than did the early American tests the normal processes in daily life. Really only the method here is simple, and this is true merely because a succession of similar responses is studied rather than the simple reactions separately. For example, Kraepelin in studying reaction time would have his subjects add single digit numbers, write from dictation, read a given selection as quickly as possible, etc., and he would time each entire series of acts. This method is obviously much simpler than measuring one's simple reaction with a chronoscope, but the responses of the subject require more complex adjustments and approximate therefore more closely the reactions in our daily work. Kraepelin's work was of course based on a rather thorough study of abnormal individuals, but his tests were supposed to evaluate certain mental qualities in normal individuals as well. It is, however, significant that his greater interest in the individual, forced by the nature of his work, is associated with less use of the sensory tests than was made in the American testing.

Binet's interest was greater in individuals than in sensations or ideas, and in this respect he but reflected the characteristic of the French psychology, interested in personalities deviating from the normal. In this relation one recalls Charcot, Ribot, Janet, and others, all of whom were little influenced by the English psychology of " deas," and by the German experimental psychology with its emphasis on sensory discrimination. The environment in which Binet had grown up was favorable to a strong emphasis on the whole individual in psychological study. Itard, Seguin, and others had led out in the line of the subnormal, too, and in Binet this tendency is combined with that of studying the dissociated personality. So in this period the new tendency to emphasize individual psychology is most **strongly** **expressed in Binet.**

ORIGIN AND PURPOSE OF THE "ANNÉE PSYCHOLOGIQUE"

In 1895 appeared the first volume of *L'Année Psychologique*, a journal founded by Binet and published by him and his collaborators up to the time of his death in 1911. The influence of this man on the testing movement in the nineties and the two following decades can hardly be overstated. He threw the weight of his influence, in the first place, definitely toward the emphasis of empirical psychology, and asserted in the first sentence of the Introduction in the *Année* that the progress of psychology dates from its separation from metaphysics. The metaphysical tendencies, he asserted, "disappeared fortunately with Taine, Spencer, and Bain, to cite only the celebrated authors." Psychology was, in his view, to become a science of observation and experimentation — that is, a verifiable science like other natural sciences; and it must put aside "all speculation on the nature and essence of the soul and of its origin and destiny." These questions are profitless for it because it is impossible to resolve them scientifically. The mission of psychology is more simple and more precise, to collect data necessary to establish a science of man on which alone the social sciences, education, and criminology might have a solid foundation. To this work the *Année* was devoted, and one is surprised to note in its successive volumes the extent of review and original work done by Binet and his collaborators during the remaining sixteen years of his life.[1]

BINET CONTENDED FOR TESTS OF COMPLEX MENTAL
FUNCTIONS

In the second place Binet emphasized, as we have said, individual psychology, and raised the important question as to what sort of differences among individuals should be

[1] Binet was born in 1857 and died in 1911.

studied, since it is impracticable to study all differences thoroughly. In the article cited above Binet and Henri objected to sensory discrimination tests, which had at that time been most extensively used from the time of Galton's beginning. They admitted that these tests are more simple and objective than the tests of the higher complex functions, and that they can be repeated by different investigators under more nearly identical conditions. Likewise they objected to various tests of particular memories, reactions, etc., as we have noted in the preceding chapter. They maintained that these elementary processes are precisely the ones in which persons differ least; that individual differences are most marked in the complex and higher processes which usually distinguish the everyday activities of one individual from those of another. While these processes are admittedly more difficult to investigate by experimental methods and will therefore give more variable results, it was maintained that tests of such complex functions are relatively much more significant and that the demand for precision is therefore not so great as it is in the case of the simple processes. In the article cited they show no data to establish this view, but simply base it on an analysis of the various tests that have been proposed or used, and on the small relationship found between efficiency in the tests and teachers' estimates of ability.

THE SHARP-TITCHENER STUDY OF THE CLAIMS
FOR COMPLEX TESTS

If now we turn to the early test movement in America, we find two reports that bear directly on the question at issue, and that probably were influential toward dampening the enthusiasm of the testers. One of these reports, by Stella Emily Sharp (*188*), from Titchener's laboratory at Cornell, is on a special investigation of the question so strongly put forth by Binet and Henri, as to the relative value "for individual psychology" of sensory discriminative and rather special tests on the one hand and of the more inaccurate tests of the higher, complex mental functions on the other. These experiments were carried out in the academic year 1897–1898. "The theory was provisionally accepted that the complex mental processes, rather than the elementary processes, are those the variations of which give the most important information in regard to the mental characteristics whereby individuals are commonly classed. It is in the complex processes, we assumed, and in those alone, that individual differences are sufficiently great to enable us to differentiate one individual from others of the same class. Many of the particular tests recommended by the French psychologists were also adopted, but were considerably modified in the general conditions of their application by the purpose of our own investigation" (page 348). The specific aim was to test the practicability of the particular tests employed, while the general aim was to evaluate the general position of Binet and Henri.

To be sure that differences obtained would represent real individual differences, and not mere chance variations; i.e., to test the reliability of the tests proposed, "it is necessary to apply them to the same individuals, not once, but several times, in order that it may be observed whether the variations in the different individuals maintain a constant relation to one another at various times and, consequently, under varying subjective conditions. Instead of single tests, therefore, series of similar tests for each activity were arranged. This necessitated, of course, a very large extension of the time beyond the limits allowed by the French investigators. The advantages of a short period of varied experimentation were, however, to a large degree attained. The experimental work of each subject was divided into periods of one hour each, and separated by intervals of one week. Within a single hour-period the tests were varied as much as possible" (page 349). Thus the tedium and fatigue of the repetition of similar operations were avoided and interest to a fair extent maintained. Certain tests "especially trying or disagreeable to the subjects" were separated by more than a week. Among such tests are given "the development of a theme" and "description of a scene or event," tests for constructive imagination.

The subjects and the tests. The subjects were advanced college students in psychology and were, therefore, highly selected as to ability and education, certainly representing the same class to a marked degree. They were grouped in twos or threes for most of the experiments, to save time. For a comparison of this group with a less highly trained group, and therefore as a control on the experiment, data on "less advanced students taking the undergraduate (junior year) course in experimental psychology" were also used. These students were tested by Titchener usually during the "first ten minutes of the lecture hour" (page 350). The tests suggested by Binet and Henri were not all used; so while those here tried out were more intensively applied, they were less extensive in the field covered, being restricted to those dealing "most directly with the intellectual processes." The "moral sentiment" and "strength of will" tests were left out, and those of the "æsthetic sentiments" were but lightly touched.

The tests used in this study were: 1. *Memory.* Memory span of letters, of figures, of words, and of sentences, and three general questions on the ability to carry and reproduce an air (really not a test at all). 2. *Mental images.* Binet's letter square test, and answers written by the subject as to the nature of the mental images from which his reproductions were made. 3. *Imagination.* (*a*) Passive. The blot test and answers to questions regarding how the subject represents to himself when they are spoken such terms as "force," "infinity," "justice," etc. (*b*) Constructive. (1) Mechanical, in which the subject was to explain the mechanism of a device shown him. (2) Literary, involving the construction of a sentence, the development of a theme, and the choice of a topic for composition; and answers to questions regarding the subject's reading, fondness for games, the theater, opera, etc. 4. *Attention.* (1) Its degree, letter cancellation, (2) its range, — the reading of a certain passage of ten lines, its re-reading while writing *a*'s, a third reading while writing *a b* repeatedly, a fourth while writing *a b c*, and a fifth while writing as far as possible in the whole alphabet. The time of each performance was noted. 5. *Observation and description.* The reproduction of a picture, the reproduction and locating of the colors on a picture of a lady brilliantly dressed, and the writing of distinctions between a pair of synonyms. 6. *Taste and tendencies.* Information tests about works of art, music, and literature, and replies to questions as in 3.

Results and conclusions. Results on the seven advanced students only can be given, some of these not being in quantitative form because the experiments did not permit this. Reliability measures that would today be required in a work of this kind and the data on which they would be based are not given, but a thorough analysis of results is made by methods then in use. The data as given are inadequate for any reliable conclusions, as we should view them with the advantage of better methods today. "The results, we believe," says the author, "have shown that while a large proportion of the tests require intrinsic modification, or a more rigid control of conditions, others have really given such information as the individual psychologist seeks. . . . In general, however, a lack of correspondences in the individual differences observed in the various tests was quite as noticeable as their presence. . . . Whether the fact indicates a relative independence of the particular mental activities under investigation, or is due simply to superficiality of testing, can hardly be decided. While, however, we do not reject the latter possibility, we incline to the belief that the former hypothesis is in a large proportion of cases the more correct" (page 389). The general thoroughness of this study and the justice of the conclusion are appealing.

The author further points out the need of repeating the tests on any individuals studied. "*Series of such tests* are necessary in order to show constant individual characteristics. The tests, to be sure, if enlarged to cover a wider range of activities, might be useful for roughly classifying a large number of individuals of very different training, occupation, etc., provided that the greatest care were taken that the conditions in the case of each individual should be as favorable as possible. And, on the other hand, certain groups of tests, especially selected for a particular purpose, and applied, once each in series, to a limited number of individuals, might yield valuable information on points which particular circumstances rendered of practical importance. As engineers, pilots, and others, who have to act upon information from colored signals, are roughly tested for color blindness, so other classes might often profitably be submitted to a psychological testing of those higher activities which are especially involved in their respective lines of duty." But "much preliminary work must be done before such special investigations can be of any great worth. This appears plainly from the present investigation, where the positive results have been wholly incommensurate with the labor required for the devising of tests and evaluation of results." Again, it is stated that the method employed by Binet is for individual psychology "the one most productive of fruitful results," but it is qualified by an assertion of the need of exhaustive studies of results of series of similar tests given to few individuals at different times and in varying circumstances, these studies to cover all the principal psychical activities.

"In fine," the statement continues, "we concur with MM. Binet and Henri in believing that individual psychical differences should be sought for in the complex rather than in the elementary processes of mind, and that the test method is the most workable one that has yet been proposed for investigating these processes. The theory of the German psychologists, who hold that the simplest mental processes are those to which the investigator should look for a clue to all the psychical differences existing among individuals, we believe would be productive of small or, at any rate, of comparatively unimportant results." Nevertheless, a combination of the two methods, the more exact German with the Binet method, is recommended; but just what is to be combined is not indicated, except that greater accuracy is suggested for the Binet method.

One thing is now clear to us regarding this study of the validity of Binet's conception and general method. However carefully and thoroughly the investigation was carried out and however judiciously the conclusions were drawn, a point of supreme importance was overlooked. The subjects tested were of so specialized and highly selected a nature, and constituted so homogeneous a group, that consistent and reliable differences would be hard to establish with even the best of tests. Where differences are very small it requires a corresponding high degree of refinement of tools and method to measure them. It is a simple matter to devise tests that will distinguish reliably between a dull and a bright boy; but such tests may prove very unreliable if applied to two geniuses, and their value may in the latter case be entirely covered up by the differences of special abilities which have little significance for general intelligence. Binet had not claimed that his early tests could indicate important differences among individuals of homogeneous groups; he explicitly stated the contrary of this. It was rather remarkable, then, that under the conditions the Cornell study supported the Binet method as much as it did, and very unfortunate that the significance of these positive results should have been obscured among repeated cautions, conditions, and recommendations of similar studies of small groups, usually highly selected. It is safe to say that the structural psychology methods then used in the same laboratory could not have come out better than, if indeed as well as, did this "test method," as it was called; but their qualitative nature did not permit of a critical evaluation. It should be noted, too, that several of the tests used in this investigation were really tests of particular abilities, not of complex mental functions, and that not a few of them were only "qualitative."

The Sharp study states also in its conclusions that investigations by means of tests will yield very little for morphological or structural psychology, because so many part-processes are involved in the complex mental activities "that it is seldom possible to tell with certainty what part of the total result is due to any particular component. It is doubtful if even the most rigorous and exhaustive analysis of test results would yield information of importance as regards the structure of mind. At all events, there is not the slightest reason to desert current laboratory methods for the 'method of tests'" (page 389). This was doubtless very consoling to many minds troubled with the feeling that they should give some of their attention to the test movement, and its effect was probably very great in America toward dampening the interest in tests. The statement, moreover, shows clearly that the interest of the investigator was in "part-processes" such as imagery, memory, etc., a point of view foreign to that of Binet. Both interests may, of course, be legitimate for different purposes.

WISSLER'S REPORT ON CORRELATIONS OF THE CATTELL TESTS

Following closely upon this study, which, though supporting Binet's conception as to the value of testing the complex processes, surrounded the positive results with so many conditions as greatly to minimize their promise, and admitted the value of the "test method" only in rather incidental connections with psychology, was another report which also doubtless had far-reaching effects toward diminishing the enthusiasm for tests in certain American laboratories. This second report was by Clark Wissler (*233*) in 1901, and consisted of an analysis by the Pearson correlation method of the data resulting from the psychological tests and anthropometric measurements in Cattell's laboratory. In this study correlations were made for the first time with a degree of mathematical precision. As a criterion of the general ability of the students the average grade of each student in all of his college studies was taken. The records and test results of 250 freshmen and of 35 seniors of Barnard College were considered. The data were classed under three main divisions: psychological tests, college grades, and physical tests. The correlations between different pairs of psychological tests ranged from − .28 to .39, showing "little more than a mere chance relation." Since there was "no evidence of any important functional relations between the activities employed" (*234*, page 540), the author concluded that the psychological tests must be measures of special abilities only. The physical tests showed a general tendency to correlate among themselves, such as height with weight, for example, but only to a very slight degree was there a positive relationship between physical measurements and psychological tests. While correlations between different pairs of college courses were appreciable, ranging from .11 to .75, the relations of these academic marks either to the psychological tests or to the physical measurements were unreliable and but little more than could be obtained by mere chance.

PROBABLE EFFECTS OF THE TWO STUDIES ON THE TESTING MOVEMENT

The extent of the effect of these two important studies on early testing in America is not easy to determine, but the studies were probably influential against the testing movement and in favor of the regular laboratory studies of sensations, imagery, memory, etc., and the more theoretical psychology represented in the two volumes of James's great work, *The Principles of Psychology*, published in 1890. While these introspective and somewhat theoretical tendencies have had certain good effects upon American education in general and while their data still constitute the major part of psychology courses in colleges and universities, it is probable that, through losing sight of the positive implications of the Sharp study and of the fact that the Wissler study only demonstrated what Binet had asserted regarding sensory tests and tests of particular abilities, American investigators were impressed with the uselessness of intelligence tests and so failed to be much influenced by the work of Binet. That is to say, though the results of these two important investigations were favorable to the position urged by Binet, they were probably interpreted by undiscriminating and little-interested psychologists as adverse to the French view. When the Binet-Simon tests later appeared in America, they took root at first mainly in institutions for subnormals. We heard little of them in college courses in psychology in the first decade of this century.

BINET FINDS ENCOURAGEMENT IN CERTAIN EUROPEAN STUDIES

While these developments, unfavorable to the testing movement in America, were taking place here, Binet found in Europe some encouragement for his own position. The earlier experiments of Oehrn under the direction of Kraepelin, while influenced in a measure by the Wundtian experimental psychology, as Miss Sharp has said in her article, were nevertheless in an important way supports to Binet's contention for the need of studying the complex processes. As we have already noted, only the method was simple, while the processes studied were actually complex and the primary interest in Kraepelin's work was in individuals. The French school received encouragement in the simplicity of the methods with which such complex mental activities could be studied, and Henri, who regularly reviewed the various German investigations in the *Année*, remarked in a review of Oehrn's experiments that his results show an increase of individual differences with the complexity of the psychic processes studied (*129*, page 796).

FERRARI'S TESTS IN ITALY

Similar encouragement (*23*, pages 296 f.) came from certain Italian studies under the direction of Ferrari, who, like Kraepelin at Heidelberg, was interested in pathological psychology. In an article (*124*) that appeared in 1896 we find a description of some of the tests used. Among these tests, which include some motor strength and skill tests and a vasomotor test (with the plethymograph), we find one test of the range of apprehension, one of description of pictures, and one test of "organic memory." In the description test, subjects are shown in succession eighteen pictures of actors in different stages of a drama. Each is to describe after each exposure what he saw and to give his judgment and interpretation of it and associated imaginations. In the last test named, the subject sees a revolving disk so marked that he can observe the several revolutions. He is told to take note of the time period of each revolution, and then with eyes closed he is to indicate by signals his estimate of when subsequent revolutions are completed. The tests are not put forth as a complete set. While nothing is established finally in these tests, they reveal interesting individual differences.

EBBINGHAUS IN GERMANY FINDS THE COMPLEX COMPLETION TEST SUPERIOR

Another experiment that encouraged Binet (*23*, pages 296 f.) and influenced him in his later devising of tests, was that carried out in the city of Breslau by Ebbinghaus (*111*). Having been called upon to assist in the solution of a problem regarding fatigue effects in school children, this psychologist, in coöperation with a certain committee of testers, applied, in the morning and before each period of the school work for only a few minutes, three tests of mental processes as follows: (1) rapid calculation, adding and multiplying simple numbers as rapidly as possible; (2) memory of digits, these being read in series of different lengths to groups of students who were to write all that they could remember; and (3) the completion of sentences by supplying, in blanks left for the purpose, letters and words which had been elided. This is the now well-known "completion test." The dashes for omitted words, syllables, and letters were to be filled out in such a way as to make sense. In the construction of this test the author asked himself the questions, What is the principal function that characterizes an intelligent act?

In what especially is an intelligent person distinguished from an unintelligent one? He concluded that it is not in mere memory. To be a good physician, for instance, it does not suffice merely to have a good memory for facts; one must be able to organize all present symptoms and other data in such a way as to deduce from them an exact diagnosis, and to combine them in such a way as to picture accurately to himself just what is wrong with the patient. This function he called "combination," and he regarded it therefore as an important element in intelligence. To test this ability he devised the completion test, in which the subject is required from the general context to determine just what the missing elements should be.[1]

While Ebbinghaus was doubtless right in the main as to the importance of the combining function in intelligence, it is undeniable that it does not necessarily involve certain elements which are very important for success in difficult pursuits. Results of these tests, however, showed the completion test to be markedly superior to the other two tests used. The children were grouped according to age, and those in each class were also divided into three equal groups according to whether their scholastic standing was good, average, or poor. With respect to age, all three tests showed superiority of old over young students, but the memory of digits and the completion test showed the greatest differences with advancing ages of groups, the latter test showing of the two, however, the greater regularity of increase in scores. Comparing the scores of the three divisions of each class, Ebbinghaus found that no reliable differences between bright,

[1] For example, text of this nature is supplied the subject, who is to fill in the blanks with words or parts of words as needed to make good sense: "Wh-- Willy --- two ----- old, he ----- -- -red farm-h---- --th - yard -- front -- --. The dandelions were ---- thi-- there, so that --- ---- lo---- yellow instead of -----." This is part of a test, slightly modified, for advanced students. It is obvious that the value of such a test depends on the nature of the elisions made in the text used.

average, and dull groups were made by scores on the memory span of digits, and that the calculation test had shown but a slight superiority of the best groups in each grade. The completion test, however, showed a clear superiority of the best over the median, and of the median over the poorest groups. Thus, though the mathematical correlation method was not used at this time, Ebbinghaus found a high degree of correspondence between scores in the completion tests and degree of intelligence as obtained by the two criteria used.

We need only add that this completion test, which certainly calls into play higher and complex mental functions, has proved to be one of our very best intelligence tests, though its value depends much on a proper selection of words or letters to be omitted and on the extent to which the constructive imagination is really brought into play. The test may be made discouragingly difficult and be reduced too much to guessing, if too many elisions are made. If too few are made for the degree of intelligence of the subjects tested, it becomes merely a speed test. The results of Ebbinghaus' test, then, while they still left open the question of fatigue effects, were a clear demonstration of the essential correctness of Binet's contention for the superior value in individual psychology of complex tests as opposed to tests of simple functions.

USES OF SOME EARLY TESTS IN AMERICA

Thus while some evidence in favor of Binet's contention was derived from studies of the complex mental processes, the results of various studies of the simpler processes were in nearly all cases negative, so far as individual testing is concerned. It should, however, be emphasized that investigations in America like those of Thorndike (*211*) on fatigue in 1900 and by Thorndike and Woodworth (*218*) on transfer effects of training, published in the following year, were based on tests of a kind that have been of great value in analytical investigations of intelligence and in group comparisons. To the genius of Thorndike in particular is due the origin or adaptation of various tests, usually of supposed special functions, which have been used in valuable researches. In the first of the studies here named the mental multiplication test appeared. Adaptations of old tests — the memory of series of numbers, of nonsense syllables, of geometrical figures of various forms; the crossing out of words containing certain specified letters, as *e* and *t* — were also made for this study, while in the investigation of transfer, the cancellation test, just referred to, a test that owes its origin to Bourdon and which was used also by Oehrn and by Cattell and Farrand, was further modified to include the crossing out of words of a given length, of certain parts of speech, and so on. In the study on the interrelations of certain perceptive and associative processes by Thorndike and Aikins (2) in 1902, the cancellation test was also employed as well as certain controlled association tests — opposites, part-whole, and genus-species — elaborated in Columbia University; and in his *Educational Psychology*, first published in 1903, Thorndike made extensive use of these several tests and many others, such as memory of related words, an alphabet test requiring the subject to write the letters which in the alphabet precede those given, and paper maze tests for motor ability. On the basis of scores made in these several tests he pointed out the advantages of quantitative methods in studies of individual differences, relationships among various mental functions, relative effects of nature and nurture, etc. In fact, Columbia University became a center of scientific work in mental testing; but the emphasis was largely on the measurement of special functions in studies such as have been indicated, not on the testing of individuals for general intelligence or general mental ability.

The study of sex differences by Helen B. Thompson (*210*), carried out in the University of Chicago from 1898 to 1900, employed, in addition to certain sensory acuity and discrimination and memory tests, a test in the rapidity of association in responses to ten given words, a general information test of 25 questions, five ingenuity tests, motor-ability tests, and certain experiments on the affective processes. The ingenuity tests were: a test in which the subject was to remove three of fifteen matches arranged to form five squares with a view to leaving only three squares and no extra matches, a sort of checkerboard problem which required the subject to arrange eight "men" on the board so that no two were on the same straight line in any direction, two mechanical-ability tests requiring the comprehension and operation of a piece of light-discrimination apparatus and of a simple combination lock, and an arithmetic problem in which the subject was to find how fast a man can swim in still water if he swims three times as fast down a stream running one mile an hour as up the stream. The extent of the group differences found and their unreliabilities were not determined, but the tests gave indications of sex differences in certain respects. The men, for example, excelled in strength, rapidity, and ease of movement, and in the ingenuity tests, while the women seemed to be superior in certain sensory-discrimination tests and memory.

No means of determining the diagnostic value of the tests as to general intelligence were, however, developed in these early Chicago and Columbia studies. It is obvious that some of the Thompson tests can hardly be supposed to measure only particular abilities.

EXERCISES

1. In what respects was the Sharp study defective in its examination of Binet's view? What valuable features did it involve? Why did Miss Sharp repeat the tests?

2. In what respects did Wissler's study fall short in the attempt to evaluate Cattell's tests as measures of general ability or intelligence?

3. List the best means you can suggest for finding the diagnostic value of any proposed intelligence tests. Which of these were used by authors of tests described in the preceding chapter? Specify as to who used them.

4. See if you can find in the literature of psychology any specific effects of the Sharp and of the Wissler study on testing in America.

CHAPTER SEVEN

THE HISTORICAL BACKGROUND OF THE BINET-SIMON TESTS

BINET'S PREPARATION AND EARLY WORK

THE adverse results as to intelligence testing, described in the previous chapter, did not, of course, stop the testing movement. Numerous special studies, both of physical and of particular mental processes, were carried out in the last decade of the nineteenth and in the beginning of this century, before the intelligence scales, now so well known, took shape. Of these investigations Binet was not neglectful; indeed, he was one of the most energetic workers in carrying out these various studies. This is particularly true in regard to the studies, of whatever nature, that were devised to throw light on individual differences or to trace relationships of physical characters and intellectual functions.

Binet at one time studied medicine and was especially interested in abnormal psychology, an interest that would be expected to result from contact with men like his instructors, Charcot and Féré. During this period he wrote on the psychical life of microörganisms, on reasoning, on "animal magnetism," and on diseased or dissociated personalities (*15, 14, 47, 16*). In 1890 he became adjunct director of the laboratory of physiological psychology at the Sorbonne, Paris, along with Professor Beaunis, and later he became, and remained during all the rest of his life, the director of this laboratory. His thesis for the *doctorat ès sciences,* which he received in 1894, was on aspects of the nervous system in insects (*17*). He tells us that in the decade following 1887, when he gave up abnormal psychology, the larger part of his experiments were made in the schools of Paris and its suburbs (*66, page 5*). Under these conditions the carefulness of scientific technique, characteristic of studies in psychological laboratories on but a few experienced subjects, had to be sacrificed in a measure for the more practical conditions found in the schools. He gives interesting accounts of attempts in this early period to experiment on and study different classes of people with a view to the determination of individual differences.

EARLY EXPERIMENTAL STUDIES OF MEMORY AND IMAGINATION

The attention of Binet and his collaborators was early directed toward memory and creative imagination. He studied the creative imagination of dramatic authors and the memories and imagery of blindfolded chess players, who play as high as six to eight games at once, and of great calculators (*18*, *19*, *48*, *55*, *56*). A number of psychologists had already made thorough studies of memory by means of scientific methods. Some of these earlier studies of memory and of imagery, as well as his own studies, are reviewed by Binet in a book on experimental psychology (*20*, Chapters 5, 6), published in 1894.

As early as 1885 Ebbinghaus had published results of a study in which he worked out certain valuable methods of investigating memory (*110*), and nine years later Müller and Schumann (*165*) had reported results of an extended study along the same line, in which they had elaborated and improved upon the technique of Ebbinghaus. These methods were, however, ill adapted to the practical testing of children as to memory ability. As early as 1887 Jacobs (*138*) had devised and used a method of measuring the "span of prehension," which was easily applicable to practical use with groups, and which has consequently been widely used. His method was to measure how many letters and digits could be correctly reproduced after two auditory presentations, with an interval of about one-half second between each two successive letters or digits in the series. He began with short series, easy to grasp, and increased the length of the series in successive trials until the subjects were unable to repeat all the members. This method differs from one of those used by Ebbinghaus — "retained members" — and later by Pohlmann (*176*) in that in the latter case the series is too long for retention immediately after one or two repetitions. The subject by Ebbinghaus' method is given several repetitions and is then required to reproduce as many members of the series as he can. Either of these methods is readily adapted to practical testing requirements, and both are found in the Binet-Simon Scale later developed. Jacobs found the nonsense syllables of Ebbinghaus unsatisfactory because of distractions of attention and such variable factors as ease of pronunciation and audibility of the syllables.

Jacobs' results showed a slight increase in span with age and also with rank in the class; so he suggested that a "standard span" be added to the items then in use for anthropological measurement. Galton in some notes supplementary to this report says that, using the method of Jacobs, he had found greater variation in prehension but a more limited average span in idiots than in normal children. Bolton, as we have already seen (*supra*, page 84), used the memory-span method in the early nineties and obtained results similar to those of Jacobs. He also applied the method to problems of fatigue, of sex differences, of the influence on any digit of relative position in the series, and of the effects of such factors as practice and attention.

Several other studies of memory developed methods suitable to apply to school children, or suggestive of means for such application. Münsterberg and Bigham (*167*) carried out experiments in which series of either ten or twenty numbers, colors, geometrical forms, words of two consonants and an intervening vowel, and nonsense syllables were presented to a number of subjects simultaneously under controlled conditions and were to be reproduced by the several subjects in a manner to determine the effects of different forms of presentation, as visual and auditory, or a combination of these. The influence of different time intervals between presentation and recollection was also investigated.

MEMORY TESTS APPLIED TO SCHOOL CHILDREN

Kirkpatrick (*146*) presented to different groups of students varying in scholastic standing from the third grade to college, series of ten words and of ten objects. One series of names of common objects was read, another was presented visually, and under similar conditions series of objects were visually presented. Both immediate recollection and recollection after three days were required. The memory of objects seen was found to be very much superior to that of the names of objects; and in the case of the latter, visual presentation gave better results than auditory presentation. The subjects were able to recognize, when present among other words, nearly twice as many words as they could recall. In general, and this point is most important from our present standpoint, memory improved slightly with successively higher school grades.

Bourdon (*73*) experimented on 104 students who varied in age from eight to twenty years, with the idea of finding the influence of age on immediate memory. To each subject separately were read series of digits, of letters, and of words of one, two, and three syllables, of which the subject was immediately to reproduce as many members in each case as possible. Only small gains with increasing age were found in the reproductions, these being hardly noticeable, if at all present, for ages of fourteen to twenty years. He found, however, that there appeared to be a close agreement between immediate memory and that which is ordinarily called intelligence, a result that was in accord with the earlier work of Jacobs and Galton. This agreement between intelligence and immediate memory was especially marked when only extreme cases of intelligence (the very bright and the very dull) were considered — cases, the author points out, on which errors in classification as to intelligence would be improbable.

To this beginning in the way of tests of memory Binet and his associates added a number of contributions. In 1894 he and Henri (*49*) published results of a study in which individual tests were given to 300 children of the primary schools of Paris, varying in ages from seven to thirteen years. Two methods, recognition and reproduction, were used in the memory of lines of varying length — presented, of course, visually. By the first method the lines shown were, after five seconds, to be recognized in a series of lines of increasing lengths, while in the second method the subjects were to draw lines the lengths of those seen. It was found that ability in the tests increased regularly with age, the younger children overestimating the lengths of very short lines (1.5 and 4 mm.) and underestimating those of the longer lines (16, 40, and 68 mm.) more than did the older ones, but the errors of all the subjects were in the directions here stated. These studies led later to investigations of suggestibility.

In this same year appeared reports of experiments by the same authors on the memory of words and of sentences (*51, 52*). These reports are of considerable importance historically because of the rather extensive use of the memory of sentences made in the later intelligence scales by Binet and Simon. The authors emphasize the importance of verbal memory, not only as the chief foundation of instruction but as a basic factor in all forms of language, both written and oral. The experiments were carried out as group tests on 380 boys in the schools of Paris, ranging in ages from eight to thirteen years. Unrelated words, such as *dog*, *ladder, virtue,* etc., were arranged in series of increasing lengths (of from five to nine words) and were pronounced to the children by the director of the school, after he had thoroughly explained the procedure to be followed and had announced in advance, in each case, the number of words in the series. The children were to reproduce in writing as many of the words in each series as possible. The experiment was also given in modified forms, individually, to ten adults.

Slightly more words were retained by the children in the long than in the short series, and no effect of age was found in the primary schools in which the ages ranged from seven to twelve years. The authors supposed that under the conditions of the test the effect of age may have been concealed, but they admit that within the age limits investigated such effect is probably small. The span of the adults was found to be somewhat larger than that of the children (average 5.7 as compared with 4.7), this difference being probably due to the fact that the adults were capable of a greater "energetic effort of attention" (page 9). Evidence was found in some studies on adults with very long series that meaning is influential in retention, a fact that was early, and is now generally, recognized.

BINET REJECTS ASSOCIATION AS THE BASIS OF REVIVAL IN MEMORY

Revival in memory is usually explained on the principle of association by contiguity and resemblance, but "in reality," these authors assert, "those who take the pains to make observations of facts (*d'après nature*) will perceive that the principles of association do not account for all the phenomena — far from that; and we propose to show, *à propos* of our experiments on verbal memory, the existence of an entirely different mental operation, which is explained neither by contiguity nor by resemblance" (page 21). They find that while words may come up by association principles, recall is in some cases made by sheer effort with apparently no association. Vaschide came to similar conclusions from a study of localization in recollection (*225*). This process of recall independent of association Binet and Henri held to be not a special but a general phenomenon in memory, being present to some degree in all cases of recall; it involves a directing of the attention and of the will toward the experiences that have taken place, with a view to recalling them. "We have an idea of the whole of the experience, an idea that is very vague since the words learned do not always have among them an analogy of sense; but all the words have the common character of constituting part of the same experience, of having been learned together, of having been pronounced by one and the same person. They form a whole, and we are able to fix our attention on this whole" and thus voluntarily to call out its several parts (page 23). This is how, according to the testimony of different persons, reproduction of memories is effected. "It appears, indeed, that the direction of attention is the primordial condition of it." Thus for Binet attention comes to play a very important rôle in the manifestations of intelligence, a subject to which we shall recur presently.

ORIGIN AND USES OF THE MEMORY-OF-SENTENCES METHOD

While the memory of isolated words was not a new field, having been studied, as we have seen, by Münsterberg and Bigham, and also by Calkins (*84*), Binet and Henri say that in their study of the memory of sentences they enter upon a field entirely unexplored (page 25). These experiments were carried out on 510 children in the elementary schools of Paris. The method was the same as that used with words. In each case the short piece of prose to be reproduced was read by the teacher of the children in the presence of Binet and Henri, after the subjects had been explicitly instructed to attend for purposes of reproduction in writing. This particular orientation of attention the authors regarded as of much importance. Prose selections varying from eleven to eighty-six words were used, and the number of ideas reproduced was determined for each selection by marking the selection off into its several ideas and checking in the reproductions all the ideas found.[1] Here is an example of a short selection of twenty words divided into eight ideas by the authors of this study:

Le petit Émile | a obtenu | de sa mère | un joli | cheval mécanique | en récompense | de sa bonne conduite | à l'école.

The authors show in numerous graphs and tables that attention is not evenly distributed over the words of the sentences dictated, and that the ideas getting most attention are best retained. While these results come out clearly in the group studies, they could not be obtained with individual tests since distracting factors would vary. The authors claim to have discovered in this experiment a method of measuring the mean relative intensities of several states of consciousness, and they enthusiastically characterized their method as "a dynamometer of attention" (page 44). Comparing the reproductions of sentences by children of different ages and classes with those of isolated words, the comparisons often being rather crude, the authors conclude that the verbal memory of sentences is about twenty-five times superior to the memory of isolated words. Words that do not give any precise significance to the tho ght of the sentence are poorly remembered, this being true irrespective of their meanings individually considered. In the case of

[1] For this and other methods of studying memory and data obtained by the different methods, the reader is referred to Whipple, *Manual of Mental and Physical Tests.*

isolated words there is but little time to attend to any single word before the next one comes to crowd it out.

Only a slight tendency is shown in the results of this experiment for the number of reproduced ideas to increase with successively older groups, or with higher classes of children, but the authors did not consider all the data that were obtained; they selected for study only thirty-three to forty-four representative children of each class. It should be noted, however, that the average ages of the lowest (9 years) and of the highest (12 years) of the five classes compared differed by only three years. The differences in the average productions of the several classes were "small but constant." That Binet attached very great, doubtless too great, importance to these memory tests as indicators of general intelligence is evident from the large use that he made of them later in his intelligence scale. While Ebbinghaus had criticized memory tests adversely as measures of individual difference in mental ability, Binet favored them for two reasons: (1) memory involves content of the higher mental functions, not mere sensations, and (2) by means of memory tests one can indirectly study the operations and nature of such higher mental processes as discrimination, attention, and intelligence, as well as the interests, tastes, and generalizations of the individual (*23*, page 297).

Binet's memory-of-sentences method was used by Shaw (*189*) in a study in Worcester, Massachusetts, published two years after the appearance of the report by Binet and Henri. Shaw makes no reference whatever to the French publication, but his work was done under the direction of G. Stanley Hall, who had evidently read the report in the *Année*. The method of conducting the experiment and of tabulating the results is precisely that used by Binet and his collaborator. Shaw tested something over seven hundred students, selected in such a manner as to leave, after discarding papers of

students who for various reasons had not responded correctly
to the instructions, at least fifty papers from each sex in each
of the following grades : the third, the fifth, the seventh, the
tenth, and the twelfth. Any excess papers by either sex in
any grade were reduced to this number by a chance process.
He also tested fifty seventh-grade students by the visual
method, the student reading from a typed sheet, and in addition he tested by the regular method twenty students of
Clark University and thirty of Miss Aiken's school at Stam-
ford, Connecticut, making in all seven hundred students
whose papers were considered. It was found that some
facts were well and others poorly remembered by all groups,
the variations agreeing markedly in all the groups tested.
While no important sex differences appeared, there was a
constant increase in the average number of words reproduced
by children from the third grade up to the tenth, inclusive.
"One of the most striking facts brought out," says the
author, "was the early age at which children reach approximately their maximum memory power" (page 64). Unfortunately the average ages of the several groups are not
given, but it appears that the maximum memory ability
was reached at about sixteen years.

TESTS OF SUGGESTIBILITY

Their study of the memory of lines, as we have already
noted, led Binet and Henri into an investigation of the
effects of suggestibility. In 1894 they report (*48*) results of
an investigation on school children of the first three grades,
with ages ranging from 7 to 9 years, 9 to 11 years, and 11 to
13 years, respectively. Three lines of different lengths were
successively shown each child individually, and after a short
time interval a chart of lines of regularly increasing lengths
was presented to him. From this chart he was then to select
lines equal in length to those which he had previously seen,

called the models. The test was then repeated with the difference, however, that this time the five longest lines, including the one equal to the third model shown the child, were lacking in the chart now used. Children who had the first time selected for line three a length shorter than those now left out were excluded from this test. Of the first-grade children 88 per cent, of the second-grade 60 per cent, and of the third-grade 47 per cent yielded to the suggestion and chose for model three, lengths still on the second (incomplete) chart. Whereas in these experiments the children were compelled to rely on memory in the comparisons, they were now in a third experiment permitted to see during the comparison both the model line and the lines on the charts in the order in which the charts were previously used. In this case only the longest of the three models was used. Errors were now considerably reduced, and there was more assurance and less timidity shown by the children.

Now another interesting modification of the experiment was tried. A line 40 mm. long was shown the child, with the request that he choose from a chart as before a line to match it, the comparison being first by memory and then by direct perception, as already explained. But now, at the moment of the child's choice, the experimenter said in a calm, even voice, without any gesture, "Are you quite sure you are right?" The result of this suggestion was that of the first-grade children in the memory comparison 98 per cent, of the second 80 per cent, and of the third 54 per cent hesitated and changed their selection; while in the direct comparison the corresponding percentages were 74, 73, and 48. Thus not only were the younger children again found more ready to yield to the suggestion, but it turned out also that those who were most accurate in the first experiments changed their selections much less often under the caution by the experimenter than did the other children. What is particularly interesting is that, of those in this experiment who changed their selection on account of the caution, 81 per cent changed it for the better and only 19 per cent for the worse, this greater accuracy under the caution being true both for the memory and for the direct comparisons.

Suggestion in experiments on small groups of children collectively was also tried. Four children at a time were allowed to see simultaneously the model and the chart, and were asked to say, all together, which line equaled the model. In this case the children usually did not all respond at once; so the slower ones were thus influenced by the answers of the quicker ones. It was found that the younger children were influenced to a much greater degree by the early answers than were the older children, yet effects of this sort of suggestibility were found to some extent in all the grades tested.

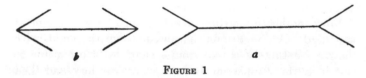

FIGURE 1

The reader will note that line *a* in Figure 1 appears to be longer than line *b*, although the lines are equal, as measurement will show. This is the well-known Müller-Lyer illusion. *a* looks longer than *b* because the small lines at its ends point outward so as to lead the observer unconsciously to make a wider sweep of eye-movements and to take note somehow of a wider space than is necessary in the case of *b*. By an arrangement of figures on the right-hand leaves of an album, so that lines of different lengths could be readily compared successively with another figure, Binet (21) studied the Müller-Lyer illusion effects on the perception of sixty school children of an average age of 12 years, and of forty-five of an average age of 9 years. He found that the illusion is stronger in the younger than in the older children, though individual variations were marked.

It is interesting to compare these results with those obtained by Dresslar (*107*) in experiments of a somewhat different kind carried out a little earlier. Dresslar studied the relations of the size-weight illusion — the tendency to perceive large objects as lighter than smaller objects of the same actual weight — to intelligence. The 173 children tested ranged in ages from 7 to 14 years, and were classified by their teachers into three groups — "bright," "good," and "dull." While the illusion was found to be constant throughout this range of ages, instead of being more marked in the dull children, as had been expected, it turned out that "The more intelligent the children, other things being equal, the stronger are the associations between the ideas[1] of size and weight of a given material" (page 462).

Binet and his collaborators carried out various other experiments on suggestibility, and in 1900 he published a volume of nearly four hundred pages on his experiments on this subject (*30*). Much work on suggestion had been done in France and elsewhere by means of hypnotism, but Binet presented his facts independently of these data and of other studies on pathological conditions. Rejecting the loose use of the term "suggestion," current at that time and even in our own day to some extent, he regarded the true meaning of this term to be a moral pressure of one individual, or of several individuals, on another, tending to produce an automatic state of mind. Moral is here used in the broad sense of the term common to French psychologists. Suggestion on this view may be effected through fear, love, charm, intimidation, respect, admiration, etc. The tests whose results are considered in this volume are, besides those on

[1] "Perceptions" would be a better term here. Why?

suggestion already considered, one dealing with the effect of a certain suggestion on weight discrimination, one on how by questions a judge may influence the witness, and one on the influence toward continuing certain subconscious movements automatically, once they have been started with the rhythm of a metronome whose movements the subject was to see and continue to count. Simple writing movements were likewise studied.

Simon, who was a student under Binet, published in 1900 a study on defectives (*192*) in which he carried into the abnormal field the work on suggestion which had been developed on normal subjects. Using the same methods that Binet had used on normal children, he applied a number of Binet's tests to twenty-seven defectives from the Vaucluse asylum. He found that the subjects were classified by the tests in a manner largely similar to that determined with normal children, except that a bizarre type appeared with reactions that were very irregular and indefinite, and that the lower imbeciles were wholly beyond suggestibility. There was, then, less suggestibility in the subnormal than in the normal children.

DESCRIPTION-OF-OBJECTS AND DESCRIPTION-OF-PICTURES TESTS

One of the means that Binet used in measuring the subject's higher complex processes, and one that was put to service in his description-of-pictures test in the later intelligence scale, was the description of an object (*23*). Binet says that as early as 1893 he and Henri had carried out experiments with this test in a primary school. A complex picture was shown to a class of children, and two minutes later the children were to describe in writing from memory what they had seen. For this writing a ten-minute period was allowed. The cards and results were put aside for a time due to occupation with other researches. In the meantime Binet discovered that Miss Bryant (*80*) had used a similar method in her more complex description-of-a-room test, much earlier than this.

Binet reports results of group tests applied to 175 children ranging in ages from 8 to 14 years. Five copies of the same picture were used in a room, and the students were grouped so that they could each see one of the pictures. A control group of twelve subjects was then given ten minutes to describe the same picture, which in this case remained before them while they wrote. Thus was determined just what, in the memory reproductions, was actually due to retention or memory and what to the selectiveness of attention. It was found, however, that many of the subjects in the smaller control group observed only for a period of from one and one half to two minutes and then wrote the rest of the time without further reference to the picture. Others looked at it again at the end of the writing, evidently to verify what they had written. The number of lines of descriptive matter was counted — a poor criterion, no doubt — and was found to increase with age, but not rapidly. Most subjects stopped writing before the end of the ten-minute period.

It was also found, both in the memory and in the observation reproductions, that objects are noted according to their importance to the child. The nature of the child more than that of the objects determines the selection, said Binet. The observation reports were in general only a little longer than the memory reports, and they gave more of the details of the pictures. Binet was impressed with the descriptions and classed the subjects, according to their dominant tendencies, into describers (who merely enumerate objects without being impressed with the events they portray), observers (who attend more to the part each object in the picture plays in the whole scene), the emotional type (who fill their descriptions with sentiment, neglecting details), and the erudite or learned type (who give a story about the picture). These differences were corroborated in a similar experiment on adult subjects.

After making his classification of the subjects into these various types, Binet attempted to determine whether his subjects of the emotional type really were emotional in practical-life conditions or whether they showed this type of reaction only under the conditions of the experiment and as a result of past training for such specific situations. He found in the estimates of the children by their teachers that of five students who had been classed with the emotional type, four were characterized by their teachers as of a frigid character, a dry nature! This was, of course, not a very adequate test of the validity of the classification, for the teachers' estimates may themselves be wrong, and also the number of cases is entirely inadequate. It is significant, however, that though Binet makes much use of the description-of-an-object test in his later intelligence scales, the "emotional type" does not occur in his classification of the responses.

It will be recalled that Ferrari published, in the year before the one that brought the article by Binet, an account of an experiment on the description of pictures of actors shown in successive stages of an act. Leclère (*156*) two years later made seven classes of the responses which he obtained by showing a watch to a class of thirty girls varying in ages from 13 to 17 years, and asking them to write what was "suggested" by the object, and he was led to believe from his results that the papers furnished a fair measure of the mental development of persons at that age, as compared with younger or older subjects.

While Binet had taken a very definite stand on the superior value for "individual psychology" of the testing of complex mental processes, he nevertheless devoted much of his time to physical tests. His early work in abnormal psychology would naturally connect up with the study of such physiological processes as circulation and blood pressure. In a review of Dumas' article on joy and sadness (*108*) Binet (*25*) shows in 1897 a broad practical acquaintance with circulatory phenomena, and refers to methods used in his own laboratory in physiological researches. He points out the error made by Dumas and all previous writers in assuming that the coldness of the extremities after prolonged intellectual work and the discoloration of the tissues are indications of vaso-constriction. A slow pulse and lessened dicrotism very high up on the line of oblique ascension shows instead, he points out, a general lowering of organic vitality; so conclusions as to vaso-constriction without a study of the force of the capillary pulse are not reliable.

In the same year appears an article in an American journal by Binet and Vaschide (*65*), criticizing the method used by Kiesow and others, and showing that only with a certain properly selected counter pressure on the fingers studied does one find an increased pulsation with mental calculation. Kiesow's negative results are shown to be due to a failure to take note of this factor. In this study, however, only one subject is used, and the statistical treatment is inadequate. Several more lengthy articles by Binet and his associates, on the influence of intellectual work, of the emotions, and of physical work on the heart action and the blood pressure, as well as on changes in these bodily processes with different hours of the day, were published in the *Année* of 1897 and

in subsequent volumes.   It was determined that the effect
of intellectual work, of talking vigorously for a period of three
minutes, of physical exertion, of excitation of the senses, and
of the physical arousal of pain was in each case increased
blood pressure, but other bodily changes were not all alike
under these various circumstances.   With joy and sadness
increased blood pressure was also found.   The effect of the
meals at midday and evening was to accelerate the pulse and
to raise the temperature of the hands and armpits.   The
influence of these changes on performance in a mental test
was not, of course, and has never been, determined.

THE FRENCH AND THE GERMAN METHODS OF INVESTIGATING MENTAL FATIGUE

It is interesting to note that studies in mental work and
mental fatigue in the latter part of the nineties differed
materially in France on the one hand and in Germany on the
other as to methods.   In the former country, largely under
the leadership of Binet, the method was physiological and
indirect, attempting to find physiological changes and sensibility changes indicative of, or correlating with, the mental
fatigue; whereas in Germany the method was direct and
attempted to measure the actual amount of mental work
accomplished in equal lengths of time before and during
mental fatigue, as well as the accuracy of such work.   Neither
of these methods, however, seems to have been very successful or productive of trustworthy results, for we are still in
ignorance concerning many essential aspects and results of
mental fatigue.   We have not yet sufficiently controlled
all the relevant factors in experiments on fatigue.   A review
of the early investigations of fatigue is given in Binet and
Henri's book on intellectual fatigue (54).

EXERCISES

1. List all the means that you can find employed by Binet for determining the validity of any test as a measure of intelligence.

2. What are the defects in tests of memory which measure memory by the amount or the percentage that can be reproduced? What is this method called? What other methods can you find listed in psychology books? Of which ones did Binet make the most use in his early tests? Specify where he used them. Which methods are probably most serviceable in intelligence testing? Why? What objections might one offer to calling reproduction tests tests of memory?

3. What do you consider the basis of suggestibility in a person? Is a person suggestible in general, or in certain respects only? What additional tests of suggestibility can you offer?

CHAPTER EIGHT

BINET ON MEASUREMENT IN INDIVIDUAL PSYCHOLOGY

In 1898 an important article by Binet appeared in the *Revue Philosophique* (*27*), in which he discusses measurement in individual psychology and gives us a good idea of the problems and methods on which he was working at that time. He points out that there is little value in studying intelligence and character traits if we confine ourselves only to descriptions without measurement, however rough and approximative this latter may have to be. From illustrations of measurement in such special functions as visual acuity, two-point discrimination, and auditory acuity, which are relatively simple, he approaches the higher functions and raises the question, "But when we come to the measurement of intelligence, what method can we use? How can we measure the richness of inspiration, the accuracy of judgment, the ingenuity of the mind?" (page 113). Recognizing that a precise and satisfactory solution of this problem must await a broader experience, he limits himself to suggestions that have come to him while at work on the problem. He says that when forced to make evaluations of mental traits and abilities, he has had recourse to empirical and provisional procedures which, though very numerous, he groups for simplicity under two main heads: first, the measurement of results obtained while the conditions of the test are kept constant; second, making such gradations in the test as will reduce the results to the maximum of simplicity.

Methods of measuring results obtained while the conditions of the test are kept constant. Several methods, more or less precise, are included under the first head. The test may be so arranged that the subject draws a line to match one shown him by the experimenter. The latter then announces that he will next expose to view a slightly longer line, which is likewise to be matched by drawing a line with its length parallel to the first one drawn. This time, however, the line shown is actually shorter. In this suggestibility test the results can be accurately measured in terms of length. Again, the results can be expressed as a definite number in tests of memory and of the rapidity of perception, consisting of a five-second exposure of fourteen familiar objects fastened to a large card and the recalling immediately afterward of the several objects, or in such cases as the description-of-an-object test, in which one counts the number of ideas or of words. Measurements of the time required in certain performances, such as mental calculations, he suggests, are also widely applicable. When it is impossible to make precise measurements, one can often succeed in making gradations in the several responses. In the crudest case the test can either be passed or not passed. Tests of this sort, however, which permit of only two grades of answers can be given flexibility by the artifice of repetition of elements of the same degree of difficulty. Thus one may require the subject to reconstruct fifteen sentences of equal difficulty, of which the words have been disarranged, or to repeat, one at a time, fifteen numbers of six digits each. The responses are then objectively divided into sixteen grades, according to whether no success, or any number of successes up to fifteen, is obtained.

An interesting example of the graded responses is the "morality test," which Binet gave, under the guise of a literary test, to pupils in a primary school of Paris. A simple story is told of a child who by accident breaks a violin belonging to a comrade, and the pupils are asked each to write down what he would do if he were the owner of the violin. Binet classified the responses, about one hundred in number, into eight groups, making a scale of the degrees of severity shown as follows :

1. Excuse the comrade, or take active steps to see that he is not punished.

2. Pardon him.

3. Pardon him, expressing strong regret and sorrow.

4. Reproach him, unless egoistic motives prevent this.

5. Announce to the comrade that hereafter he cannot borrow anything.

6. Ask a small indemnity, some sous.

7. Make him pay the whole price of the violin.

8. Seek to get revenge on him.

Binet points out that even though differences would doubtless arise as to classifications, the method is objective. He does not insist on its value as a morality test, this being a matter of interpretation, but is interested fundamentally in the method. Here, then, we see clearly the idea of a scale, but the reactions of all subjects are made to one and the same circumstance.

In all such cases as the foregoing ones Binet preferred to leave off the arbitrary or the subjective elements and to develop a purely objective means of evaluation. He gives finally, also from his experiences, two examples of complex methods of measurement which he says have been very puzzling. The first is a method of measuring a person's comprehension of a difficult text. A selection of five lines from John Stuart Mill's *Logic* is used. In this test Binet shows his keen insight into human nature. He points out that to ask a subject to say what in the text he does not understand would be unsatisfactory and would serve to embarrass him ; so he chooses the indirect method of having the subject read it over once and then reproduce in writing as much as he can remember of it, at least of the sense of the passage. The selection is purposely so long that only those with remarkable memories can recall the words if they do not get the meaning. He reports that those who do not understand the text either reproduce nothing at all or only a few words in fragments. By this indirect method Binet would measure the comprehension power of the subject and save his self-respect, not having him directly confess his inability to understand. He adds that subjects will generally say that they understood the passage perfectly well when it was read but forgot it before reproduction, for as La Rochefoucauld said, "A person will complain of his memory, but never of his judgment."

Now when these data — the subjects' "memories" — have been obtained, how can their several comprehensions be measured? Evidently not absolutely as one would measure the length of a line with a ruler, or weigh something on the scales, but relatively; that is, by classification of the subjects, according to the completeness of their reproductions, into two, three, or more groups. This is a measurement in the sense that it classifies the individuals, putting one ahead of another and behind a third one. In this respect the comprehension test comes out to be similar to the morality test, and it was Binet's hope that after a thorough study of the difficulties in the passage a scale like that of the latter might be arranged.

The other complex test mentioned involves exactly the same difficulties of measurement as the one just considered. It is the well-known paper-cutting test, which later appeared in all three of the Binet-Simon intelligence scales. Binet here calls it a test of visual memory, and says that it was first suggested to him by Henri. The results are provisionally handled as in the comprehension test, although the goal of a scale comparable to that of the morality test is held in mind.

Measurement by gradations in the test itself. The second general procedure suggested in this article toward a method of measurement in individual psychology relates to a gradation in the test itself rather than in the results obtained with it, as illustrated above; and in this regard it comes nearer to the plan first adopted in the intelligence scale, in 1905, and retained to some extent in the later revisions; but the several units of the scales are made up almost completely of the first class of tests here illustrated by Binet.

The most usual way of varying the test with the idea of reducing the results to the simplest form, as seen in Binet's own work, is to make it progressively more difficult until the subject fails on it. To illustrate this method, a test of the memory of objects is described in this article. The subject is first shown a small number of objects, say three, for five seconds, and is then asked to write them down. Next he is shown for the same period of time four objects, then five, and so on, until a number is reached which he cannot retain completely. The maximum number of objects remembered yields a simple, precise measure of the subject's memory of this kind of content. This test resembles closely the digit-span test, also cited, which was first used by Jacobs, and which consists in reciting to the subject increasingly long series of digits to be reproduced.

Two more examples are chosen, these from the study of motor skill. One is the now well-known steadiness test, then already in use by psychologists, in which the subject inserts a needle into successively smaller holes until the side of a hole is touched and indicated by some means, such as the making of an electric contact. The other test, originated by Binet to measure steadiness of hand and skill in the balancing of objects, consists in successively increasing the displacement of the center of gravity of a piece of apparatus up to the point where the subject can no longer keep the object in equilibrium.

Instead of giving a test in a form more and more difficult, one may repeat it without change until the subject has attained some definite goal in a learning process, or otherwise has arrived at some objective and easily determined end. This method is mentioned as especially applicable to various sorts of suggestibility experiments in which one, two, or three preliminary tests are given to create a habit, followed by a blank test to see how much of the suggestion of the preliminary tests is carried over. The example given is one of Seashore's experiments. A white screen is illuminated in such a way that the intensity of illumination can be gradually lessened by pulling a cord. The subject, who thinks he is undergoing a test of perception, is to announce at what moment he becomes aware of the change in brightness. The test is made several times without deception, and then, by means of a special arrangement, the experimenter pulls slowly on the cord as before, but now without causing any change in the lighting. The smaller the number of preliminary tests required to produce enough suggestion to cause the subject to announce a change when none takes place, the greater his suggestibility. Binet also tells us of attempts, then but recently made, to measure by a similar method the intensity of mental images; but the results were too uncertain for consideration.

Several tests mentioned in this article were employed later by Binet and Simon in the construction of their intelligence scales, as the reader will see if he will examine in order the several tests of these scales.

Binet closes with two general remarks. The first one is that measuring by any of the methods described, even though the results are expressed in precise figures, is not measurement in the physical sense of the term. When we measure the length of three beams of 6, 7, and 8 meters, respectively, we get differences which are equal in an absolute sense, but this is not true of psychological measurements because no absolute zero point is known. Thus if one subject scores 6 digits, one 7, and one 8 in the digit-span test, we cannot say that the differences between the second and each of the other two are equal, or that the first subject is three fourths as good as the last. Attempts have been made since Binet's day to determine an absolute-zero point in test scales, but with little success, and the cautions here given are still valuable. The second remark deals with qualitative differences in individuals, predisposing some of them toward literature and similar imaginative pursuits, others toward the sciences and callings which deal with the more stubborn realities of life. Certain individuals are endowed with very strong emotivities of different kinds — æsthetic, moral, egoistic, etc. — and, Binet reminds us, it is a problem for the future to determine the various physical signs and manifestations of these several types of personality. Individuals do not differ by degrees only ; this is the essence of the second remark.

ATTENTION AND ADAPTATION : RELATIONS TO INTELLIGENCE

The year 1900 brought an article by Binet (29) on the subject "Attention and Adaptation," the aim of which was not to find out what attention is, a question that he regarded as solved, but rather the very practical one of devising methods by which to measure the force of voluntary attention in any person. From a class of thirty-two children in a primary school in Paris, he had the class teacher and the director of the school select for him the five "most intelligent" and the six "least intelligent," and these children he studied carefully as to the force of their voluntary attention. His method of study was to give to these two groups of children numerous tests, in a search for those which would prove most fit to measure voluntary attention. The tests that gave about equal results for the two groups were rejected as bad, while those that showed up the greatest differences between these groups of children were regarded as good. The children averaged 10.7 years and 11.25 years of age for the "intelligent" and the "unintelligent" groups, respectively.

Binet's experiments on attention. The experimental work was rather extensive and involved the following tests: 1. Tactile sensibility on the back of the hand together with effects of practice. 2. Simple and choice reaction times. 3. Counting dots in groups of varying sizes and in series. 4. Perception of changes in the rapidity of strokes made by a specially devised metronome. 5. Counting periodic sounds of five impulses per second. 6. Copying a long series of digits, an easy and a hard sentence, unrelated words, and a complicated design. In the case of digits, sentences, and words the number of digits or words for each look at the copy was noted; in the case of the design, which was composed entirely of straight lines, the number of acts of looking at the copy was recorded. The copying in this latter case could not be aided by "interior language," so the number of acts varied from eight to sixteen. 7. Memory of letters and of numbers. 8. Quick perceptions, the test consisting of the reproduction of certain words after momentary exposures, and of the copying, after successive momentary exposures, of the Greek design now well known because of its use in the Binet-Simon scale. 9. The cancellation of letters from a printed page. Five letters were written at the top of the page and the subjects were to cross out as rapidly and accurately as possible all letters included in this group and occurring in the printed words. The experiment was then changed by designating five new letters to be crossed out, and later six letters, of which, however, only two were new. 10. Simultaneous addition to three given numbers, 6–28–43. The subject was to write results of successive additions of one to each number and continue with this process without seeing his figures, which were covered by the experimenter with a small card as soon as they were written. Thus he would write 7–29–44, 8–30–45, etc., both for speed and accuracy. 11. Speed in reading columns of twenty numbers formed by adding mentally the number one to each of a list of twenty numbers. The subject calls, for example, eight for seven. Also speed of counting two series of dots (test 3) and of copying sentences (test 6). The time taken to count dots and to copy a given sentence was noted for each subject, who, however, was not aware that he was timed. Thus his natural time was obtained.

In all these experiments the tests were repeated once at least, generally more times, being modified in certain particulars in the repetitions.

What is attention? In the conclusion Binet tells us that after spending four months in the testing of attention he must still ask if it is really attention that he has measured, and he admits that he may be criticized for having missed the end that he started out to reach; for attention is not a thing on whose meaning all can agree as on that of memory or imagination. His own assumption has been "that attention consists in a mental adaptation to a state that is new to us." The idea was that of finding how persons of different degrees of intelligence differ in their reactions to conditions presenting difficulties. He avoided being involved in the usual dualistic speculations regarding voluntary attention, and admits that one may attempt to measure attention by means of tests very different from those employed by him — such, for instance, as the effects of distractions on mental work. The difficulties presented to the subject in Binet's tests were intended to be difficulties not of reason or of comprehension but of adjustment to a situation that is of such a nature that the errors committed depend on the mental constitution of the subject and not simply on his good will.

How Binet selected the best tests for his purpose. Now, having results on the two groups differing in estimated intelligence, he is able to ascertain which ones of the tests make the clearest discrimination between individuals as to their general mental ability. The tests which were found by this means to be of no value in making such discrimination are those of perception of increase or decrease in the strokes of a metronome, quick perception of words, reaction time, and speed of work. Binet says that he has arrived at the conviction that speed in his tests has no relation to the intelligence of the several pupils (pages 390 and 396), but he is not willing to assert that this will be true in all tests.

All the other tests showed clear discrimination between the group of intelligent and the group of unintelligent children. In the first test it was found that the children in the intelligent group, as he called it in contradistinction to the unintelligent group, showed much the finer tactile sensibility in the first trial, but they did not improve as much through successive trials as did the duller children. He believed, however, that this was due rather to a greater finesse of judgment than to a finer tactile sensibility.

Binet discusses the several tests that made a clear difference between the two groups of children, considering their naturalness, the sort of apparatus or materials necessary for their use in practical testing, and other points which add to or detract from their merit as intelligence tests. It is very clear that his main object is that of selecting valid and suitable intelligence tests, though in these experiments he has approached it through a study of attention as adaptation, which, as we have already seen, he now regards as an essential characteristic of intelligence. In the present article Binet devotes some space to the consideration of the influence of practice and habitude, and finds that his data show a much more rapid adaptation by the intelligent than by the unintelligent subjects. It is not improbable that these data and Binet's opinion have influenced Stern in his definition of intelligence as a general power of adaptation. This question of the relation of quickness of adaptation to intelligence Binet hoped to treat more fully in later researches, but these researches were apparently never carried out.

EFFECTS OF DISTRACTION ON ATTENTION

The article is a long one and the work on it was doubtless influential on his later activity of intelligence-scale construction. The report is followed by another, by the same author (*28*), in which he gives results of studies of tactual sensibility in two girls and a young man, the girls being his own daughters. Compass contacts on the back of the hand, as before, were made, while the subjects, as a means of distraction, were asked to add numbers and give aloud each progressive step. Results were now compared with similar discriminations made without such distraction. Differences were not very significant with respect to the problem investigated, for it was discovered that subjects varied in the extent to which they tended to set up verbal automatisms and so to generalize their answers. Therefore the answers "one point" and "two point" did not express the actual degree of sensitiveness under these conditions of distraction.

BINET'S "EXPERIMENTAL STUDY OF INTELLIGENCE"

Binet's extensive testing of his two daughters, results of which were published in 1902 in a separate volume entitled *The Experimental Study of Intelligence* (*34*), was doubtless a most important step in his preparation for the later construction and establishment of the intelligence scale. In this book Binet characterizes the psychology of Fechner and Wundt as having borrowed from physiology its apparatus, its stimuli, and its methods. Attention has been given mainly to material conditions of the experiment, and the rôle of the persons serving as subjects has been reduced to the minimum. On the other hand, the new movement to which Binet has contributed with all his energy, with the collaboration of several of his students, especially of M. Henri, he tells us, consists in giving a larger place to introspection and in carrying the investigations into the higher mental phenomena, such as memory, attention, imagination, and the orientation of ideas. He then criticizes the narrower sense in which "stimulus" has been used, even by Ribot, and defines stimulus as not simply the application of a material excitant to our sense organs but as changes which the experimenter provokes at will in the subject's consciousness. He calls attention to the important and subtle rôle of language as a stimulus in this sense. Any stimulus, whether a physical object or a verbal symbol, he points out, produces a complexity of reactions, which continue in complicated forms for some time and of which the immediate sensation is but a small part. Instead of limiting the study to the sensations, one should take into account the larger and more far-reaching reactions of the individual, including the various aptitudes which they reveal. For this broader study no specifically new technique is necessary, but it is important to study not just the simple movements of the subject and the reports on the sensations experienced, "but the whole group of reactions for which the individual is the stage" (page 4).

Binet then proceeds to a very extensive qualitative analysis of his two daughters, Marguerite and Armande, 14½ and 13 years of age, respectively. A number of other subjects were also used to some extent. He begins with simple exercises, such as having each subject in separate sittings write a series of twenty words, just any words that come to mind. He notes the time, or the quickness, of these responses and studies the words given, going over the lists with the subject

so as to get their significance and their settings in the subject's
own thought; he notes the frequency of words referring to
self and to things relating to self, to external objects, to recent
and to remote memories, to fantasies; he follows up the
various evidences of tendencies to neglect sense objects and
to dwell on imaginary content, or the reverse; he studies
vocabularies and interests as manifested in the words given;
he investigates the connections between successive pairs of
words, finding that a number of words in immediate succession relate to some general "theme" and that changes of
theme occur more often in the responses of the one subject
than in those of the other; he quizzes the subjects gently
and patiently on what lead from one word to the next. Day
after day he studies new series of words. He rejects the laws
of the associationist as adequate explanations of the connections between successive words. Sentences are called
for in the same manner, and investigated in similar detail;
he observes the incipient movements of the subjects in writing
these words and sentences, without letting them know that he
is doing this, so that their reactions will be natural; he notes
the exact time taken for deliberation before the writing of
each of the sentences called for; and he traces out the
various tendencies and natural dispositions of each subject
as revealed in these various responses and corroborated in
test after test, far beyond the point sufficient to satisfy one
of less genius.

Continuing his studies, he presents word after word to the
subject, who is required to give the ideas and images suggested by each stimulus; he studies images, tendencies to
subvocal speech, etc., in these young and inexperienced
subjects, devoid of a knowledge of psychology and of its
various theories of imageless thought, and concludes that
images are not essential to thought. As many as sixty-seven
pages are given in the book to images, with probably more

attention to imageless thought than to the subjects' characteristics. Whether meanings are general or particular is
found to be determined not simply by the nature of the words
given, but by the significance they have to the subject at the
time and in the particular setting. He leads on further into
the force of voluntary attention (as already given above in
the consideration of distraction effects), and finds that attention can be measured only with a group of tests, and not with
any single test or device. The completion of sentences,
the description of objects and of events, the evocation of
various sorts of memories, and the development of themes —
these are topics that are each studied in a similar intimate,
natural, and thorough manner. The materials and methods
used are the simplest; there is no apparatus of the showy
and costly kind. As a consequence of this simplicity Binet
has been charged with being unscientific, but his work is
thorough, painstaking, and persistent; difficult things are
attacked with the marvelous simplicity of a great artist,
and tangled problems yield gradually as they are examined,
turned over, and scrutinized from all angles by means of
ever multiplying data.

Finally he emerges with beautiful pictures of personality
differences, not in terms of simple numbers or even of graphs,
but in terms nevertheless so objective and so well verified
that his results are in the main indisputable. Through all
this search Binet has shown a master's hand in discovering
realities in human nature and in *letting facts lead*, rather than
being determined by prejudices and theories.

Marguerite he finds to be better oriented than Armande
to the immediate, objective world, to be a good observer,
to have a good literal memory; she is precise, preoccupied
with things relating to herself, practical-minded; her attention is regular and her effort constant; her images are definite and intense, notwithstanding the obvious fact, as the

experiments show, that her involuntary imagery is poorly developed and that she has little aptitude for reverie. While her space perceptions are exact, those of temporal relations are poorly developed. The picture of Armande is very different. She is detached from the real world, imaginative, vague in her ideas, and has tendencies to verbalism. Her attention is inward, but yet not as much turned toward her immediate self as is that of the older sister; it dwells on the more remote past, and on the future, and yet her images are faint and poorly defined. Her involuntary imagery is well developed, and she delights to live in a world of fancy.

But these pictures are to Binet only a proof of his method; they show that individual psychology is possible, that simple tests in sufficient variety can discover individual differences. No attempt is made to evaluate the amount of intelligence, however. What a disappointment this study would be to those who ask merely *how much* in general! That was of course not the problem in this research, but Binet shows how much of value a thorough analysis of the several tendencies and traits can reveal. While his conditions for study were very good, — the sisters were his own daughters, — this study at least shows what is possible; it holds up an ideal as to qualitative results. It also gave Binet invaluable experience for the work on the intelligence scale which was still before him, although in the latter case he came closer to the determination of quantitative differences in mentality.

PHYSICAL MEASUREMENTS AND THEIR RELATIONS TO INTELLIGENCE

Binet and his collaborators carried out in the latter part in the nineties a large number of physical tests, with the idea of measuring "the physical force of an individual from a special point of view" (*66*, page 1). They attempted to measure separately certain aspects of physical strength and then to determine what sort of correlations exist among these several physical qualities of an individual. They point out that while the testing of different physical traits had advanced a good deal, the study of intercorrelations among these traits had hardly passed its beginning stage. The reason for this unequal development of the study of the two aspects of physical traits was, in their view, that the measurement of traits does not require large numbers of subjects, whereas reliable correlations do require large numbers. They themselves did not know this latter fact in advance of their study, and found it out by their own mistakes, for, alas! "it is only after having completed a piece of work that one knows how it should be done" (page 2).

The subjects and the tests. The tests were first carried out on forty-five boys in the Paris public schools of an average age of 13 years, the results of only forty being considered, but they were later applied also to forty young men 18 to 20 years of age, these subjects being students in the Versailles normal school. The tests used include strength of grip of both right and left hands as measured by the oval dynamometer, strength of back by vertical pull, strength of arms by climbing a rope, strength of legs by broad and high jump (only for older boys), and two tests on endurance with the use of the dynamometer and the Mosso ergograph; tests of the quickness of reaction, both simple and choice reactions being determined, of rate of tapping in a period of five seconds, of quickness of pressure on the dynamometer, and of speed of running; tests of respiration as measured by lung capacity with the spirometer, by finding the normal and the expanded chest measures, and by determining the maximum distance at which the subject could blow out a candle; and tests of circulation, measured by the pulse records under various conditions of mental attitude and physical exertion. Photographs of standing position and of the profile, and various anatomical measurements were also taken. These measurements were weight, height, length of trunk; girth of shoulders, of arm, and of wrist; length of limbs, of medius, and of stride; and five head diameters. The head of the school also furnished information as to social status of the parents and gave certain moral characterizations of the boys. He also ranked the boys according to estimated intelligence. In addition to the physical measurements of the subjects, their memory span of digits was also determined.

Binet's methods of correlation and his results. The results are not treated very scientifically. No measures of variability from the averages are given, and in many instances slight errors in calculation are made. The degree of variability of the scores in each test is roughly shown by dividing the subjects into four equal groups according to their rank in a given test and then getting the percentage relationship between the first and the last divisions. The work shows evidence of hasty and superficial treatment.

Correlations are not, of course, calculated by methods now in use, but are indicated approximately by two other methods devised by the authors. In the first of these the names of the forty subjects are divided into four equal groups according to the ranks of these subjects in some one test, and opposite each group is then placed the average of their ranks obtained in some other test with which this one is to be correlated. If the correlation in the two tests is high, these averages will, of course, increase rapidly for successive groups from the first to the fourth. An illustration will make this method clear. In Table 1 the letters A to L represent the names of subjects, and the Roman numerals indicate the different tests. The numbers of the subjects represent their respective ranks. The correspondence between the ranks in Tests I and II is obviously rather close because the averages of the successive quarters of the ranks in the second column,

TABLE 1

SUBJECTS	TESTS		AVERAGE
	I	II	
A	1	2	
B	2	1	2⅓
C	3	4	
D	4	3	
E	5	5	4⅔
F	6	6	
G	7	8	
H	8	7	8
I	9	9	
J	10	11	
K	11	12	11
L	12	10	

TABLE 2

SUBJECTS	TESTS				TOTALS
	I	II	III	IV	
A	1	2	1	3	7
B	2	1	5	1	9
C	3	4	3	6	16
D	4	3	4	2	13
E	5	5	6	4	20
F	6	6	8	7	27
G	7	8	7	10	32
H	8	7	2	9	26
I	9	9	12	8	38
J	10	11	9	12	42
K	11	12	11	5	39
L	12	10	10	11	43

Test II, increase regularly from 2⅓ to 11. The correlation is high whenever the averages in each case are just equal to the similar averages in the first column, Test I. The first and the second average is each out by only a fraction and the third and forth agree with those of the first column; but the absolute amount of the divergences is not a reliable index of the degree of correlation.

The second correlation method used in this study was to arrange the names of the subjects according to the rank of the scores in one of the tests, and then to write opposite the name of each subject his rank in each of the other tests. This method is illustrated in Table 2. When these ranks are added, the correlation is high if the totals of the ranks of each subject increase rather regularly from the first name to the last. If the several totals remain practically constant from the first to the last name, there is no correlation. The illustration shows only three exceptions to a constant increase in the totals from the first to the last number; hence the correlation is positive and somewhat marked. While the difference between the first and smallest total and the largest one is 36 (43−7), it is not as large as it would be if the correlation were perfect, — i.e., 44, or 48−4. Even such a difference, however, would not prove that the correlation between each successive pair of tests is perfect, a fact that is probably obvious to the reader.

These methods of correlation, while somewhat superior to a general estimate based on the ranks alone, are obviously far inferior to a method developed in its essential features by Galton and later perfected by Pearson and others. This method, now commonly in use, expresses the correlation in a single number, the percentage of correlation between the two columns; and while it is applicable in a strict sense to only two series of measurements or test scores at a time, there are a number of ways now developed of expressing the correlation of one test with several others combined. This more accurate correlation method was probably first applied in 1901 to the results of intelligence tests by Clark Wissler, one of Cattell's students. By Binet's method the relative standing of any individual could at once be seen by taking note of the relative size of his total of the ranks in all the tests; the smaller the size of this total, the higher was the standing. Thus, in Table 2, A is seen at once to have the highest standing and B is close to A, while J has nearly as low standing as L.

By the methods indicated Binet and Vaschide found a considerable degree of correlation among the various physical measurements of the group of younger boys, and somewhat less correlation in the case of the older subjects. Only a slight correlation was found between memory span for digits and the combined physical tests, and also between the latter and estimated intelligence, this latter positive relationship existing only in the extreme groups as ranked for intelligence — that is, in the best and the poorest one fourth of the subjects.

PHYSICAL DEVELOPMENT AND INTELLIGENCE IN THE
FEEBLE-MINDED

In 1900 Simon published an article giving records of anthropometric measurements of 223 abnormal boys ranging in ages from 8 to 23 years (*191*). This research was carried out under the direction of Binet, in the colony of Vaucluse on persons with various degrees of feeble-mindedness down to and including idiocy. The object was to find out whether there is any correlation between the physical traits measured and intellectual capacity. The following measurements were made : height, chest, breadth of shoulders, maximum circumference of the head, weight, and reach of the arms. Correlation tables are given to show the interrelations of these several measurements, and age comparisons of these children are made with data from normal children obtained by numerous other investigators. Comparisons of the data obtained from extreme degrees of intellectuality within the colony itself are also made. Results show no general correspondence between physical development and degree of intelligence, although there is evidence that certain of the feeble-minded subjects had a general lack of physical development, rather than significant defects of a particular kind. Simon therefore disagreed with both extreme views then held as to the relationships between physical and mental development — with the one held by Galton, for example, that physical development in mentally abnormal persons is independent of their intelligence, and also with its opposite extreme, held by Porter, as we have already seen, that physical development in children corresponds to the degree of their intelligence. No such general conclusions as either of these could be arrived at from the data obtained. In his doctorate thesis, Simon studied correlations between the physical (height and weight) and the intellectual develop-

ment of 167 of the subjects of this study, comparing children
of successive years of increase in age (*193*).

CEPHALIC MEASUREMENTS AND THEIR SIGNIFICANCE AS TO INTELLIGENCE

In 1901 Binet pointed out that it had apparently been
established by the researches of various authorities (*67*) that
the average cephalic measures of intelligent individuals are
greater than those of unintelligent persons. He tells us that
he had long desired to study this problem closely himself by
actual measurements of the heads of various children of
different mental capacity. In a series of five articles (*33*) he
reports results of investigations on the technique of head
measurements as well as of actual measurements of the head
capacity of about 250 children. Binet suspected that a
person making head measurements might be influenced by
his knowledge of the classification of the subjects, as to
whether they were rated as "superior in intelligence" or
"inferior in intelligence," tending unconsciously in decisions
on finer points — e.g., as to whether a true measure is nearer
122 mm. or 123 mm. — to favor the larger of two possible
measures in the case of the intelligent and the smaller in the
case of the unintelligent subjects; that is, he looked for
a slight suggestion effect on the results, even in the case of
such physical measurements. His experience with tests and
measurements had given him grounds for such suspicions,
and he desired to keep the results free from subjective elements. The results of his experiments on this problem
with respect to the head measurements showed that the
suspicion was well founded; that the knowledge that a given
child had been classed by his instructors as very intelligent
did actually carry with it a tendency toward a constant
error of increase, whereas the awareness that a child had been
selected as being unintelligent carried with it a tendency to

a constant error of decrease in the size of the measurements of the head. It was therefore decided that in his own tests Binet was to be ignorant, for the time, of the classification of each subject. It was also found that different testers differed among themselves in the same way, some getting slightly larger measures than others, as a general tendency. Thus Binet found that Simon, who had had considerable experience with Broca's method, constantly obtained slightly larger dimensions on the same subjects than he did himself; but he also found that this difference was reduced when the testers had a knowledge of the nature of their own deviations. Thus by training and by comparing results, different testers would finally drop off any subjective tendencies and arrive at more accurate results.

In the work of obtaining the cephalic measurements of the school children, Binet had instructors select for him only children of extreme differences in estimated intelligence, so that any existing correlations between size of head dimensions and degree of intelligence would be most evident; but during the process of measuring he was himself ignorant of the classification of the several subjects, at least in some of the schools. Only 11- and 13-year-old children were chosen, these being selected independently of grade classifications. To give an idea of the severity of selection for the extremes of intelligence, Binet tells us in one of his articles that about five intelligent and five unintelligent children were chosen from each group of forty. During the summer vacation and early in the fall Binet tested large numbers of children of the primary grades in Seine-et-Marne and in Paris, reporting the results of each group in a separate article in the *Année*.

After taking the various precautions against errors that his experiments had shown him to be necessary, he concluded from the measurements of about 250 children, that those of superior mental ability have on the average the greater head dimensions. There were, however, irregularities in these results, so that it would not be safe to select children for superior intelligence on the basis of head measurements. That is to say, head measurements could not be regarded as safe tests of intelligence for purposes of individual selection, and the size and shape of the head must be considered, according to Binet's results, as unsatisfactory indicators of intellectual capacity. Indeed, Simon found in a study (*194*), published also in 1901, that among feebleminded children idiots are characterized, from the point of view of cephalometry, by excessive variations in the size of the head, their head measures being usually considerably greater or less than those of morons, and thus tending toward extremes in this class of subjects. Binet's results have been supported in general by subsequent investigations.

LATER STUDIES BY BINET OF PHYSICAL SIGNS OF INTELLIGENCE

As late as 1910 (*43*) Binet contributed an extended study of the physical signs of intelligence. Head measurements of blind, deaf, and backward children were compared with those of normal children, and various so-called signs of degeneracy were considered, such as irregular teeth, strabismus, malformation of the ear and palate, extreme facial asymmetry, as well as speech defects. A study of the hands of both normal and abnormal children was made by means of photographs in different positions, and physiognomies were similarly studied from both profiles and front views. No important relations were found, and Binet says in conclusion that nothing is as deceiving as the physical appearance of intelligence, and that it is necessary to react consciously against our instinctive impressions in this regard.

TWO-POINT DISCRIMINATION AND INTELLIGENCE : RESULTS UNRELIABLE

Wide differences had developed in the data of different investigators in tactile sensibility. Binet attempted to reduce these differences and to prepare the way to more uniform methods and results, by describing an esthesiometer which he had devised (*31*), and, in another article, by outlining methods to be followed in esthesiometry (*32*). In the early part of the present century Binet published a number of articles on this subject, and he developed a "method of irregular variations," consisting of the arrangement of a series of stimuli ranging by irregular steps from a certain minimum to the maximum employed on the test. The point differences thus succeed each other irregularly, but each difference occurs a number of times that is just equal for all differences. He also showed in other articles (*35–38*) the effect in actual experiments of changes in attitudes due to exercise and to suggestion from the experimenter, bringing about apparent modifications in the subject's sensibility; and he warned against overlooking effects of factors of this kind. He contends in these articles, from the results of his experiments, that it is impossible to determine the individual's threshold for the discrimination of two points. For "it varies from one moment to another, and the more it is sought, the more difficult it is to discover; moreover, it is related so closely to the method of interpreting sensations that even in the cases where it seems to have a definite position, we cannot be sure that it represents the degree of acuity of the organ" (*38*, page 252). His attempts thus to measure effects of voluntary attention and to show differences between the five most and the five least intelligent in a group of thirty-two children therefore failed to give any positive results.

EVEN HANDWRITING AND PALMISTRY INVESTIGATED BY
BINET AS POSSIBLE TESTS

Individuality in handwriting had been an inviting subject
for students of psychology as well as for graphologists. Even
before the beginning of this century handwriting had been
studied from several points of view, both in normal and in
abnormal subjects (*105*). Binet did not overlook this type
of reaction, so infinitely variable from individual to individual, as a possible indicator of the aspects of character in
which he was interested, particularly of intelligence. In
1903 and the following year he published (*39*) certain analytic
studies of handwriting, and in 1906 his book, *The Revela-
tions of Handwriting under Scientific Control*, appeared (*40*).
This last study was an attempt to determine whether sex,
age, degree of intelligence, and character are revealed in
handwriting. The natural writing, taken mostly from en-
velopes that had passed through the mails, was submitted
both to graphologists and to other persons. Sex was judged,
it was found, somewhat better than by pure guess; age also
was determined with a small degree of accuracy, the determinations averaging within about ten years of the true ages
of the subjects. From the writing of some very well-known
geniuses and a few inferior persons as well as from that of
persons nearer the average and of some well above this
average, he found slightly positive results in attempts to
estimate intelligence, but many persons did not show their
degree of intelligence in their handwriting. Character
determination as estimated from the writings of certain
notorious criminals, on the one hand, and of men of recognized character, on the other, was even less successful than
intelligence determination. On the whole the professionals
proved themselves in these determinations to be superior
to the other judges. "It does not appear to me impossible,"

he said, "that graphology may yet contribute to experimental psychology a good test of intelligence" (*39*, page 210).

Binet examined so wide a range of possible intelligence indicators that even palmistry did not escape his experimental study (*44*). When professional palmists were allowed to see only the hand of subjects or pictures of their hands, their estimates of their intelligence were but little above expectations based on pure guess, or chance. Thus Binet showed his open-mindedness in being willing and ready to canvass the whole range of possible indicators of intelligence from palmistry, for the study of which he felt obliged to apologize, to the most complex psychological tests. His studies of various physical traits in relation to intelligence continued, along with the improved revisions of the intelligence scales, right down to the time of his death; but the physical signs of intelligence promised to be meager indeed, as we have seen, while the scale of psychological tests, the development of which we shall presently trace, brought a revolution in educational and social service methods and made the name of the authors familiar to nearly every teacher and social worker in the civilized world.

EXERCISES

1. List the tests and devices in Binet's article on "Measurement in Individual Psychology" (as reported in the text) that were later used in the intelligence scales as described in Chapters 9, 10, and 11.

2. Now take the article on "Attention and Adaptation" and do with it what you were directed to do with the article on measurement.

3. Why are persons who are ranked on any test not measured in the sense that three pieces of wood measured by a rule in inches are measured? If A gets 10 points, B gets 20, and C gets 30, why may we not say that B is twice as good in the ability tested as A, and two thirds as good as C?

4. In what sense do the ranks of individuals on the basis of given scores fail to show something as to the comparative abilities that is contained in the scores? Illustrate with the scores 29, 18, 23, 22, 15, 21, 35.

5. If the averages of Table 1 had been, respectively, 2, 5, 8, and 11, would this necessarily have indicated perfect agreement, or perfect correlation, between the results by the two tests? Show why.

CHAPTER NINE

BINET'S FIRST INTELLIGENCE SCALE

INTELLIGENCE TESTS NEEDED IN THE STUDY OF SUBNORMALS

INTEREST in defective children and in their education arose first in France, where Esquirol (1772–1840) had made the important distinction, now generally recognized, between the idiot, whose intelligence does not develop beyond a very low level, and the demented person. Distinctions were early made between different degrees of feeble-mindedness, idiocy being the term applied to the lowest degree of mentality, imbecility to the next lowest, and debility[1] to the highest degree, or the degree next to the lowest cases of individuals classed as normal. But these terms had no precise significance, and before the contribution of Binet and Simon no exact standards for comparison existed. What one alienist called idiocy another would call imbecility, if his standard differed from that of the first, while a third, paying attention to yet other traits of the defective person and interpreting them differently, would probably class him as a moron. Dr. Blin (68), at the colony of Vaucluse, complained of just such differences in standards. So great uncertainty in

[1] In England "feeble-mindedness" is used to designate the higher class of defectiveness in these three degrees of subnormality, and "amentia" or "mental deficiency" is used to cover all three degrees. "Deficiency," however, seems also to include certain forms of instability, and is technically not as good a term as "amentia." In America "feeble-mindedness" is used as the general term to include all three degrees, and the term "moron" (*mōros* = foolish), suggested by Goddard, is used to designate a person of the upper grade of feeble-mindedness. Thus in the English usage aments include idiots, imbeciles, and the feeble-minded, while in the American usage the feeble-minded include idiots, imbeciles, and morons. In this book we shall adhere to this latter meaning of the terms, and we shall use the term "moronity" as coördinate with "imbecility" and "idiocy." In all quotations and references to foreign works changes in the names used will be made to conform to this usage. "Moronity" then replaces "debility" as here used in the text.

163

classification and so great variation in the use of terms to designate the several classes of defectives existed that statistical reports could be of little scientific value. In America, Kuhlmann, then a fellow in psychology in Clark University, pointed out (*150*) the lack of consistency and the need of a common terminology in classification. He criticized the earlier systems of questions by Seguin and Voisin, Möller, Sollier, Sommer, and others, and stated his belief in the possibility of basing a system of classification chiefly on experimental methods; and he himself carried out a few experiments on imbeciles and higher grades of defectives. He adds a valuable bibliography on the subject.

Binet and Simon held that, contrary to the general practice of medical alienists, it was possible to formulate precise definitions which would enable competent persons to agree on the diagnoses of idiocy, imbecility, or moronity. "We have made a methodical comparison," they tell us in a later work, "between the admission certificates filled up for the same children with a few days' interval by the doctors of Sainte-Anne, Bicêtre, the Salpêtrière, and Vaucluse. We have compared several hundreds of these certificates, and we think we may say without exaggeration that they looked as if they had been drawn by chance out of a sack" (*60*, page 76).

These differences in classification were attributed by Binet to ignorance on the part of some physicians, to variability in the meaning of terms, and to lack of precision in the discrimination of symptoms. In the work of the alienist exact standards for classification were not so essential as in schools where different educational treatments were to be given children of different degrees of ability and where large numbers compelled a uniformity of procedure. While even the ancients undoubtedly recognized the fact that some children could not learn well in comparison with normal children, the maladjustments in the schools were naturally more explicitly forced on the attention of educators when education became more nearly universal among the children. A society for child study was organized in Paris, and it studied, under Binet's leadership, the practical problems of child adjustment in the schools. In the early part of this century a great deal of preliminary work in this line was under way. A number of books on abnormal children appeared (*97, 223, 155, 10*), indicating a growing interest in the problem at the time Binet and Simon took up the work of the first scale. As early as 1896 Binet wrote on special classes for arrested children (*22*).

THE FRENCH COMMISSION TO STUDY SUBNORMAL CHILDREN IN THE SCHOOLS

In the early fall of 1904 the Minister of Public Instruction appointed a commission to study measures to be taken in the education of subnormal children in Paris, who were unable to profit by the instruction regularly given in the public schools. It was decided that children of this kind should be eliminated from the normal work of the schools and that they should be taught in a special school. Admission to this school was to be on the basis of pedagogical and medical examinations. It was specifically to meet this emergency that the first intelligence scale was constructed (*57*). The need of an objective means of selecting the subnormal children from the normal was obvious, for without such means great injustices would be done, and subjective opinions more or less influenced by personal advantage would be the basis of choice.

EARLY TESTS WITHOUT STANDARDIZATION

As we have already seen, this intelligence scale was not the first case of the devising of intelligence tests. Indeed, the

testing movement was even then so well advanced that Binet
and Simon tell us that "The use of tests is today very wide-
spread; there are even some contemporary authors who have
made a specialty of organizing new tests. They organize
these tests according to theoretical views without pre-
occupying themselves with trying them out at length"
(58, page 195). The tests then used did not clearly distinguish between innate and acquired abilities, and they were
as a rule poorly constructed and involved large elements of
personal judgment in the evaluation of results. Dr. Damaye,
a student of Dr. Blin, published, only about a year before
the first Binet-Simon scale was prepared, an article in which
he showed in detail how the method of mental examination
used by his teacher could be applied to defectives (see 57).
He made up a list of numerous questions covering twenty
different topics concerning the subject's name, his parents,
age, knowledge of bodily parts, sensations, ideas of objects and
of time, space, country, etc. A number of questions also dealt
with military service and occupations. But these tests
were not simply questions; they also comprised observations
by the examiner on the subject's manners, habits of cleanli-
ness and dress, language, and his ability to calculate, to write,
and to read. Simple commands were also carried out, such
as, "Show me your hands; your tongue. Close your eyes.
Put your finger over your right ear."

The questions were poorly formulated in many cases, and
responses to them were weighted arbitrarily and not standardized, even though the test had been applied to 250 abnormal children; but the study was praised by Binet and
Simon, despite faults of the specific questions formulated,
and was referred to as "superior in precision to anything we
have read." They said it was "the first effort to apply
a scientific method to the diagnosis of mental defectives"
(57, page 182). These tests undoubtedly suggested to them

some of the tests they later used in their own intelligence scale.

THE SPECIFIC OBJECT OF THE FIRST BINET-SIMON INTELLIGENCE SCALE

Binet and Simon limited themselves in the construction of their scale to the practical end of devising a measure of the intellectual capacities of the children in school, with the avowed purpose of knowing of each child ?whether he was normal or was mentally retarded. They specifically denied any intention of determining with the scale whether any given defectives were curable or not, or could be ameliorated; and they limited themselves strictly to one thing, the determination of the mental state of the subject. Moreover, they explicitly state that in their determination of defectiveness they restrict themselves to the mentally retarded and do not attempt to deal with forms of neural instability, which they admit are very hard to distinguish from certain attitudes in normal individuals.

Various types of the mentally disorganized, such as those subject to impulsions and obsessions, and degenerates, as well as dements, whose intelligence has actually suffered diminution under certain diseased conditions, are excluded from their consideration. This must be kept clearly in mind by the reader. "Our purpose," these authors inform us, "is by no means to study, to analyze, and to disentangle the aptitudes of persons inferior in intelligence. That will be the object of a later work. Here we limit ourselves to the evaluation and the quantitative determination of their intelligence in general; we shall determine their intellectual level; and to give an idea of this level we shall compare it with that of normal children of the same age, or of an analogous level" (page 193).

Binet and Simon do not fall into the error of supposing that the intellectual condition of mentally defective individuals is described merely by indicating the age level to which they belong. "It appears, indeed, that the intelligence of these beings has undergone a certain arrest; but it does not follow that the arrest, that is to say, the disproportion between their degree of intelligence and their age, should be the only characteristic of their condition" (page 192). The idiot of 15 years who has a mental level of the 3-year-old child and is just in the early child-stage of verbal language, is not to be completely likened to a child of 3 years. The child is normal while the idiot is an invalid (*infirme*); there are necessarily differences between them, either apparent or hidden. In idiots, as careful studies have revealed, certain mental functions are almost absent while other functions are better developed. These individuals, moreover, frequently show certain well-marked special aptitudes, as in music, in mechanical activities, or in calculation.

These investigators assert that there is no unique method to follow in making a scale to test intelligence. Binet's broad experience with numerous tests of different kinds on large numbers of both normal and abnormal subjects had qualified him thoroughly to recognize that a variety of tests and methods was necessary. In previous writings he had emphasized the fact that no single test, however good it may be, is sufficient to test the intelligence of an individual, because of the great complexity of the intellectual functions. The method in tests like these must be objective and free from the influence of what the parents say about the child's condition, and of any preconceived notions of the tester. The authors saw certain merits in the "medical method," evaluating the anatomical, the physiological, and the pathological signs of inferiority, and also in the "pedagogical method," estimating a child by what he has learned, as well as in the "psychological method," based on direct observation and test. Each of these methods can render some service, but the psychological method is the most, and the medical method the least direct, the latter judging intelligence from physical signs. Binet's attitude toward the indirect method is certainly liberal in view of his failure to find in numerous experiments any very significant relations between intelligence and physical, sensory, or physiological measurements.

A METRICAL SCALE THE FUNDAMENTAL IDEA

The fundamental idea in their psychological method Binet held to be what he called *a metrical scale of intelligence.* "This scale is composed of a series of tests arranged in order of increasing difficulty, beginning at one end with the lowest intellectual level that one can observe and extending at the other to the level of average and normal intelligence. To each test corresponds a different mental level" (page 194). Binet asserted that this scale will not, properly speaking, permit of a measurement of intelligence — because intellectual qualities are not measurable in the way that lengths are, since they are not superposable — but only of a classification, an arrangement into a hierarchy of different intelligences. In practice this classification approximates a measure. Thus in testing any two individuals we can determine with the scale not only which of them is higher in intelligence and how many degrees, but also how each one compares with the average of other individuals considered as the norm and how much he is above or below this average. Thus, knowing the intellectual development of normal children from year to year, or having the norms of their mental growth, we shall be able to determine in the case of any child how many years he is behind mentally, or in advance, at a given time; and we can determine, moreover, to what degree on the scale idiocy, imbecility, or moronity belongs.

The authors assure us that the tests which they propose in this scale have been tried out many times and retained, while others, after similar trials, have been discarded; but unfortunately they give us neither the complete results nor the methods of these experiments.

PRACTICAL LIMITATIONS OF THE SCALE

The construction of a practical scale of this kind imposed upon Binet and Simon certain limitations. "We have desired," they say, "that all our tests shall be simple, rapid, convenient, precise, heterogeneous, maintaining the subject in contact with the experimenter, and bearing principally on the faculty of judgment" (page 195). As to rapidity, we are told that this is a necessity in this sort of examination. It is impossible to continue the tests for a period of more than twenty minutes without fatiguing the subject, and during this time it is necessary to probe him from all angles and to carry out at least ten tests, which leaves only about two minutes for each test. So they were obliged to omit any use of long exercises, however good these might be. It will be helpful to the reader to keep in mind that this was the idea in view, and the situation, in the construction of the tests.

Then, the tests must be of great enough variety to explore all the important forms of intellectual capacity. Binet in his earlier articles has repeatedly stressed the impossibility of testing adequately with a single test so complex a thing as a person's intelligence. The authors recognized, however, that it would be futile to attempt to measure all the sensory, perceptual, and other aspects of the intellectual processes. "A little reflection has shown us that this would be a great waste of time. There is in intelligence, it appears to us, a fundamental organ, any defect or alteration in which is of the greatest consequence to the practical life. This basic factor in intelligence is judgment, otherwise spoken of as good sense, practical judgment, initiative, the ability to adapt oneself. To judge well, to comprehend well, to reason well, these are the essentials of intelligence. A person may be a moron or an imbecile if he lacks judgment; but with good judgment he could not be either" (pages 196 f.). This shows us the conception that the authors had of the intelligence which they attempted to test. Binet knew very well from his previous experiments that particular and special sensory and motor functions carried very little general import as to one's intelligence, and in the present article the authors refer to Laura Bridgman and Helen Keller as persons who, though deprived of certain senses, had very good general ability. On first thought, memory would seem to be of capital importance in mental processes and therefore to demand a good deal of attention in the construction of a test of intelligence, and Binet so considered it ten years earlier; but it was clear to him in 1905 that it is distinct and independent of judgment. One may have "good sense" and be lacking in memory, and the reverse condition is also frequently found. Hence, we are informed, the first place has been assigned to judgment in the intelligence scale. In this scale the authors have even taken special pains to lay traps to lead the subject into making absurd responses, thus to test his capacity for sound judgment. It was, of course, impracticable to hold exclusively to this guiding idea of what the tests should stress, and to isolate clearly the judgment element. With children below two years of age, for example, the tests had to take into consideration the degree of accuracy in motor coördination, and the manifestations of attention, since the infant cannot overtly express judgments.

The thirty tests of this 1905 scale follow.[1]

1. Visual coördination. Noting the degree of coördination of movement of the head and eyes as a lighted match is passed slowly before the subject's eyes.

2. Prehension provoked tactually. A small wooden cube is to be placed in contact with the palm or back of the subject's hand. He must grasp it and carry it to his mouth, and his coördinated grasping and other movements are to be noted.

3. Prehension provoked visually. Same as 2, except that the object is placed within the subject's reach, but not in contact with him. The experimenter, to catch the child's attention, encourages him orally and with appropriate gestures to take the object.

4. Cognizance of food. A small bit of chocolate and a piece of wood of similar dimensions are successively shown the subject, and signs of his recognition of the food and attempts to take it are noted carefully.

5. Seeking food when a slight difficulty is interposed. A small piece of the chocolate, as used in the previous test, is wrapped in a piece of paper and given to the subject. Observations are made on his manner of getting the food and separating it from the paper.

6. The execution of simple orders and the imitation of gestures. The orders are mostly such as might be understood from the accompanying gestures alone.

(This is the limit for idiots as experimentally determined.)

7. Verbal knowledge of objects. The child is to touch his head, nose, ear, etc., and also to hand the experimenter on command a particular one of three well-known objects: cup, key, string.

[1] For a fuller description of the tests and for instructions for giving them the interested reader must go to the original article or to an abbreviated translation, such as that given in Whipple's *Manual of Mental and Physical Tests* (1910), pages 475 ff.

8. Knowledge of objects in a picture as shown by finding them and pointing them out when they are called by name.

9. Naming objects designated in a picture.

(This is the upper limit of the 3-year-old normal children. The three preceding tests are not in order of increasing difficulty, for whoever passes 7 usually passes 8 and 9 also.)

10. Immediate comparison of two lines for discrimination as to length.

11. Reproduction of series of three digits immediately after oral presentation.

12. Weight discrimination. Comparison of two weights — of 3 and 12 g., of 6 and 15 g., and of 3 and 15 g.

13. Suggestibility. (*a*) Modification of 7: an object not among the three present is asked for. (*b*) Modification of 8: "Where [in the picture] is the *patapoum?* the *nitchevo?*" (These words have no meaning.) (*c*) Modification of 10: the two lines to be compared are of equal length.

(Test 13 is admitted to be a test not of intelligence but of "force of judgment" and "resistance of character.")

14. Definitions of familiar objects — *house, horse, fork, mamma.*

(This is the limit of 5-year-old normal children, except that they fail on Test 13.)

15. Repetition of sentences of fifteen words each, immediately after hearing them spoken by the examiner.

(This is the limit of imbeciles.)

16. Giving differences between various pairs of familiar objects recalled in memory: (*a*) *paper* and *cardboard*, (*b*) *a fly* and *a butterfly*, and (*c*) *wood* and *glass.*

(Test 16 alone effectively separated normal children of 5 and 7 years.)

17. Immediate memory of pictures of familiar objects. Thirteen pictures pasted on two pieces of cardboard are presented simultaneously. The subject looks at them for thirty seconds and then gives the names of those recalled.

18. Drawing from memory two different designs shown simultaneously for ten seconds.

19. Repetition of series of digits after oral presentation. Three series of three digits each, three of four each, three of five, etc., are presented until not one of the three series in a group is repeated correctly. The number of digits in the highest series which the subject repeats is his score.

20. Giving from memory the resemblance among familiar objects: (a) a *wild poppy*[1] (red) and *blood*, (b) *an ant, a fly, a butterfly*, and *a flea*, and (c) *a newspaper, a label*, and *a picture*.

21. Rapid discrimination of lines. A line of 30 cm. is compared successively with fifteen lines varying from 35 down to 31 cm. A more difficult set of comparisons is then made of a line of 100 mm. with twelve lines varying from 103 to 101 mm.

22. Arranging in order five weights — 15, 12, 9, 6, and 3 g. — of equal size.

23. Identification of the missing weight from the series in Test 22 from which one is removed. The remaining weights are not in the right order. This test is given only when Test 22 is passed.

(This is given as the most probable limit of morons.)

24. Finding words to rime with a given word after the process has been illustrated.

25. Supplying missing words at the end of simple sentences, one for each sentence. This is the Ebbinghaus completion method simplified.

26. Construction of a sentence to embody three given words: *Paris, gutter, fortune.*

27. Making replies to twenty-five problem questions of graded difficulty; such as, "What is the thing to do when you are sleepy?" "Why is it better to continue with perseverance what one has started than to abandon it and start something else?"

(Test 27 alone reveals the moron.)

[1] Some of these objects were evidently more familiar to the French children than they are to American children. Whipple changed them to (a) milk and snow, (b) a mosquito and a bee, and (c) a table, a chair, and a door. Binet said that there were Paris children who had never seen wild poppies or ants and cautioned the tester to use objects familiar to the children.

28. Giving the time that it would be if the large and the small hands of the clock were interchanged at four minutes to three and at twenty minutes after six. A much more difficult test is given those who succeed in the inversion; namely, to explain the impossibility of the precise transposition indicated.

29. Drawing what a quarto-folded paper with a piece cut out of the once-folded edge would look like if unfolded.

30. Giving distinctions between abstract terms; as between *liking* and *respecting* a person; between being *sad* and being *bored*.

THE SUBJECTS ON WHOM THE SCALE WAS STANDARDIZED

The authors arranged these thirty tests into what by preliminary testing they had found to be an ascending order of difficulty. The scale was applied to normal children in the primary schools and also to subnormal subjects both in the Salpêtrière and in the primary schools. The normal children tested were selected by their teachers for normal intelligence — those who were neither retarded nor advanced. They were children who were placed in the grades just right for their ages and who were just at the exact ages desired (*59*, page 246). While many such children were tested, the descriptions of the reactions of normal children to the scale and the norms given by the authors are based on the records of fifty children of just even 3, 5, 7, 9, and 11 years, about ten cases in each group.

SOME TENTATIVE STANDARDS

The following standards were set up as a result of these tests: Tests 1 to 9, inclusive, were passed by all 3-year-olds. Tests 10 to 12, and 14 in addition, were passed by the 5-year-olds, but these children required help on 12 and repetitions of Question 10 to sustain the attention. Test 13 showed that the youngest children were most suggestible. Test 16 separated absolutely the 5-year-olds from the 7-year-olds.

While for the 3- and the 5-year-olds there are certain tests called "frontiers" which effectively check the group in question but are passed by practically all normal children of higher groups, the distinction between the 7- and 9- and the 9- and 11-year-old levels, successively, is made upon the basis of performance in certain tests which permit of answers of a wide range of efficiency, and for which norms computed from very scant data are given. These tests include three memory tests: verbal memory of sentences, 15, memory of pictures, 17, and memory of figures, 19; four sensory tests: comparison of the length of lines, 21, arranging five weights in order, 22, identification of the missing weight in a series of five, 23, and drawing what a quarto-folded paper with a piece cut out of the once-folded edge would look like, 29; five tests in which language plays a great part: abstract-questions test, 27, finding rimes, 24, giving distinctions between abstract terms, 30, using three given words in a sentence, 26, and the sentence-completion test, 25. The suggestibility test, 13, was also found useful.

The reader may be surprised, knowing Binet's depreciation of the factors of intelligence involved, to see that the majority of these thirteen tests are tests of memory or sensation. However, in tests of this kind, attention is paid by the experimenter to details which may indicate the degree of judgment possessed by the subject. Thus for verbal memory of sentences, the number of absurdities committed is held to be just as significant as the total number of sentences repeated correctly, and in this, as in the language tests particularly, the number of absurdities figures in the norms given. In Test 19 the child was to indicate after each repetition of a series of digits whether or not he was satisfied with his response. Satisfaction with a repetition involving several grave errors was considered indicative of low intelligence. In the arrangement of weights, the method adopted, or the lack of method, was held to be very important. This test, together with Test 29, is classed by Binet as a sensory judgment and reasoning test. Moreover, the authors attach importance to the sensory tests because of the fact that "they will certainly be very useful in the analysis of the aptitudes of defective persons" (page 273).

THE TEST LIMITS OF IDIOTS, IMBECILES, AND MORONS

On the basis of this intelligence scale the authors found it possible to classify idiots, imbeciles, and other feeble-minded persons in a somewhat objective manner. For the convenience of the reader, we have inserted in the scale here outlined the upper limits both of certain normal age-groups — where such limits were sufficiently clear cut — and of the subnormal groups. Binet and Simon found that idiots could not go beyond Test 6 and that imbeciles could not go beyond Test 15. For the morons, no such precise limit can be given. If some definite point on the scale were to be cited as the high level, that between Tests 23 and 24 would be chosen. Yet at rare intervals persons of this class were found who could make rimes (Test 34) or compose a loose compound sentence to include the three words of Test 26. It is therefore probable that these nearer normal persons would have passed Test 25, although this test was not given them in the regular routine testing.

The procedure was, in the case of school children, to begin with Test 16. This being passed, the thirteen tests (or more often the twelve tests, that of suggestibility being omitted) enumerated above for children of primary school age were administered. Morons were found who had normal memories, normal visual memory of pictures being, indeed, the rule. Many of these children had excellent "sensory intelligence." The five language tests differentiated them distinctly from normal children, Test 27 being particularly valuable in this regard. Binet and Simon tell us that "In a rapid examination, it might be sufficient to ask them seven or eight of these abstract questions; they would be classified at once" (page 336). As we shall see, however, this method was not intended to be used upon adult subnormals without change; it applied to children of from 8 to 13 years of age.

Within each of the three main divisions of the mentally deficient, sub-classes were designated and their limits tentatively determined, but the reliability of the results is not great enough to warrant our consideration of these limits. These three classifications of feeble-minded persons are recognized by the authors as being purely practical, since no sharp, exact line can be drawn anywhere. Each class gradually shades off into the next above it. It was in conformity with medical usage to make three main divisions, and the terms already in use were retained.

Idiocy. Idiocy is the term applied by the authors to persons of so low a grade of mentality that they are without a vocabulary or make no use of language. This does not mean that they cannot pronounce certain words, but that they are incapable of substituting words for objects in their behavior. Thus in the scale, tests 7 and 8 present impassable obstacles to the idiot because he cannot pass readily from objects or pictures to their names. Idiots can, of course, learn to use certain names often met or specifically taught in connection with a few familiar objects, but their language function is very narrowly limited. The characterization thus given by Binet to idiots agrees, he reminds us, with the etymological sense of the word *idios*, meaning "alone" or "isolated." The individual who cannot use spoken language is certainly limited very much in social participation. Binet regarded the aptitudes of idiots as roughly equal to those of normal children of 2 years of age or less.

Imbecility.   While the line between imbecility and moronity could not be as closely drawn as it was between idiocy and imbecility, the authors found that these two upper classes of feeble-mindedness are separated by the following tests : giving differences between two known objects recalled in memory, arranging the weights in a series, and repeating a series of six digits (page 300). The morons did not give the series of digits in any random order and in absurd orders when they were asked to repeat them, as did the imbeciles. These tests and others like them, which call for precise comprehension and demand a degree of judgment, do not fall within the range of the powers of the imbecile as this term was defined by Binet. He estimated that the aptitudes of imbeciles equaled roughly those in normal children of about 2 to 5 years of age.

Moronity.   These studies on the two lower grades of defectives were made on children in the Salpêtrière. Morons were studied in the primary schools, where they were known to shade off by degrees toward normality. Since the selection of these moron children in the schools for purposes of special instruction was the chief object in the construction of the scale, it was necessary that children of different ages be studied and that norms be established for the several ages. A young mentally retarded child could not be expected to go as high in the test scale as an older child of an equal number of years of retardation. No general method of diagnosis of moronity independent of age is therefore attempted at this time. That, we are told, would go beyond the authors' pretensions in this study. The morons studied ranged from 8 to 13 years.

The selection of morons in the schools.   In order to select the children to be tested individually for moronity, a list of the ages of all the children was compared with a list of their school marks. Those children were then chosen who, while being among the oldest in the class, were consistently marked low in school work. The authors then asked that the children thus selected for tests be so distributed among normal children that they would not be known as inferior except as a result of the tests applied. Thus the testers would not be influenced by a knowledge of the child's status in advance of the testing, and a control on the validity of the tests was secured.

In some cases the head of the school and the teacher of the child held conflicting opinions as to the mentality of the child, and in others similar conflicts arose between teachers of the same child in different years. These differences of opinion were settled beyond doubt by the tests. In a general way it may be said that the morons showed their deficiency in dealing with abstract matters, especially with verbal abstractions. They were able to state differences and resemblances between familiar objects, to pass the memory tests, 17, 18, and 19, and to arrange in series the lines and weights; but they failed on the higher tests dealing with the selection of certain abstract elements.

Since normal 12-year-old children were as a rule found able to respond to abstract questions — a fact that Binet seems either to have inferred from the responses of the 11-year-olds or to have obtained from data not reported — the authors decided that morons were below the 12-year level of intelligence (page 300). However, we are informed, this inability to respond to abstract questions applies only to persons not above 14 years of age; it would be an insufficient criterion for distinguishing normal children from morons 20 years of age or older, who would have gained enough knowledge by experience to resemble normal children in responses to abstract relations. "It may be that certain differences are concealed under these resemblances and that we shall some day succeed in analyzing these differences so clearly that we shall be able to find signs of mental retardation entirely independent of any consideration of age. It would evidently be a great advantage to know such signs, but for the present that which strikes us most often is the resemblances between very young normal children and older abnormal persons. The resemblances are so numerous and so curious that on reading the description of the reactions of a child of which the age had not been given, one could not say whether the subject is normal or subnormal" (page 321).

THE PROCEDURE IN TESTING THE SUBJECT

The number of persons tested was recognized to be too small for reliable standards, however, and the authors' general conception of the procedure to follow is better than their practical results show. The general idea favored by them was to give each subject every test in the scale and then to compare his score with the scores of normal age-groups without at first taking note of his age. Thus, having a scale of tests and a series of standards for the several ages, derived from tests of normal children, it is easy to find in this series the place of any person whose test score has been obtained. Then by taking into consideration his age, — that is, by comparing the age of the subject with that of the group whose normal score his just equals, — one can easily determine whether or not he is retarded, and how much. The authors supposed that one could also find at the same time in what particular mental functions he falls down (page 326). For more rapid work the subject could be started on tests appropriate to his age, and he could thus in a very short time be given the tests in the neighborhood of his limit. The longer method is strongly recommended, however, as the more reliable and the one to be followed, in view of the great importance of the results to the subject.

The far-reaching importance of perfecting an intelligence scale, as viewed by these authors, is shown in their statement of its possible uses, once it has been constructed on a satisfactorily objective basis. "When the work, only outlined here, shall have taken on a definitive character, it will doubtless permit of the solution of many unsettled questions, since its object is nothing less than to measure intelligence; thus it will be possible to compare differences of intellectual level not only according to age but also to sex, to social status, and to race. Applications of our methods will be found to normal anthropology and also to criminal anthropology, which touches closely the study of abnormal persons and of which the principal conclusions of this study will become a part" (page 246).

THE CONCEPTION OF MENTAL-AGE LEVELS

In this report the authors have clearly developed the idea of having a series of tests of increasing difficulty and of establishing limits on the scale within which different classes of feeble-minded subjects will be ranged. They have also definitely grasped the conception of mental age levels — that is, levels of performance normal to children of the different ages who are neither retarded nor accelerated in mental development; and they have attempted to define the three degrees of feeble-mindedness in terms of these mental age levels, so that the classification of any subnormal individual can be known once his mental age is determined. Thus if a feeble-minded person makes a test mental age of six years, or scores equal to the average 6-year-old normal child, he will be classed, if he is not young, as an imbecile.

Binet and Simon clearly recognize the advantage of stating a person's retardation or advance in terms of the number of years that he is in retard or in advance of the norm for his age; but they do not yet face fully the question of how to classify defective children who, because of youth, still have before them some possibilities of growth. For instance, a 10-year-old child scoring an age level of 6 years is evidently to become superior with greater age to an adult who just reaches this same mental age level. The authors point out that the younger defective has possibilities of further mental growth, but at the same time they are unable to suggest any one measure of universal application — such as the intelligence quotient later adopted by Stern and Terman — to designate the degree of intelligence of the subject irrespective of his age. Absolute retardation or acceleration in terms of mental-age units is obviously faulty as a description of one's intelligence, because it means different things at different chronological ages — two years' retardation, for instance, being much more serious in a young child than in an adolescent.

Early references to mental age. The comparison of a person, defective in knowledge or in intelligence, with a normal child of a specific age did not originate with Binet. It seems to have been made in 1828 by Esquirol, in a general and somewhat vague manner, when he pointed out that an idiot is incapable of acquiring the knowledge common to other persons of his own age (*112*). Duncan and Millard said in 1866, "It is a very striking method of showing the mental deficiency of a member of any one of these classes to compare its mental gifts with those of children of perfect mind at younger ages"(*109*, page 13). The classes referred to are the three degrees of feeble-mindedness, idiocy, imbecility, and moronity. Down likewise suggested comparing the mental condition of backward children with that of normal children two or more years younger, but he believed that in the case of an idiot child "there is no amount of imaginary antedated

age to which the present condition of the child corresponds"
(*104*).[1]   Pintner (*174*, page 33) calls attention to a report by
Hall in 1848 of the trial of William Freeman, colored, charged
with the murder of four persons unknown to him and for the
killing of whom there was no provocation, in which Dr.
Dimon, a psychiatrist, said that the accused "in point of
knowledge was equal to a child of 3 years" (*125*).   There is,
however, a long way from such more or less casual comparisons without any standardizations to a definite use of mental
age as a unit of measurement in a scale.

WHAT THE FIRST SCALE ACTUALLY ACCOMPLISHED

Binet and Simon recognize in this article that they have
really as yet set up no satisfactory standards.   They have
taken but small numbers of normal children for their norms,
the groups of these children representing successive age
differences of two years — 3, 5, 7, 9, and 11 years; and they
have used only children who are neither retarded nor advanced in school.   They recognize that all the children of
any age, however classified as to grade in school, would have
given more satisfactory norms, and that their scale must
eventually be completed on age-norms of this sort for every
year within certain limiting ages, each age group numbering
above a hundred individuals, instead of approximately ten
as in the present study.   Thus they seem at this time to have
anticipated rather clearly the principal changes that were
to come in their later scales.   The giving of more tests and
the inclusion of each age within the limits of the scale are
matters that embody no new principle, but simply assure
greater accuracy and finer units of measurement.   The
year units, or units of a fraction of a year, later used were
inevitable with further refinement.   The authors are feeling

[1] These cases are taken from Woodrow's *Brightness and Dullness in Children* (1919), page 25.

their way ahead in a truly empirical manner. Their own statement at the end of their report on the first scale and its use is both modest and promising of future progress :

"We may be excused for not developing here a lengthy conclusion. A word will suffice. We have wished simply to show that it is possible to determine in a precise and truly scientific way the mental level of an intelligence, to compare this level with a normal level, and consequently to determine by how many years a child is retarded. Despite the inevitable errors of a first work, which is of a groping character, we believe that we have demonstrated this possibility" (page 336).

EXERCISES

1. Trace in earlier chapters the origin of as many of the thirty tests in the first Binet scale as you can. Indicate your results in the manner shown in Chapter 11 with the 1911 scale, except that you may refer to article and date instead of place in earlier scales. Be as careful as you can to get the real origin in every case. Go to the various sources if they are available to you. Which of the tests are traceable to sources outside of Binet's own work?

2. What processes does the standardization of a test involve? State as many methods of standardization as you can, and point out the one essential thing in all of them.

3. Write out your best possible definition of "mental age."

CHAPTER TEN

LATER DEVELOPMENTS AND THE 1908 SCALE

BINET's work on the intelligence scale was only a part of the many contributions of his day to the advancement of experimental psychology, a part that developed mainly, as we have seen, in work with subnormal individuals. Consequently many psychologists paid little or no attention to this work in applied psychology. Even the experimental work in the various psychological laboratories dealing directly with tests was concerned with such problems as the interrelations of different mental functions, transfer effects, fatigue effects of continuous work, individual differences in particular tests, relative effects of heredity and environment, etc. Studies seeking to devise tests for the differentiation of persons according to their degrees of intelligence in a general way were few, outside of the laboratory conducted by Binet.

TERMAN'S STUDY OF GENIUS AND STUPIDITY

One piece of work on normal subjects, however, that approached the work of Binet previous to his preoccupation with the construction of an intelligence scale, was the study by Terman (*206*) of "genius and stupidity," carried out in 1904 and 1905 on seven boys judged to have superior intelligence and seven dull boys. These subjects were selected for extreme abilities by the teachers from about five hundred boys in the Worcester schools, near Clark University, the idea being to determine whether the tests used could make the discrimination between the two groups, that selected for mental superiority and that selected for the greatest stupidity. Terman's idea regarding the importance of testing the higher complex processes, very much like that of Binet, is expressed as follows: "It is reasonable to suppose that the decisive intellectual differences among men are not greatly dependent upon native retentiveness or mere sense discrimination. Far more important than this mass of raw sense data is the correct shooting together of the sense elements in memory and imagination. This is invention. It is the synthetic or apperceptive activity that gives the 'seven-league boots' to genius. It is a kind of ability that all great minds exhibit. Why so great spontaneous relating activity in one mind and so little in another, is the ultimate problem in this portion of individual psychology" (page 15).

While he admitted the similarity of all genius, he nevertheless marked out tentatively three kinds of inventive genius, leading toward mechanical, artistic, and scientific or philosophical invention, respectively. Eight more or less different types of tests were used: tests (1) of "inventive or creative imagination"; (2) of logical processes; (3) of mathematical ability; (4) of "the mastery of language"; (5) of "insight, as shown in the interpretation of fables"; (6) of "ease of acquisition, as shown in learning to play chess"; (7) of memory abilities; and (8) of "motor ability both in general and in the acquisition of bodily skill" (page 13). The inventive ingenuity tests consisted of the finding of a method of putting together into one long chain five short chains of three links each by means of only three weldings; the Thompson match test (see *supra*, page 115); the working out of a method by means of which a man traveling with a fox, a goose, and some corn may cross a river in a boat, taking only one of these at a time in any direction, so that neither the goose (by the fox) nor the corn (by the goose) will be eaten while he is away from them; thinking out a method by which two boys and two men traveling together could get over a river in a boat that is capable of carrying only one man at a time or two boys; showing how a boy could measure out exactly four pints of water with a three-pint and a five-pint vessel; and arranging six pennies into two rows of four in each row. Material objects were used with some of these problems to aid in imaging the situation, and in the last problem the subject was told after a short period of failure that two coins might occupy the same place, one on top of the other. The "logical problems" were tracing a figure of two squares overlapping at one corner of each so as to form a small square common to each of the larger ones, the tracing to be done without crossing a line, lifting the pencil off the paper, or tracing any part of a line twice; tracing by the same rules the figure earlier used by Lindley (*157*) in his study of puzzles; solving different forms of the checker-puzzle test, which has recently been described by Haught (*128*); solving various arithmetic problems, some of them involving simple fractions; making change, a test used by Binet soon after this in his 1908 scale; finding the relative amounts for two or more men to pay for a carriage rented at a fixed price, each of the men riding a different distance; finding the costs of two articles when the total cost and the excess cost of the one over the other article are given; and developing a general rule in the Binet paper-folding test. The language tests consisted of reading for accuracy and speed, making words from certain sets of given letters, the Ebbinghaus completion test, a sort of composition test of "expression," and the execution of thirty commands with respect to the moving of chessmen on a chessboard. Other tests used, which are now well known, were the interpretation of fables; a number of tests of memory — reproduction of a complex geometrical figure (from Binet), oral and written reproduction of stories, and the solution of a mechanical puzzle after seeing the operation performed by the experimenter; and a number of tests of motor ability.

In the mental tests the seven boys selected for superior ability clearly excelled as a group the seven dull boys, the difference, however, being least in the case of the ingenuity tests; but in the motor-ability tests the dull boys were superior. "On the whole," says the author, "the standing of the individual subjects through the separate tests is strikingly uniform. This is only another way of saying that intelligence in these subjects does not show a decided tendency to develop along special lines" (page 68). The possibility of constructing tests of general mental ability was thus shown.

Terman sent a copy of his monograph to Binet[1] in 1906. It is not known whether the work embodied in this monograph influenced the 1908 scale, but it seems probable that the making-change test and the executing-commands test, first appearing in this scale, came from Terman's work.

When the Binet scale first appeared, a number of psychologists were employed in work of such a nature that they found in it much that was of value to them. Indeed, so pressing were the needs for an intelligence scale by which to classify children according to different degrees of defectiveness that developments toward scale construction, as we have already seen, were going on in several quarters.

THE DE SANCTIS TESTS

Sante de Sanctis, of the University of Rome, published, in the year following the appearance of Binet's scale, a series of six tests (*98*) to be used especially on feeble-minded children from 7 to 16 years of age. The author of these tests believed that they would enable one to discover in the child his capacity of adaptation to situations, his memory of colors, recognition of certain forms, persistent attention, judgment of the number, size, and distance of objects, reasoning on relations of objects not present to sense and on their several qualities, and his quickness in such mental

[1] This information was obtained from Professor Terman in a letter.

operations as perception, action on commands, and thinking. The tests, which the English reader will find in Whipple's *Manual of Mental and Physical Tests* (1910), consist of (1) giving the tester one ball of five at hand when asked to do so, the balls all having different colors; (2) immediately indicating from memory which ball was taken when the five are again shown the subject; (3) selecting five cubes from a collection of these cubes with three pyramids and two parallelopipeds; (4) selecting or indicating all the squares on a test card containing different printed forms (squares, rectangles twice as long as wide, and equilateral triangles); (5) counting twelve cubes and indicating the largest and the most distant one; and (6) answering these questions: (*a*) Are big things heavier or lighter than small things? (*b*) How is it that small things are sometimes heavier than big things? (*c*) Which looks bigger, a thing that is close by or a thing that is far away? (*d*) When things are far away, do they just look smaller or are they really smaller? The time is recorded with a stop watch in each test, and speed and accuracy of responses are taken into consideration in rating the subject tested.

These tests were not standardized well either as to procedure in giving or in scoring the tests, but it was asserted that inability to pass tests 1 and 2 indicates a high degree of defectiveness, while inability to pass the next two or three tests shows but slight mental deficiency. Normal performances, including time and number of errors for the several ages, were not given by the author. These tests, as well as those by Binet and Simon, were used in Europe and in America and promised to give good results for the purposes of certain rough classifications by non-literary tests; but they soon became so much overshadowed by the revised Binet scales that at the present writing — less than twenty years after the appearance of the De Sanctis tests — it is probable that only a very small per cent of persons using tests, but not specially trained in psychology, know anything about them or have ever heard the name of their author.

REACTIONS OF PSYCHOLOGISTS TO THE 1905 BINET SCALE

Despite the recognition that Binet had attained by 1905, his first scale was to become known to the world mainly through the use made of it, and the criticisms of it, by workers with defectives. The year after its appearance brought out a long critical article by Decroly and Degand (*94*) of Belgium, who had applied this test scale to defective children. Their analysis of results showed that, while there was a rather close correspondence between the ranking of these children by the test and the ranking based on their school success, on clinical determinations, and on general observations of their behavior, certain modifications and additions were desirable. Aside from various changes suggested for adapting the tests for use on deaf-mutes, these authors urged that tests stressing "active intelligence, alertness, or logic in action" be added to supplement those putting stress principally on memory. They also suggested modifications in some of the tests to reduce their length and the amount of needless repetition required by them.[1] They found that the tests in this scale were not arranged in an exact order of increasing difficulty so far as abnormal subjects are concerned, a fact that the authors of the scale had themselves in a measure discovered, and also that the scale was least serviceable for children of but slight defectiveness.

Dr. Goddard translated this scale into English for use in the Vineland school (*118*), but in this same year a revision, or a new scale, by Binet and Simon had already appeared.

---

[1] A good summary of their results with twenty-five children is found in Whipple, *op. cit.*, page 491.

THE APPEARANCE OF THE NEW INTELLIGENCE SCALE

This new scale bore the significant title, *The Development of Intelligence in Children* (*61*). The interest has now shifted from defectives to normal children. Intelligence is now a subject of wide interest. The authors tell us that there has been no more often repeated expression in psychology the last few years than "the measurement of intelligence." They say that their earlier work in attempting an approximation to such measurement was much less elaborated or perfected than that which they now present. The purpose in the report now before us is, first, to become acquainted with the law of the mental development of children and to devise a method of diagnosing their intelligence; and, second, to study the diversity of their intellectual aptitudes. Their interest is, however, still pedagogical to a large extent, for they hope to show that certain parts of the instructional program for children is not well adapted to their receptivity. "The child differs from the adult not only in degree and in quantity, but also in the very form of its intelligence" (page 2). They found the problem relating to intelligence more complex than they imagined it to be: "our minds always simplify nature."

It now appears to these investigators that making the program of studies of children agree with the development of their intelligence constitutes a new problem; but they repeat that their tests are useful not only to psychology but "to mental medicine and to medico-legal surveys" as well (page 3). The three methods of exploring intelligence — the medical, the pedagogical, and the psychological — are again pointed out, although as before, and even more strictly here, only the last method can be considered. The idea of a metrical scale of intelligence is clearly stated, and the importance is stressed, above all, of describing the tests with a precision so exact that every person who takes the pains to understand and use them may give them correctly.

While for the history of the scale the reader is referred by the authors to their earlier articles of 1905, we are told that "M. Decroly and Mlle. Degand have undertaken to verify our first researches with a care that pleases us," and that the Pedagogical Society of Brussels has included these researches on intelligence testing in its program of work. It is important to note that all the experiments on this new scale were carried out in two mental hospitals and in the primary and maternal schools of Paris on children of the working class.

We shall here give only an outline statement of the new scale in question, as English translations are easily accessible to interested readers (*119; 231*, pages 493–517; *151*).

THE 1908 BINET-SIMON INTELLIGENCE SCALE

AGE 3 YEARS

1. Points to nose, eyes, mouth.
2. Repeats sentences of six syllables.
3. Repeats two digits.
4. Enumerates objects in a picture.
5. Gives family name.

AGE 4 YEARS

1. Knows sex.
2. Names certain familiar objects shown to him; *key, pocketknife,* and a *penny.*
3. Repeats three digits.
4. Indicates which is the longer of two lines 5 and 6 cm. in length.

AGE 5 YEARS

1. Indicates the heavier of two cubes (of 3 and 12 g. and also of 6 and 15 g.).
2. Copies a square, using pen and ink.
3. Constructs a rectangle from two pieces of cardboard, having a model to look at.
4. Counts four pennies.

AGE 6 YEARS

1. Knows right and left as shown by indicating right hand and left ear.
2. Repeats sentence of sixteen syllables.
3. Chooses the prettier in each of three pairs of faces.
4. Defines familiar objects in terms of use.
5. Executes a triple order.
6. Knows age.
7. Knows morning and afternoon.

AGE 7 YEARS

1. Tells what is missing in unfinished pictures.
2. Knows number of fingers on each hand and on both hands without counting them.
3. Copies "The little Paul" with pen and ink.
4. Copies a diamond, using pen and ink.
5. Repeats five digits.
6. Describes pictures as scenes.
7. Counts thirteen pennies.
8. Knows names of four common coins.

AGE 8 YEARS

1. Reads a passage and remembers two items.
2. Counts up the value of three simple and two double *sous* (or one- and two-cent stamps in American scales).
3. Names four colors — red, yellow, blue, green.
4. Counts backward from 20 to 0.
5. Writes short sentence from dictation, using pen and ink.
6. Gives differences between two objects from memory.

AGE 9 YEARS

1. Knows date — day of week and of month, also month and year.
2. Recites days of week.
3. Makes change on four cents out of twenty in simple play-store transactions.
4. Gives definitions superior to use. Familiar objects.
5. Reads a passage and remembers six items.
6. Arranges five blocks in order of weight.

AGE 10 YEARS

1. Names in order the months of the year.
2. Recognizes all the (nine) pieces of money.
3. Constructs a sentence to include three given words — *Paris, fortune, gutter.* Two unified sentences are acceptable (passed by only about 50 per cent).

4. Answers easy comprehension questions.
5. Answers hard comprehension questions. Only about half of the 10-year-olds get the majority of these correct.

AGE 11 YEARS

1. Points out absurdities in contradictory statements.
2. Sentence construction as in 3 for age 10 years. Hardly one fourth pass the test at 10 years, while all do at 11 years of age.
3. Names sixty words in three minutes.
4. Defines abstract terms — *charity, justice, kindness.*
5. Puts words, arranged in a random order, into a sentence.

AGE 12 YEARS

1. Repeats seven digits.
2. Finds in one minute three rimes for a given word — *obedience.*
3. Repeats a sentence of twenty-six syllables.
4. Answers problem questions — a common-sense test.
5. Gives interpretation of pictures.

AGE 13 YEARS

1. Draws the design that would be made by cutting a triangular piece from the once-folded edge of a quarto-folded paper.
2. Rearranges in imagination the relationship of two triangles and draws the results as they would appear.
3. Gives differences between pairs of abstract terms, as *pride* and *pretension.*

RELATIONS OF THE NEW TO THE OLD SCALE

It is not clear that Binet and Simon regarded the 1908 scale as a revision of the earlier scale, which they largely disregarded in the discussion of the later one. It is probable that they regarded it as a development and refinement of the first scale. That the new scale, moreover, is not simply independent of the first one, and therefore to be used only for normal subjects, is evident from the fact that the authors have applied it to subnormal as well as to normal subjects and that they define in the present article the different degrees of feeble-mindedness much more precisely than they had done in connection with the first scale. Under these circumstances it is probably best to regard the second intelligence scale as a substitute for the first one, this view being supported by the fact that it is arranged into tests for all the different year levels from 3 to 13 years, inclusive.

It will be recalled, too, that in the 1905 article the authors had set their problem rather to show *that a scale could be constructed* for the measurement of the level of any given intelligence and the determination of the amount of its retardation; and this they claimed to have demonstrated, even though all the year-levels were not represented in their tests. The task undertaken in the later work was, therefore, to do what they had earlier shown to be a possibility. It cannot be denied, however, that the 1905 scale was regarded as a means of practical helpfulness in researches until the perfection of the better tool had been accomplished. It was but natural, then, that their attention should go to the new scale to the practical exclusion of the old one, once the former was worked out.

HOW THESE TWO SCALES DIFFER

As we noted in the previous chapter, the concept of mental age had been clearly arrived at in the articles published in 1905, but it was not worked out completely in the first scale even for the year-levels there represented. These two scales differ most, therefore, in the fact that in the second one groups of tests for each age-level within the limits mentioned are given; that is, different groups of tests have been located experimentally in the different year-levels so that the mental age in exact years can be determined for any subject tested. Thus there are tests in one group which the normal 3-year-old child should pass, tests which the normal 4-year-old child should pass, tests for the 5-year-olds, and so on, up through the 13th year. But it is important to note that an equal number of tests had not been provided for each year-level, an irregularity that was, with a single exception, corrected in the 1911 scale. This arrangement of tests suitable for the different ages is known as standardization of the tests. Simply devising the tests is quite a different matter from standardizing them, and it was on this latter point in particular that Binet went beyond other test makers of his time.

THE STANDARDIZATION OF THE TESTS

How were these tests standardized? The authors of the scale leave us no very definite answer to this question, but their data and comments on the placement of different tests make two things clear: first, that no very precise method was used, and, second, that roughly speaking, any test was considered to belong in the year in which it was passed successfully by about a half to eight or nine tenths of the normal children. Obviously, if 75 per cent of the children of a given age passed a certain test, this would mean that the middle 50 per cent had just passed, and it is not a bad practice to judge any group by what can be accomplished by the middle half of them when they are arranged in an order ranging from the most to the least able. Thus in Figure 2 each hundredth of the area under the curve represents a child of a given age, say of 9 years. The imaginary hundred children are supposed to be fair representatives of all children of just 9 years of age. Since they do not all have equal ability, they are distributed all along the scale of

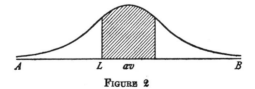

FIGURE 2

ability from the low point of efficiency, *A*, to the high point *B*, and just fifty, or half of them, are located between the vertical lines limiting the shaded area. There are very few extremely inefficient or extremely efficient children, and the number at any point constantly increases from these extremes toward the position *av* on the scale, which marks average ability. At this point is found the greatest number of children of any single degree of ability, as is shown by the fact that here the curve is highest. Now, it may be maintained that a test situation which all the children to the right of the vertical line *L* can pass, but which cannot be passed by the children to the left of this line, will theoretically be a proper test for 9-year-olds; for such a test will be just passed by the entire middle half of the group, and also, of course, by the one-fourth who are above this middle group in ability.

It was evidently this situation which Binet had in mind in a general way in his work of standardization of the scale, but it is to be noted that his tables show a wide variation in the percentage passing any test at age. Why, then, did he not approximate more accurately a passing percentage of 75 for each test in the year appropriate to it? The answer is based on a purely practical matter, which will hardly occur to readers who have not had some experience in standardizing tests, but which forces itself upon one with the first experience of this kind. It takes a good deal of thought and work to devise tests that are suitable for the measurement of intelligence, and even when they have been prepared it is only a rare test that will happen to be just hard enough to let 75 per cent of the children of any age-group pass. Most of the tests will let a greater or a smaller percentage through. If only 40 or 50 per cent of, say, the 6-year-olds pass the test, it may happen that nearly 75 per cent of the 7-year-olds will pass, but rarely will this percentage be just right, and whether or not it will approximate 75 very closely no one can say in advance of trying it on the children. So the experimenter must throw aside the hope of getting enough tests that are just correctly placed, and must resort to approximations. That is what Binet did, but he doubtless tried to get into each age level tests which would on the whole be about right, some being slightly too easy and some too hard — that is, some being passed by too large and some by too small a percentage.

Other difficulties confronted him. It was not easy, for instance, to select children who were just representative of the age groups to be considered. How could he know just what children it would be best to take? Two conditions sent him to the public schools of Paris for the children. One of these was his strong interest in getting some tool that would be helpful in the educational process, an interest that is everywhere prominent in his work, and the other one was that it would be very hard to get subjects for his tests if he did not go to the schools. We shall consider later the accuracy of his selections as norms for the different age groups, saying here only that the children selected were largely from the poorer classes. Despite Binet's distrust of theoretical procedures in scientific work, he was in this case forced to adopt a theoretical point of view in the construction of this year-scale, or "metrical scale of intelligence," and to select subjects and standardize his data of the tests in accordance with the requirements of this point of view.

Nevertheless, the tests in the scale were arranged into year groups and into their general order by an empirical procedure, by actual trials of what children could do, and not by any ideas of the authors as to what they ought to do at different ages. "First," they tell us, "it is to be noted that our tests are really arranged in the actual order of increasing difficulty. It is only after many trials that we have established this order, and we did not at all conceive it as it now stands. If we had left the field open to our conjecture, we should certainly not have admitted that the span of time between 4 and 7 years is necessary for a child able to repeat three digits to become able to repeat five digits. Likewise, we should never have believed that not before 10 years of age are the majority of children able to recite accurately in order the series of months without forgetting more than one of them, or that not before this age is reached does the normal child know all the pieces of our money" (page 71). That is to say, when they came down to actual tests under controlled and constant conditions, they found that the abilities of the children were much more limited than they had supposed. This discovery has been supported in later testing work. In practical life each person is free to lead out, in conversation and in performance, in the things that he knows best or can do best; so, judging him by these performances, we overrate his ability.

Aside from the practical limitation on the accurate placement of the tests in the scale, which we have noted, it should be mentioned also that Binet and Simon did not employ enough children to standardize their scale accurately. "We have made the experiment at length," they tell us, "in the primary schools and maternal schools for boys in Paris on children who were within two months of the ages 3, 4, 5, and so on, to 12 years; we have studied individually 203 children, each of whom was examined in a sitting which lasted at least half an hour" (*ibid.*). This number of children we now know from numerous experiments to be far from sufficient for all these several year groups, so that the authors' standardization of the tests, and their placement of the several tests in the scale, was by no means as exact as might be desired.

PRACTICAL CHECKS ON THE ACCURACY OF THE SCALE

The authors suggested and tried several checks on the accuracy of their scale. One of the simplest of these, they said, would be to find the number of children missing the tests of a given age and passing those of a higher age. Their scale was confirmed by the fact that of over seventy children examined with this check in view not one was found who passed a higher age than one he missed. Another test of the accuracy of the standardization of the scale proposed by them is this: Do a large percentage of the children tested by the scale pass the tests of the age corresponding to their own chronological ages? They found that all the children of a given age did not get equal rating and thus test true to age, some being advanced and some retarded. This, however, favors the scale, for, as they say, a test that would make equal all the children of a given age would be known to be wrong, for it is well established that children of equal age vary considerably in ability. But, as a third test of the accuracy of the scale, we should expect to find that the number of children testing below age, or retarded, would equal the number testing above age, or advanced; and, as a fourth criterion of accuracy, we may expect that in the comparison of successive ages the retarded children of the higher age are fewer than the number testing normal of the next lower age, and that the accelerated of any age are also fewer than those testing normal of the next higher age. Or, stated differently, their fourth criterion amounts to this: If the scale is accurate, we should expect that the number of children testing just normal at any age will be greater than the number testing either above or below normal.

The data offered by the authors do not show their scale to be perfect on all these criteria, but the number of subjects in the several age groups is too small for a reliable evaluation of the scale. Of the whole group of 203 children, the authors found that 103 got mental-age rankings by the tests that agreed with their true ages; that 42 were given a mental age one year in advance of their true, or chronological, age, and 2 were two years advanced, while 44 were retarded one year and 12 two years. This shows more retarded than advanced, but the children were probably hardly up to the standard of ability that would be represen.ative of the age groups studied.

THE VALIDITY OF THE SCALE

These were not all the tests of the validity of their scale that the authors attempted. They also had children selected for their superior ability by the teachers and found that these children were invariably ranked as advanced by the tests. On the other hand, 14 children who were three years behind their normal grades in school were tested and found to be retarded mentally by an average of 2.5 years, or by amounts ranging from 1 to 6 years. However, Binet did not believe that scholastic ability is just the same thing as intellectual ability. The former, he held, depends a good deal on attention to school work, on will, and on a certain kind of character, — e.g., a degree of docility, a regularity of habits, — and above all on continuity of effort. Not all intelligent children have these traits, and therefore many of them do not do as well in school as they could do with better application; but all apply themselves well in the test under the conditions of the shortness of time and of the presence of the tester. "The insufficiencies of attention, of character, and of will do not," the authors say, "appear to give trouble in our intelligence examination; the test is too short and the child is not sufficiently abandoned to himself. In fact, we have never in our examinations come across an inattentive child, save in the case of those of 3 or 4 years of age. All gave good effort; they were close to us and our very presence would suffice to prevent a deflection of attention" (page 75).

There is therefore reason to believe that the ranking of subjects by the tests is in most of the cases of disagreement more accurate than that based on school work. It was found that even abnormal children, presumably weak in attention, did not fail to respond in a whole-hearted manner to the tests; but while the difference in concentration between such individuals and normal children did not show up in the tests, it did appear when groups of children were seated around tables in a cancellation test and were given the problem of crossing out certain specified letters in a page of print. The authors did not, however, make any effort to determine by suitable control tests whether the differences thus brought out between children of poor and of good concentration were really not due to other factors than intelligence — such, for instance, as speed or previous training of some sort.

EFFECTS OF ENVIRONMENT AND TRAINING ON THE SCORES

The authors of the scale admit that responses to certain of their tests are considerably influenced by the previous training of the subject, especially when tests call for information of some sort that children might learn to the extent of their opportunities or school training; and they point out such tests as naming colors and giving the days of the week as most subject to the influence of general experience and training, chiefly extra-scholastic. On the other hand, the arrangement of the weights, the giving of definitions superior to use and definitions of abstract terms, and the interpretation of pictures are mentioned as the tests least under the influence of these factors. These tests were held to give the most adequate expression of spontaneous intelligence in the child (page 79). Other tests, such as counting backwards from 20 to 0 and giving memories from a selection read, are mentioned as most influenced by specific scholastic training, and we are informed that children most often test at age on these because such tests require a basis of scholastic training that is received just at the age in question.

It is not so important to us nowadays to keep in mind which tests were put into each group by Binet, as his conclusions were often arrived at on too meager data; but it is important to note that he explicitly recognized that the scale was not independent of the amount of opportunity that the subject has had to learn some of the things called for in the tests. While it is true that responses to informational tests depend on opportunity as one factor — and Binet's tests were not all, and very few were markedly of this sort — it was supposed that with environment nearly equal, as it generally is among children of the same class and neighborhood, the child with the best intelligence would naturally have gathered the most information, so that, otherwise stated, the child with the greater intelligence would have as a consequence of this a greater store of information and skill. In other words, Binet held definitely, and he explicitly so stated, that the intelligence measured by the scale is not independent of a group of concrete circumstances; it is a complex of (1) "intelligence pure and simple," (2) extra-scholastic acquisitions, (3) scholastic acquisitions which have in each child's experience a date somewhat fixed by the curriculum, and (4) acquisitions relative to language and vocabulary, both scholastic and extra-scholastic.

Would the scale, then, do injustice to one of a high intelligence level who had been deprived, or largely deprived, of scholastic culture relative to his degree of intelligence? "We do not think so," the authors say. "The person of great innate qualities shows his superiority in the repetition of numbers, the repetition of sentences, the drawing of a design cut in a quarto-folded paper, the arrangement of weights, the interpretation of pictures, etc.; and it is especially the province of these tests, when this need is evident, to isolate from the scholastic effects the real native intelligence" (page 80). But even granting this superiority of the tests named, we must note that they are not sufficient in variety or number to make an adequate scale, and that therefore to get very accurate results allowance would have to be made for marked differences in the environment of children; and the authors in their practical testing did make such allowance, a fact of which their writings show ample evidence.

MATURITY AND RECTITUDE OF INTELLIGENCE

Binet held that we should distinguish two aspects of intelligence usually confounded — maturity of intelligence and rectitude of intelligence (pages 80 ff.). The former of these is the result of mental growth with age, but it may appear early in a child, when he is termed precocious. It is the opposite of a childish quality of intelligence. Maturity of intelligence, or its lack, is revealed by four tests particularly : the giving of definitions, the construction of a sentence to include three given words, the explanation of pictures, and the arrangement of weights. The definitions given by a child with a fair maturity of intelligence are superior to those which merely give the use of the object or its relation to oneself. Such a child makes a sentence possessing unity, not one consisting merely of three distinct ideas, one for each word, connected with "and." In explaining a picture, he interprets instead of merely enumerating. He displays method and efficiency in arranging the weights.

Rectitude of intelligence, on the other hand, is not incompatible with the most early age and shows itself in the meaningfulness and accuracy of responses and in the avoidance of absurdities. A good illustration of a response revealing maturity of intelligence with a lack of rectitude was given by a feeble-minded adult who declared that the picture shown him represented a scene which took place in the month of February, an entirely unwarranted detail which, of course, could neither be confirmed nor denied. It is probable that the distinction here made by Binet is more or less artificial. He himself regarded it as tentative.

These and many other ideas and incidental problems raised by Binet show how tentative and expanding his conception of intelligence was, and how far he was removed from a certain dogmatism and finality manifested in the work of testers of less insight, many of them even of our own day.

SOME APPLICATIONS OF THE SCALE

With respect to applications of the scale to the realm of normal children, Binet and his colleague urged that the curriculum should be adapted to the degree of intelligence of the children of the different grades, so that at each stage the tasks assigned the children would not be beyond the abilities possessed by them to do and to assimilate. They deplored the system according to which history is taught to children who, as the tests show, do not yet know morning from afternoon (page 28). "Instruction," they say, "should be designed to follow the march of the natural development of the child, at the same time hastening it a little; but it is a vain effort to precede it by three or four years, as is actually being done through ignorance, by trying to inculcate in babies of 5 or 6 years what only boys of 9 years can retain" (page 38). Moreover, teachers adapt the work to the children in a general way, getting one sort of evidence of the fitness of the adaptation from this child and another from that one, but not making the work suitable to the several abilities of the particular children. As a consequence great maladjustment in school work results, and many children have tasks that are not suited to their requirements. The value, both to parents and to teachers, of accurate mental tests of children is pointed out clearly.

But the authors believe that the greatest service of the scale lies not in the application to normal but to subnormal children, or children inferior in intelligence. The very great benefit of the tests to children of super-normal intelligence was not at this time clearly perceived, but the recognition of this benefit has been one of the contributions of the testing movement in our own day. In the 1908 article the discussion and characterization of the three degrees of feeble-mindedness is considerably advanced over that in the earlier Binet publications, and are worth considering here in some detail. The value of the scale in this realm is shown by the helplessness of authorities without it. Conscientious physicians trying to classify feeble-minded cases speak of light and of profound morority, but give not a word of the real difference otherwise. "It is as if one should say that we have in Paris 43 per cent tall and 42 per cent short men, without defining either class; or as if the law on military recruiting decided that to be enrolled the conscript ought to have a *reasonable height*" (page 85). These vague notions of classification are then accompanied in certain statistical publications by figures, as if they meant something very definite. We are told that if a normal child, by some mischance, is presented to a clinic the alienist is unable to recognize it as normal.

CHARACTERIZATIONS OF IDIOTS, IMBECILES, AND MORONS

Binet and Simon now attempt definitions and characterizations of the three degrees of feeble-mindedness and also a statement of their limits in terms of the scores on the scale.

The idiot. The lowest grade of feeble-mindedness is idiocy. "An idiot is a person who is not able to communicate with his fellows by means of language. He does not talk at all, and does not understand. He corresponds to the intelligence level of a normal child ranging from early infancy to 2 years of age" (page 87). To differentiate the idiot from the imbecile it suffices to employ the following tests: the carrying out of such orders as to touch nose, mouth, eyes; and the naming and indicating of some familiar and easy objects shown in a picture.

The imbecile. The line between the imbecile and the moron, they say, is just as easy to establish as that between the two lower grades. "The imbecile is a person who is incapable of communicating with his fellows by means of written language; he is unable therefore either to read, comprehending what he reads, or to write intelligently, either under dictation or spontaneously" (page 87). Were it not for the possibility of the subject's being illiterate because of the lack of schooling, two 8-year-old tests would suffice to distinguish between imbecile and moron, — reading a passage and remembering two items, and writing short sentences with pen and ink; but to these must be added, for the reason suggested, other 7- and 8-year tests, — describing pictures, counting up the value of some simple coins, and giving differences between two objects recalled in memory.

The moron. It is difficult to make the distinction between the moron and the lower grade of dull persons who would be called normal, as the borderline is not fixed but varies with circumstances. "The most general formula we can adopt is this: An individual is normal if he is able to conduct his affairs of life without having need of the supervision of others, if he is able to do work sufficiently remunerative to supply his own personal needs, and, finally, if his intelligence does not unfit him for the social environment of his parents" (page 88). Binet held that the son of a lawyer, for instance, who is reduced by his limitation of intelligence to the condition of a small-job employee, is a moron, as is also the son of a master mason who at the age of thirty is still a mason's assistant. A peasant may be normal in his simple environment in the country but be a moron in the city, where conditions are more complex. In other words, retardation was regarded as a relative affair, dependent on many circumstances, and the authors prefer tentative distinctions because of this fact. Twenty cases tested by them in hospitals for defectives had given intellectual levels not passing 9 or 10 years. A 14-year-old imbecile of a 5-year mental age level, they pointed out, may recite without error the names of the days of the week and of the months of the year, and may name colors and pieces of money — some of which tests, the reader will note, were in the 10-year group — because he has profited more by his longer experience in these things, which he can learn, than has the normal 5-year-old child.

Tests to detect moronity. If, then, we leave out of consideration these tests of simple notions which the adult moron has usually acquired, there remain certain tests which he cannot pass. The authors name the following ones as forming, for the population of the Paris district studied by them, the line between moronity and normality : arranging weights, giving correct responses to questions of difficult comprehension, constructing sentences containing three given words, defining abstract terms, interpreting pictures, and finding rimes. These tests, taken from the 9- to the 12-year levels, were found by experiment to be too difficult for persons properly classed as morons. None of the twenty morons they tested passed even three of these tests, though some passed one or two. It is important to note that with these defectives they did not hold simply to the tests of a certain year-level for making the distinction. "All our work has shown that intelligence is measured by a synthesis of results," they say, and not by a special localized success (page 89). They hesitate to give even these six crucial tests, fearing that they may seem to suggest a dangerous precision; for there are many conditions to consider, and it is only in a general way that it may be said that passing at least four of these tests shows one's normality. Moreover, normality as thus established may exist with accentuated instability, or with certain irresistible impulsions or other pathological conditions grave enough for the subject's internment.

In the diagnosis of a young defective person, whose mentality is not yet mature, it is necessary to take into account age as well as present mental ability. How shall these factors be combined? "We shall not know the answer for certain," say Binet and Simon, "until a broad experience will finally have taught us what we do not yet know, — how the idiot, the imbecile, and the moron develop, and what prognosis can be made on the basis of a particular amount of retardation at a given age" (pages 90 f.). The results of tests of supposedly normal children indicated that a mental arrest of one year, as determined by the tests, is so frequent as to lose significance. A retardation of two years, however, is sufficiently rare to be met with in only 7 per cent of the cases and may therefore indicate a probability of defectiveness.

Their procedure, then, is to class those children who test two years or more under the mental level of their chronological age, with the adult defectives who pass the same tests, while those children who by the tests are found to have only one year of retardation are considered normal. The groupings of feeble-minded persons by mental age are : 0 to 2 years, idiots; 2 to 7 years, imbeciles; and above 7 years, morons.

This system of determining feeble-mindedness and its degree of mental age is obviously unfair in certain particulars, especially to the younger children. A child of 5 years of age who just passes the 3-year tests would be classed near the lower limits of imbecility, while another child but a year younger who passes the same tests would be considered normal. Recognizing this injustice, Binet and Simon admit that the classification has no prognostic value for any child, but only a present value. "He who is an imbecile today may perhaps become a moron with the progress of age, or he may, on the contrary, remain an imbecile all his life. One cannot tell" (page 91).

SCHOLASTIC STANDING AS SUPPLEMENTARY
TO RATING BY TESTS

These investigators used the scholastic standing as a check on the test classification of children. They regarded as feeble-minded any child who was three years or more retarded in the school grade, provided that frequent absence or irregularity in attendance could not account for the failure of normal promotion. Therefore Binet considered that taking the school standing into consideration in connection with the test rating it would be possible in most cases to arrive at a fair conclusion as to whether a given individual should be classed as a moron or not. He and Simon cite cases of children who were three years retarded in school but whom the tests showed to be arrested mentally but one year, and who could therefore not be considered morons. The reverse condition, serious mental retardation with a normal scholastic progress, was apparently more rare, and it would need more study, for often teachers promote children in the lower grades largely on the basis of age.

Thus in the 1908 report Binet and Simon bring down their definitions and characterizations of the degrees of feeble-mindedness to more strictly drawn points in terms of the tests than formerly, but they still fail to deal successfully with the matter of age in relation to the degree of defectiveness in children. It is obvious that the absolute amount of retardation, whether mental or scholastic, is not a safe guide ; for a retardation of, say, two years is certainly much more grave in the case of a 10-year-old child than in that of one who is 15 years old. This point Binet never did solve satisfactorily.

SOME WEAKNESSES OF THE 1908 SCALE

This 1908 scale was not itself free from important weaknesses. Aside from the imperfect standardization made evident in subsequent work with the scale, both in Europe and in America, there was the fact, indeed noticed but not corrected by the authors, that certain tests were considerably dependent on school and extra-school experience. With such tests in the scale it was very important that the results be taken seriously only when the subjects tested had all had approximately equal opportunities. This defect, though obvious enough, is not easily removed, as any one acquainted with modern testing knows ; but it is important to emphasize it here, because it so often happens that inexperienced testers leave out of consideration the element of unequal opportunity to learn the things called for in certain mental tests. The desirable thing would, of course, be to have tests that measure only pure intelligence, whatever that may be ; but such a scale we do not yet possess, for no mental function is independent of external influences of some sort. There are, however, tests that are probably very little influenced by the subject's past experiences.

Another defect of the 1908 scale is the inequality of the number of tests in the different year levels, this number ranging from three in the 13th to eight in the 7th year. This scale, like the 1905 scale, is also defective in the fact that instructions for giving and scoring the several tests were not standardized satisfactorily. Various children can be compared on the same set of tests only when the latter have been administered in a thoroughly objective manner, and when the instructions have carried the same meaning to all of them. The problem of securing a satisfactory degree of objectivity in tests is a very important one, and is not fully settled even in our own day.

DIRECTIONS AS TO METHODS OF SCORING

With the 1908 scale Binet and Simon gave definite instructions as to how to find the mental age of the subjects tested, even though they neglected to standardize satisfactorily the responses to many of the tests and to indicate what sort of response to each would be considered a pass. They found that rarely will a subject be able to pass all the tests up to the end of any one year and fail in all above this point. How, then, shall the mental age be determined? The rule adopted is this: The subject is first to be given the mental age of the highest year level in which he passes all the tests, with a possible exception of one test. To this basic year level is to be added an additional year for every five tests that he passes in higher levels. In the application of this last part of the rule the error of having a variable number of tests in the several year-levels becomes obvious. Let us take an example to make the rule for scoring clear. If a child passes all but one of the tests in the 9-year level and likewise all but one in the 10-year level, then on this record alone he would have a mental age of 10 years. If, in addition to this, he should also pass three tests of the 11-year group and two of the 12-year group, his mental age, or "intelligence level," would be 11 years. But if he should pass only four tests above the 10-year level, his mental age would be but 10 years. In the 1911 scale, presently to be considered, the rule was so modified as to permit of the addition of a fractional part of a year.

TWO STRONG POINTS OF THE SCALE

We must not overlook the important fact that the completion of this scale marks a step in the progress of intelligence testing that is surpassed only by the appearance of the 1905 scale, which not only established the possibility of such a scale, but outlined the general plan to be followed in its construction. The correction of the inevitable errors in such a work is but a secondary matter, and was sure to follow. The two things about this new scale that gave it the advantages which subsequent years have shown it had over all other mental-testing devices to the date of its appearance, are doubtless these: first, the adoption of the method of simple mental age units, easily understood, even by non-technically trained persons; and, second, the application to each subject of several tests calling into play a variety of mental functions.

EXERCISES

1. In a second column, as illustrated in Chapter 11 with the 1911 scale, give the origin as far as possible of the several tests in the 1908 scale. Go to the sources if they are available.

2. With respect to the principles, what are the differences between the scales of 1905 and 1908? Is the conception of mental age involved in the 1905 scale? Explain fully. Could mental age be the unit of measure in a very complete scale after the order of the scale of 1905? Why?

3. What is the difference between the validity, or the diagnostic value, and the reliability of a test of intelligence? Which presupposes the other? Illustrate by supposing that height should be tried as an intelligence test. Discuss its possible validity and reliability.

4. Compare the percentile method of standardizing a test with that of letting approximately the middle 50 per cent of children of any age pass the test normal to that age.

CHAPTER ELEVEN

EVALUATIONS OF THE BINET METHOD OF TESTING AND THE SCALE OF 1911

CRITICAL EVALUATIONS OF THE 1908 SCALE IN DIFFERENT COUNTRIES

THE publication in 1908 of a scale more accurate and complete than the first one had stimulated a good deal of investigation in various localities. There was opposition to the use of the scale in certain fields, this coming chiefly from alienists who had doubtless felt themselves antagonized and discounted by the criticisms that Binet had made of their own methods and by the evidence of the inefficiency of these methods, as applied to feeble-mindedness, that Binet and Simon had shown by the use of their tests. One alienist, by the arbitrary judgment method characteristic of a good part of their opposition, had declared the intelligence scale worthless. On the other hand, wherever the scientific method of criticism or evaluation was undertaken, — that is, wherever the scale was put to actual use in the solution of practical problems, whether in the field of education proper or in the dealings with feeble-minded individuals, — the scale was at once recognized as an unusually helpful instrument. It was of course to be expected that many weaknesses in the scale would develop and that suggestions for improvement would come from different workers. To such criticisms Binet seems to have had an open mind, so that he could profit by them and improve the efficiency of the scale.

Results in Belgium and an analysis of them. In 1910 Decroly and Degand (*95*) tested with the scale forty-three boys and girls in a private school in Brussels, directed by them, and published their results in detail. These investigators regret the omission in the new scale of some tests in the 1905 series which they regard as valuable, and they find that tests unduly influenced by school and home training have not been sufficiently eliminated. They hold also that certain of the tests, such as those calling for the names of the days of the week and the months of the year, are too mechanical. Furthermore, the tests were in general found to be too easy at the lower end and too hard at the upper end of the scale, thus failing to make sufficient differences between extreme abilities. In addition to this general defect in standardization, certain tests were somewhat misplaced. These critics also suggest the need of norms in the digits test for the years between the 7th and the 12th, though it is obvious that the performance differences through this range of years would be too small to make the suggestion practicable.

Binet seems to have been somewhat confused as to whether their data actually confirmed or disagreed with his own results, and to have supposed that a mere superficial examination of these results obtained in Belgium would lead to their being interpreted as unfavorable to the scale. He therefore got these investigators to let him have their own notes and unpublished tables for the purpose of making an analysis of them himself (*45*, pages 187 ff.). The data indicated that the Belgian children were of a superior class as compared with those tested in Paris. On the average they were one and one-half years in advance of the norms published by Binet, eleven of them being advanced mentally over two years.

To what is this considerable difference due? Binet suggests three probable causes : (1) He finds evidence to believe that these authors have tested with an excessive indulgence, that without being conscious of it they have aided their subjects. He regrets that they had not come to Paris to see his own use of the scale ; for, he says, "they knew our technique only through our publication" (page 189). This in itself is an admission of the presence of subjective elements in the scale, due to a lack of sufficient standardization in the administration and scoring of the tests. The difference due to this factor, however, he holds to be small and too insignificant to account for the differences between their results and his own. (2) There is ample evidence that the Belgian subjects were from a higher social class than the subjects tested by Binet in Paris, the former being children of the professional class — doctors, professors of the University, lawyers, etc. (3) The Belgian children had not only had superior educational and social opportunities in their homes but they were trained in small classes in school, eight to ten in a class; whereas the Paris children were taught in classes of around sixty individuals, so that for the Belgians contact with their instructors was more intimate, and personal acquaintance and stimulation was close.

Intelligence and social class. In view of these conditions of differences in the homes and the schools it became evident to Binet that the Belgian investigators had opened up a very important problem, that of relative effects of heredity and environment on the intellectual status of children of the poor, on the one hand, and of the rich and the professional classes, on the other, as measured by the scale.

In view of the different training of children in these two classes, Binet attempted to compare the results on the Paris children with those on the Belgian children in such a manner as to determine the probable effect of diverse early training; so he asked himself the question, What are the tests on which the Belgian subjects were most in advance of those tested in Paris, and what are the tests showing the least difference? He found the greatest superiority in the description and interpretation of pictures, the counting of thirteen sous, repeating five digits, naming four colors, comparing objects by memory, pointing out what is lacking in unfinished pictures, arranging weights, naming the days of the week, defining abstract terms, knowing pieces of money, giving names of months, giving sixty words in three minutes, criticizing absurd sentences, and repeating sentences. An examination of these tests and of those in which the least difference was shown led Binet to conclude that the Belgian children excelled most in cases in which better language and home training counted most, and least in the matters involved in regular school training — copying a sentence, reading, counting nine sous, counting backward, writing under dictation, copying a diamond, giving change from twenty sous, making a sentence to contain three words, making rimes, and explaining problem questions. This interpretation he offers tentatively, and, indeed, on rather slim evidence, his idea being that the children of the professional classes have superior opportunities of personal contact, and so express themselves with greater ease. He believed, however, and recent studies support this view, that better native ability was also a factor.

To verify these views he went back to some of his earlier test records of children of well-to-do parents and compared them with records of children of the poor class. Here he found little evidence of superiority of the former group. M. Morlé tested fifty children of a school in Paris, of which he was in charge, and turned his data over to Binet, having classified the children in four classes according to social conditions described respectively as misery, poverty, mediocrity, and ease. Very little evidence of correlation between scores in the tests and social class was found. But these children were all in the same school with its very large classes; and Binet says that the parents "in ease" in this case were mostly merchants or "alcoholics," whose children were neglected, being left to themselves without supervision and seldom seeing their parents. These parents were away while the children were awake, and they "came home late and did not occupy themselves with their children " (page 194).

Very different results were obtained, however, from tests of eighteen children by Mme. Thévenot in a special school under her charge, in a commercial part of Paris. Her classes were small, consisting of about fifteen students each; so the children compared favorably with those in Mlle. Degand's school. They were a select group, as were the Belgian children. Here again the children tested on the average 1.7 years mentally in advance of their ages.

In further study of this problem, Binet and M. Morlé tested thirty primary school children of one of the poorest parts of Paris and an equal number from a primary school in a section where the parents belonged to the class living "in ease." Of these children sixteen in the better group were mentally in advance of their age to the extent of one or more years, and only four of the poorer group were in advance, while the numbers found to be mentally retarded one or more years in the same groups were four and twelve, respectively.

Uses and results of the scale in England. Miss Katherine Johnston, of the University of Sheffield, England, visited Binet's laboratory in 1910 and became acquainted with his method. On her return home she tested two hundred children in Sheffield schools (*143, 144*). The children were of very unequal status, and those of the better parentage were in classes of fifteen to twenty, whereas those of poorer social standing were in classes numbering forty to sixty. In her report before a section of the British Association for the Advancement of Science she had lost these differences in averages. Binet (*45*, page 196) urged her to compute new averages, making separate groups of the children of different classes.

A widely recognized defect in the scale. Her results, which were sent to Binet for analysis, showed that in the ages below 10 years too large a per cent of the children were rated by the scale as superior mentally, whereas in the higher ages a majority of the children received mental ages below normal, indicating that the tests in the lower age-levels as standardized by Binet and Simon were too easy and that those in the higher levels were too hard. Early reports of tests by Goddard (*121*) and by Terman and Childs (*209*) in America, by Mlle. Descœudres (*100*) in Geneva, and by Bobertag (*70*) in Germany, all published too late, however, to influence Binet in his 1911 revision, agreed essentially in this regard with the work of Miss Johnston and with what Binet had already found out himself.

In this agreement among investigators of different countries, working under different circumstances, Stern (*202*, page 49) saw one of the strongest evidences of the validity of the tests. To quote: "That, despite the differences in race and language, despite the divergences in school organization and in methods of instruction, there should be so decided agreement in the reactions of the children — is, in my opinion, the best vindication of the *principle* of the tests that one could imagine, because this agreement demonstrates that *the tests do actually reach and discover the general developmental conditions of intelligence* (so far as these are operative in public school children of the present cultural epoch), and not mere fragments of knowledge and attainments acquired by chance. And this confirmation of the principle may also lead us confidently to expect that the discrepancies that have been revealed at the same time in some of the details of the system can be obviated in the future."

Binet gets valuable data for revision of the scale. Miss Johnston also arranged for Binet the tests of each year-level in the order of their difficulty. These data were useful to him, because her groups of different ages were large enough to be of some significance, — 41, 22, 30, 38, and 24, for ages

7, 8, 9, 10, and 12 years, respectively. In the 7-year group the hardest tests were the incomplete pictures, the naming of four pieces of money, and the repetition of five digits; in the eighth year, counting out change and giving two items remembered from a reading made by the subject; in the ninth, giving definitions superior to use and arranging weights; in the tenth, comprehension of difficult questions, making two sentences to include three given words, and knowing nine pieces of money; and in the twelfth year, defining abstract terms. In each year these harder tests are named in decreasing order of difficulty. This investigation was undoubtedly of much use to Binet in making the 1911 revision of his scale. He analyzed the data and discussed them carefully in the *Année* in connection with the presentation of this revision.

Miss Johnston's tests were the first use made of the Binet-Simon scale in England, and they were followed closely by others carried out on defectives by Shrubsall (*190*), whose work has probably not received the recognition that it merits.

In 1911 Abelson (*1*) published an article on some experiments which he had carried out to determine the reliability and the diagnostic efficiency of certain practical tests, and also to solve certain problems relating to the nature of mental defect. He used certain of the Binet tests and some tests based on geometrical figures probably suggested by the De Sanctis tests. The geometrical figures were overlapping circles, triangles, and squares, and the subjects were to indicate places that were within the circle and triangle and outside the square, for instance, to show that he grasped space relations as involved here. This test has been utilized and made well known by Otis in his group tests, and has also been used in the Army Alpha. In addition to these tests Abelson also used a number of simple quickness-of-reaction and sensory-discrimination tests. Borderline or slightly defective subjects were used as most useful for the purposes of this study. Results showed that any one of the tests had about as high diagnostic effectiveness as any other. "For instance, the simple test of 'tapping' showed itself to have (for these defective children) just about as much diagnostic value as the far more plausible test of 'interpreting pictures' " (page 310). The need of a variety of reliable tests, or tests that would yield consistent results, is emphasized in the conclusions, and it is asserted that "tests practically valueless in isolation become remarkably trustworthy in pools of from ten to twelve." Yet we are informed that "The reason for applying a large number of tests is not to gauge a number of different factors in ability but merely to obtain multiple evidence as to the one factor, the general level " (page 311). This study therefore found no support to the faculty view of mind, which would test memory, observation, judgment, reasoning, etc., and little importance was also attached to the use of "a scale of tests graduated [as are the Binet tests] to the ages of the persons tested."[1] The essential nature of intellectual deficiency "seems to be a general lowering of that class of performances which is characterized by the need of clear consciousness" (*ibid.*). The author shows clear leanings toward the Spearman theory of intelligence as a general factor.[2]

Uses of the scale in Italy. In 1908 Ferrari (*113*) translated the Binet-Simon scale of that year into Italian, but he held that his own tests for defectives gave a more helpful picture of the subject than did the Binet mental age. To this criticism and to others by Baroncini and Sarteschi, Binet replied in 1910 (*44*). Treves and Saffiotti began in 1909 a very

[1] Myers (*168*) sounded an early warning against deducing conclusions from a "hodge-podge of statistics" and declared the scale faulty because it lacks the element of introspection. With this position Abelson found himself in accord.
[2] See page 270.

extended investigation with the scale, one that later led to a radical modification of it (*184*). They translated the scale in 1910–1911 (*222*) and made some preliminary criticisms. At Binet's request they wrote an article for the *Année* (*183*), which, however, had to be completed by Saffiotti alone, for during its preparation Treves, as well as Binet, died. These two Italian investigators found in the lower grades a noticeable superiority of the scores of children from the higher social classes; but in the higher grades, where a selective process by higher schools had left only the duller children of the better parentage, this superiority disappeared, and was indeed partly reversed in favor of the poorer children.

Uses of the scale in Germany — Origin of intelligence quotient. In Germany the intelligence scale had to meet in competition other methods of testing which had become rather extensively developed. Binet himself seems never to have learned the German language (*75*, page *252*), and had followed psychological progress in Germany through the reviews regularly made by Henri in the *Année*. Stern, one of the best-known psychologists in the field of tests, had in 1900 published his well-known book (*200*) on individual differences, a book that was completely revised in 1911 under the title *Differential Psychology* (*201*). Meumann published an extensive review of the test literature in 1905 (*163*), which of course could not at that date include the Binet tests. Bobertag early appreciated the value of the new method in the Binet scale, and in 1909 published (*69*) a summary of Binet's contributions to this subject up to that time. A couple of years later he published a version of the 1908 intelligence scale (*70*) that became a standard work in Germany. He made a number of changes and improvements in the tests, which, however, appeared in print too late to affect Binet's last scale. Bobertag, Kramer (*149*), and Chotzen (*92*) early pointed out the fact that absolute retardation as measured by Binet in terms of mental age increases with age so that a given amount of retardation is less serious in the case of an old than of a very young child. This demonstration of a relation between age and degree of retardation led Stern in 1912 (*202*, pages 79 f.; *203*, page 143) to suggest the *intelligence quotient*, later adopted by Terman in the Stanford revision of the Binet scale, a measure that is found by dividing a subject's mental age by his actual or chronological age.[1]

INTELLIGENCE TESTS IN AMERICA

In America, as we have seen, there had been a vigorous movement in mental testing over a decade before the Binet scale was introduced, and a good deal of refinement in methods had developed in connection with the use of correlation methods worked out in England by Galton, Pearson, Yule, Spearman, and others. The tests were various measurements more or less independent of one another, not forming a scale in the Binet sense of this term. Valuable studies, in addition to those mentioned on foregoing pages, had been made by Bagley (*7*) and Seashore (*185*) on tests of school children, by Cattell (*89*) on the measurement of individual differences, in merit, by Thorndike on statistical methods in testing (*213*) and on the application of various mental tests to the measurement of resemblances and differences in twins, a study in heredity (*214*), by Norsworthy (*169*) on tests of

---

[1] It is interesting to note that in Russia the alienist Rossolimo (*182*) attempted so to combine a series of tests as to give a profile picture of an individual. The profile is constructed by erecting an ordinate for each test score, the height of each ordinate being determined by the test score in the mental function it is supposed to represent. Stern says that "on the whole, the principle of the construction of the profile is too superficial and the co-ordination of certain tests to certain mental functions — e.g., to volitional acts — is not precise enough to allow us to hope for much success" (*202*, page 26). Other articles have since been published by Rossolimo, and the profile tests of Downey (*106*) in America have become well known, though their diagnostic value for the traits they propose to measure is still in question.

mentally deficient children, and by Bonser (72) on reasoning in school children. These investigations were, however, little related to the education of children in the elementary schools, and to the care and treatment of feeble-minded children.

There was another line of development in America, which was very similar to the one that had served as the immediate stimulus in Paris to the construction of the Binet scale. The formal educational process was not successful with all the children. Retardation in the schools was drawing serious attention, as expressed a little later in Ayres' well-known book, *Laggards in Our Schools*, published in 1910. Moreover, institutions had been formed in a number of places, such as at Vineland, New Jersey, at Faribault, Minnesota, and at Lincoln, Illinois, for positively feeble-minded children, and these schools had developed problems of their own relative to means of classification of the inmates and to the determination of their several capabilities as to training. These schools for feeble-minded children furnished the richest soil at first for the transplanting of the Binet tests to America. Later the testing movement reached the public schools.

The interest in child psychology which G. Stanley Hall had fostered at Clark University seems to have been rather closely related to the practical use of the Binet scale in America; for it is significant that in the early part of this century, when the majority of our universities were teaching and making investigations in the academic psychology only, Clark was training men like Goddard, •Huey, Terman, and Kuhlmann, who later became leaders in the development of the Binet tests in this country.[1]

[1] Dr. J. P. Porter, however, has informed me that Hall was opposed to the test method at this time, and that he objected to Terman's study (206). In reply to a question on this point, Terman has sent me the following statement under date of January 14, 1925: " It is true that Dr. Hall stren-

While the early Binet scale was known to experimental psychologists in America and was reviewed in the *Psychological Bulletin* in 1906, it was doubtless regarded by most readers as being of only passing interest. The Sharp-Titchener study, it will be recalled, had found the tests for which Binet had argued in the nineties to be of very limited value to psychology, their value having been compared to that of tests of color blindness. Goddard, who went to the Vineland Training School in 1906 to conduct researches on the feeble-minded inmates of this school, received little aid on his new problems from the psychologists to whom he appealed for advice; so he turned to the literature of experimental researches and worked out some twenty-five tests, or "stunts," to be used in the diagnosis of mental defectiveness. Some of these tests were standardized, among them being the well-known Seguin form board.

The introduction of the Binet intelligence scale. At this time Goddard did not know of Binet's early work on the intelligence scale, but was told of it by Decroly, whom he saw while on a trip abroad in 1908. Decroly gave Goddard a copy of the 1905 scale, which the latter used to a limited extent on his return to Vineland. "He did not think it contributed much over and above what he obtained by the use of his own series of separate tests. In 1909, the *Année Psychologique* for 1908, containing the 1908 revision, reached him. He writes of this: 'When I read Binet's *Measuring Scale*, I rejected it as too formal and exact. I thought "mind" could not be measured in that way. A second thought showed me that my impression or feeling was of no value compared to the serious declaration of a man like Binet. I accordingly set about trying out the scale on our

uously opposed my taking up a mental test problem at Clark University. I have always felt that his advice was honestly and sincerely given. He was constitutionally incapable of appreciating the type of work mental testers attempted to do. I received so much inspiration from Hall that I have never held his stand on this matter against him."

children. The more I used it the more amazed I was at its accuracy' " (*242*, page 35).

In 1908, as we have already noted, Goddard published a translation of the first Binet scale, and two years later one of the 1908 scale (*119*). Whipple included in the first edition of his *Manual of Mental and Physical Tests*, in 1910, a translation and criticisms of both these scales. In the same year Huey (*135*) published in the new *Journal of Educational Psychology* a translation of the 1908 scale, and also a paper (*134*) suggesting the application of the scale to dull children in the schools, with a view to finding the extent of their mental retardation. In 1909 a special committee of the National Education Association reported (*78*) on books and tests to be used in the study of exceptional and mentally deficient children. The report contained both the Goddard revision of the 1908 scale and the De Sanctis tests. Even though Terman, who was to become the most influential authority in America on the application of the Binet scale to children in the schools, had published results of a study of genius and stupidity (*206*) in 1906, he did not become acquainted with the Binet scale until the following year, and "did not turn his attention to the tests until he went to Stanford University in 1910" (*242*, page 37).

Kuhlmann (*151*) in 1911 published a condensed and slightly modified English version of the 1908 scale. In this article he gave more fully than had been done in other American translations of the scale, the various comments of the authors, Binet and Simon, and thus hoped evidently to contribute toward a more nearly uniform administration of the tests and scoring of results, as well as to enable persons who were "not necessarily trained in psychology" to use the tests. Wallin published a similar version (*226*) in 1911.

The early developments in the use of the scale in America were reviewed and commented upon by Binet in the *Année* in 1911, but most of the reports appeared in print too late to have any effect on his revision of this year. He noted, with possibly a little amusement, the fact that in the Whipple translation some of his tests were regarded as too cruel for the children. After mentioning the necessary changes in the tests to adapt them to English-speaking children, such as those in tests dealing with money, Binet adds: "But the curious thing is that the author has considered it useful to substitute for our sentences to be criticized, some new ones, under the pretext that ours are too cruel. We do, indeed, speak of a woman cut into pieces, of a train wreck resulting in forty-eight deaths, and of a man who commits suicide; it appears that these stories seem frightening to young Americans. Our young Parisians laughed at them. However that may be, we think Whipple's new sentences cannot be accepted before being tried experimentally. There is nothing to prove that they present a difficulty of comprehension equal to that in ours" (*45*, note, page 145). Goddard's use of the scale on large numbers of feeble-minded children (*120*) is also noted by Binet in this article. One of the early results (*121*) of the tests of American children was evidence, in agreement with the results by Miss Johnston in England, that the tests for the earlier years of the 1908 scale were too easy while those for the higher age levels were much too hard; that is, that the scale tended to bring too near together the children of the range of ages from 3 to 13 years. The full effect of the American tests did not reach Binet to influence him much if any in his final revision, but may nevertheless be briefly indicated here in connection with a few other facts and views, to show the reader how the testing movement was taking hold of this country before the death of Binet in October, 1911.

Criticisms and evaluations of the scale. In general it may be said that wherever the scale was put to practical use in connection with the classification of defectives it was received with enthusiasm as a very useful instrument, even though imperfections in minor details were noted. Ayres (*5*), however, in 1911 published a criticism of the 1908 scale which seems to have been based on *a priori* considerations rather than on experimental work, and which was not well received by those who had used the tests most. While he expressed appreciation of the idea of arranging the tests into a scale of increasing difficulty and of giving the score in terms of mental age, he adversely criticized the tests adopted by Binet, as depending too much on the child's ability to use words fluently, on the child's recent environmental experiences, on his ability to read and write, to repeat words and numbers, to solve puzzle tests, and to define abstract terms. Some of these criticisms were not ill founded, but when Ayres objects to some of the tests as being unusual to everyday life, particularly to the counting-backward test as being "educationally vicious," he has clearly confounded the testing with the training of a child.

Kuhlmann (*152*), in a vigorous defense of the scale, points out that certain of Ayres' specific criticisms are founded on misconceptions and are not based on extensive use of the tests, which, we are told, contradicts these criticisms. Miss Lawrence (*154*), trying the definitions test on 748 pupils in the St. Cloud, Minnesota, elementary schools, finds that this particular test taken alone is but "a coarse sieve," with some significance.

Binet insisted on a variety of tests. This result does not, of course, contradict Binet's view of the test, for at about this same time he was himself writing this statement: "One test has no significance, we repeat with emphasis, but five or six tests do mean something." And on the same page, at the close of the article on the 1911 scale, he says in almost his last words on these tests, that the principle of using a multiplicity of tests must be a good one, for even in the case of Dr. Ferrari's method of measuring intelligence, which a review by Mlle. Diroud had shown to contain only a small proportion of good tests, satisfactory results were obtained. "The attention of psychologists must, then, be called to this principle of the multiplicity of tests. Without any doubt these methods will be drawn upon to a large extent in the future in the study of aptitudes, of character, and even of the physiological state — in brief, for the realization of measurement in individual psychology" (*45*, page 201).

Terman's early impressions of the Binet scale. As early as 1911 Terman published an article in which he gave his impressions of the 1908 scale as gained on its application to four hundred non-selected children, thus making a notable start toward using the scale for the testing of normal children. He reported that the Binet type of intelligence scale is feasible and of great practical and theoretical value. In this article he draws an interesting comparison between work with this scale and with the tests used in his earlier study on genius and stupidity, saying that he had spent nearly two years before in the use of various "tests of intelligence" and that he "could hardly count value received. My present belief is that the field is one that will richly repay any careful and well-directed effort" (*207*, page 199). The need of a radical revision of the scale was, however, indicated, for it was found that young children are rated too high while those in the upper age levels of the scale are rated too low; that is, that the scale was far too easy at the lower end and too hard at the upper end. These findings agreed with those of Miss Johnston in England.

Terman mentions in this valuable article several tests of his own that he has tried as supplementary to the scale — a generalization test (the interpretation of fables), a graded completion test (from Ebbinghaus' method), a vocabulary test, and a test of practical judgment (the ball-and-field problem) — and he also suggests that there should be tests for higher levels than those at the upper end of the Binet scale. He urges the importance of intelligence tests, and the need of more attention to them. "Everything else is relative to intelligence" (page 203). Teachers' estimates are subjective and unreliable, while tests are objective. He shows clearly a realization of the fact that with test results at hand, even though the tests are not perfect, there is something concrete with which to work, so that in comparisons of test scores with other available data on the child's ability and training, we are bound to get down to a factual basis and to consider the influence of this and that factor on the subject's responses.

Thus Terman sees so clearly the possibilities of the use of a good intelligence scale that the present imperfections in the one under consideration are but minor matters, and he characteristically sets himself at once to the work of revision. Several problems loom up in the solution of which the scale will be of great service. He mentions the effects on mentality of adenoids and of other defects, the relation of mental to physical age, of mental growth to pedagogical progress, of incorrigibility to retardation in intelligence, heredity factors in intelligence, and the effects on intelligence scores of prolonged and unfavorable social conditions. A number of these problems had earlier been raised by Binet. In spite of the many imperfections and inadequacies of this scale, Terman says: "I believe that by its use it is possible for the psychologist to submit, after a forty-minute diagnostication, a more reliable and more enlightening estimate of the child's intelligence than most teachers can offer after a year of daily contact in the schoolroom" (page 204).

Thus the stage was set in America for a real testing movement, and while the separate tests for different functions and the more accurate and analytical correlation methods, already in use in America, were proving themselves of value in various useful investigations, the Binet tests were found to be superior in the practical fields of education to any existing methods of intelligence testing, both on feeble-minded and on normal children.

The danger of ignorant and unskilled use of the scale. Naturally there was great temptation for persons to rush into this testing work with very little preparation in the way of psychological training, and with meager notions of the ideas of the originator of the scale. Against the tendency thus threatening to injure the testing movement Clara Harrison Town sounded a timely warning (*220*). After quoting some of Binet's cautions, she says: "Unfortunately the American public has not read these paragraphs, and the result which is threatening is a wholesale use of the scale in an unscientific manner, which will do nothing but postpone the time of its real usefulness" (page 240). She answers some of Ayres' objections to the scale by quoting from Binet's 1908 article, which Ayres had apparently not read, and points out that several of the defects mentioned have been recognized by Binet himself and have been corrected in a new (1911) revision, which, she points out, has appeared, and of which later she became the translator (*64*).[1]

The revised scale as put forth by Binet in the *Année* article follows. We have indicated in connection with each test, on the right side of the page, its origin and position in earlier scales. It may be well here to say that in giving these tests to any child, one must follow strictly the procedure under which they were administered in securing the data for their

[1] The 1911 revision by Binet and Simon appeared in April in the *Bulletin de la Société libre pour l'Étude psychologique de l'Enfant*, under the title (translated) "A Method of Measuring the Development of the Intelligence of Young Children." It also appeared, over the name of Binet alone, in the *Année* under the title, "New Researches on the Method of Measuring the Intellectual Level of School Children."

standardization. For these details the reader must go to the various manuals now available, or to the Town translation (*64*). A recent statement by Woodworth (*238*) expresses so well the cautions against a misuse of the scale that it is worth quoting here: "The Binet scale, it must be understood, is an instrument of precision, not to be handled except by one who has been thoroughly trained in its use. It looks so simple that any student is apt to say, 'Why, I could give those tests!' The point is that he couldn't — not until he knew the tests practically by heart, not till he had standardized his manner of conducting them to agree perfectly with the prescribed manner and till he knew how to score the varying answers given by different children according to the scoring system that goes with the tests, and not till, by experience in handling children in the tests, he was able to secure the child's confidence and get him to do his best, without, however, giving the child any assistance beyond what is prescribed. Many superior persons have looked down on the psychological examiner with his (or her) assortment of little tests, and have said, 'Certainly no special training is necessary to give these tests. You simply want to find out whether the child can do these stunts. I can find out as well as you.' They miss the point altogether. The question is not whether the child *can* do these stunts (with an undefined amount of assistance), but whether he *does* them under carefully prescribed conditions. The child is given two, three or four dozen chances to see how many of them he will accept; and the whole scale has been standardized by try-out on many children of each age, and so adapted that, when given according to instructions, it will give a correct measure of the child's mental age. But when given by superior persons in ignorance of its true character, it gives results very wide of the mark. So much by way of caution" (note, pages 273 f.).

THE 1911 REVISION OF THE BINET INTELLIGENCE SCALE[1]

AGES 3, 4, AND 5 YEARS	PLACE IN THE 1908 SCALE
These tests remain as in the 1908 scale, the 3- and the 5-year level each having five tests, and the 4-year only four.	No change

AGE 6 YEARS

1.	Distinguishes between morning and afternoon.	No change
2.	Defines familiar objects in terms of use.	No change
3.	Copies a diamond.	7-year group
4.	Counts thirteen *sous* (pennies in American translations).	7-year group
5.	Distinguishes between ugly and pretty faces.	No change

AGE 7 YEARS

1.	Shows right hand and left ear.	6-year group
2.	Describes pictures.	No change
3.	Executes three commissions given simultaneously.	6-year group
4.	Counts the value of six *sous* (stamps used in America) three of which are double.	8-year group
5.	Names four colors — red, green, blue, yellow.	8-year group

[1] In his book *Les Idées modernes sur les enfants*, published in 1909, and reprinted in 1911 with a few minor changes, Binet also gives a reproduction of the complete scale, slightly different from either of the two well-known revisions. This scale includes tests for infants below three years of age, as follows:

AGE 3 MONTHS

Shows visual coördination.

AGE 9 MONTHS

Attends to a sound of an object behind the head, or out of the field of vision.

Seizes an object after contact with it or after visual perception of it.

AGE 1 YEAR

Recognizes foods.

AGE 2 YEARS

Walks without aid.

Executes a simple commission, as "Go and find a ball."

Indicates own natural needs.

Most of these tests are evidently taken from the 1905 scale. They are not usually regarded as a part of the 1911 scale, and no definite statement as to their standardization is given.

AGE 8 YEARS

PLACE IN THE
1908 SCALE

1. Gives differences between objects from memory. — No change
2. Counts backward from 20 to 0. — No change
3. Notes omissions from pictures. — 7-year group
4. Knows date. — 9-year group
5. Repeats five digits. — 7-year group

AGE 9 YEARS

1. Gives change from twenty *sous* — No change
2. Defines familiar words in terms superior to use. — No change
3. Recognizes all the (nine) pieces of money. — 10-year group
4. Names in order the months of the year. — 10-year group
5. Answers easy "comprehension questions." — 10-year group

AGE 10 YEARS

1. Arranges five blocks in order of weight. — 9-year group
2. Copies two designs from memory. — Test 18, 1905
3. Criticizes absurd statements. — 11-year group
4. Answers difficult "comprehension questions." — No change
5. Uses three given words in not more than two sentences. — No change, but modified

AGE 12 YEARS

1 Resists suggestion as to length of lines. — Test 13 (c), 1905
2. Uses three given words in one sentence. — 11-year group
3. Speaks sixty words in three minutes. — 11-year group
4. Defines three abstract words. — 11-year group
5. Puts words arranged in a random order into a sentence. — 11-year group

AGE 15 YEARS

1. Repeats seven digits. — 12-year group
2. Finds three rimes for a given difficult word in one minute. — 12-year group
3. Repeats a sentence of twenty-six syllables. — 12-year group
4. Interprets pictures. — 12-year group
5. Interprets given facts. — 12-year group

ADULT

1. Solves the paper-cutting test. — 13-year group
2. Rearranges relationship of two triangles in imagination and draws result as they would appear. — 13-year group
3. Gives three differences between a president and a king. — New
4. Gives differences between pairs of abstract terms. — 13-year group
5. Gives the main thought of a passage after it has been read to him. — New; from article in *Rev. Phil.*, 1899

In this scale Binet made the number of tests in each year five, so that each would count .2 year, though he did not stress the use of fractions of a year in the determination of mental-age. The only exception to the rule of five tests in a year was the 4-year level, which was left — probably by an oversight, as Burt says (*83*, page 3) — with the same four tests assigned to it as in 1908. The rules for scoring, slightly changed in this revision, are as follows: First take the highest year of which all the tests are passed. To this age add one fifth of a year for each additional test passed in any higher age level. Thus if a child of 8 years passes all the tests of the sixth year, 2 tests of the seventh year, 3 of the eighth, 2 of the ninth, and 1 of the tenth, he will have a mental age of six years plus $\frac{8}{5}$ of a year, which amounts to 7.6 years. "But let it be well understood that fractions in so delicate an appreciation do not merit absolute confidence, because they would probably vary from one examination to another" (page 149).

This illustration, which is actually given by Binet, is of a very unusual case, since the subject passes more tests in the eighth than in the seventh year, and since the range of year-levels in which part success is attained is wide. The child in this case would be mentally retarded .4 year if he is exactly 8 years of age. The more usual practice seems to have been to disregard fractions and simply to add one year for every five tests passed in levels above that in which all are passed (*64*, page 69).

A normal child testing at age is *regular* in intelligence, according to Binet;[1] one getting a higher mental-age score than his chronological age is *advanced* to the extent of this

[1] For a detailed statement of conditions necessary for a satisfactory examination, the taking and utilizing of notes by the tester, etc., see pages 63–70 of Town's translation.

difference, and one getting a lower mental-age score is *retarded* in intelligence to the extent of his deficiency.

THE CHANGES MADE IN THIS REVISION

Binet's own experience, as well as that of certain investigators in other countries whose reports reached him before the final revision was made, convinced him of the need of certain general changes in the 1908 revision. In the first place, it had become evident that the higher levels were too hard; so he raised four of the 11-year tests to the 12-year level, and all of the 12-year tests to the level for 15 years. The three 13-year tests of the 1908 scale now, with the addition of two new tests, became adult tests. In the second place, certain tests, as Binet had recognized at least three years earlier, depended too much on the subject's scholastic training or on knowledge incidentally gathered, which did not, as he had wrongly supposed, correlate much with intelligence. These tests, with certain others that were repetitions of tests coming at another level in the scale, were eliminated. Thus, repeating a sentence of sixteen syllables and giving one's own age, in the 6-year level; giving the number of fingers, copying "The Little Paul," naming four common coins, in the 7-year level; reading a passage and remembering two items, and writing from dictation, in the 8-year level; and giving days of the week, reading a passage and remembering six items, in the 9-year level of the 1908 scale, — these tests are all omitted in the last revision. Small changes are also made, such as putting certain tests in a higher age level and others in a lower one, and adding certain tests not found in the previous scale. These changes we have indicated in the 1911 scale as we have here reproduced it, so that the reader can readily see what they are. Some of the omitted tests have come back in revisions of the Binet scale by other investigators, indicating that the judgment against them was not founded on sufficiently broad experimentation.

THE RELIABILITY OF THE SCALE

Binet did very little in the way of checking directly the reliability of the intelligence scale. It is true that high validity, or a high degree of correspondence between the ranking that a test gives individuals and their ranking by some good independent criterion, indicates the probability that the test is reliable; but more direct measures of reliability are possible and desirable. By the reliability of a test we mean the degree of agreement in the ranking of a group of individuals by it in successive applications. An order of merit established but once by a test may be due to chance, but if nearly the same order is regularly obtained in different applications of this test (or of different "forms" of it) to the same group, under conditions that have been reasonably controlled, it is evident that the test is measuring something, whatever it may be, rather constantly. In such a case we say that the test has a fair or a high degree of reliability, as the case may be. A simple way to test the reliability is to correlate the scores made by a group of individuals in the first test with scores made by them in a second or later test with the same scale. This method was not used by Binet with reference to his scale.

SOME EMPIRICAL MEASURES OF RELIABILITY AND VALIDITY

He did, however, raise the problem and he attempted by a more empirical method to solve it. A Belgian teacher, who had tested all his students with the scale, wrote Binet that it would be desirable to have different forms of the test so that the mental growth of each child could be found annually for a number of successive years. Binet says that it would, in his opinion, be easy to find substitute tests to make a new form of the scale, and that this would require only patience and a good deal of coöperation. He had thought of making experiments to determine whether the same tester, determining the intellectual level of a number of children at intervals of fifteen days, would obtain approximately identical results on the same individuals. "On this point I had but vague conjectures," he says. "I knew from previous researches on attention and adaptation that children make rather rapid gains in such experiments, especially when they are tested individually so that chances of distraction and ennui are avoided; I therefore supposed that if the measurement of the intellectual level were made in this way each student would gain more or less from one test period to another" (page 164).

In 1910 M. Jeanjean carried out for Binet an experiment of this kind, using the 1908 scale. He tested five children twice, with an intervening period of fourteen days. Gains in the second scores over the first ones were obtained, which averaged an amount equal to five months. Binet admits this gain to be rather serious, but notes that the greatest gain was made on certain tests which were omitted from the 1911 revision and that if the successive applications of the tests were made at intervals of a year, instead of at intervals of fifteen days, the effects of repetition would probably be considerably reduced. This bit of evidence, on five subjects, is of course entirely inadequate for so important a problem, and if Binet had lived longer he would probably have worked out more satisfactorily the questions of reliability and of transfer of training here involved.

Results on ninety-seven children tested at age. In their researches on the 1908 scale Binet and Simon had studied the responses to the tests of children whose grade classifications agreed with their actual ages. Now with a view to studying the relationships of mental and scholastic standing, Binet gives data in the present report on ninety-seven children who were tested within two months of their birthdays — that is, children who were practically at ages which could be expressed in a whole number of years — and who were unselected as to mental status. The deviation of the grade of each child from the school grade normal to his age, and also that of his mental age from his actual age were found, and these deviations of the ninety-seven children were averaged. The difference in the two averages was found to be .7 year. There is no reason to believe that important discrepancies would not be covered up in such mere averages. However, a correlation table also constructed shows a "remarkable correlation," though not a perfect agreement, between the scholastic and the mental level of each child. Some of the children who were normal mentally were retarded simply because of poor educational opportunities; so a perfect correlation could not be expected.

The study not only indicated a high degree of validity on the part of the tests, but it also justified the rule that Binet had proposed for a rapid sectioning of the children of superior intelligence in any school; i.e., to "take in every class the youngest, because they are the most advanced in their studies" (page 160).

AMERICAN REVISIONS ARE BASED ON ALL THE BINET-SIMON SCALES

It should be noted that most of the early testing in America by the Binet method was based on translations of the 1908 scale. The movement had got so well under way, and several investigators had begun so early to collect data for their own modifications of this scale and for the solution of other problems, before Binet's final revision appeared in available form, that the latter did not readily, or indeed ever, replace the 1908 scale. In certain respects, moreover, this earlier scale was superior to the last one. Consequently those investigators who have worked out revisions of their own since 1911 have drawn freely on all three of Binet's scales and have added new tests as necessity demanded. On the whole this has been a fortunate procedure.

INTELLIGENCE RATINGS IN DANGER OF BEING OVERSIMPLIFIED

It must be clearly understood that while the scales developed by Binet and his colleagues have been very useful in practical testing and have indeed almost revolutionized the procedure in the education of children in most progressive communities, they nevertheless have many weaknesses. Binet was as ready to admit this as any one. Intelligence is not a homogeneous, simple thing that can be measured as one measures distance with a yardstick or weight with the scales. Binet repeatedly urged that no one test alone can give an adequate measure of intelligence; that such a measure can be obtained only by the use of a diversity of tests. When we consider that any one child tested is given as a rule the tests in from two to four year-levels, it is obvious that several of the individual tests may contribute to rather accurate total results and yet be very poor tests themselves. Then, too, many of these tests stress largely the same functions, — such as memory span, for instance, — functions that often, as in the case given, are not of very great importance.

However, since memory is not independent of judgment, attention, comprehension, etc., and since these functions are not discrete and independent things as faculty psychology has wrongly held, all being only different forms or manifestations of the adjustment of an infinitely complex organism, it must be admitted that the Binet scale, simple as it is both in conception and in construction, has not the weakness due to an unequal stress on different functions in successive years that such critics as Pyle (*178*) have supposed.

The success of the intelligence scale has very greatly added to our conceptions of intelligence. Binet's dominant idea of getting away from theoretical speculations on what mind is and of proceeding in a thoroughly empirical manner to study the possible responses of different individuals, has certainly been a most fruitful one. His general thought seems to have been this : formulate to yourself some practical working conception of mind, and then proceed experimentally to work on this conception, modifying it from time to time as the facts thus obtained seem to require. He was very strongly opposed to introducing into psychology notions which could not be subjected to experimental investigation, speculations based on such notions being rightly regarded by him as obstructive to progress in psychology. It is probable also that experimental work with no obvious bearing on questions of efficiency in general behavior was regarded by him as of relatively little value.

EXERCISES

1. Secure a good modern version of the Binet scale and test a few children of different ages, recording carefully all results. Compare the intelligence ratings based on the tests with independent estimates of intelligence by teachers.

2. Trace the origin of the tests given in this chapter for children below 3 years of age. Which of the recent American revisions of the Binet scale includes tests of very young infants?

3. Devise an intelligence test of your own and try, by giving it to several children, to find to what year-level it belongs. Test its validity by some of Binet's criteria.

CHAPTER TWELVE

THE MANIFESTATIONS OF INTELLIGENCE

PROBABLY every person at some time or other passes judgment on certain of his fellows as to their degree of intelligence. Some men are known in their communities as being very capable and their opinions on problems involving complex relationships are valued highly, while others are regarded as unfit for dealing with any but concrete perceptual situations. In the complex world of human relationships some persons seem to be born to lead humanity to constantly higher and higher levels of behavior, while others are as evitably constituted to follow the well-marked trails in the humdrum of daily life.

This fact seems to be taken for granted by all thoughtful individuals, and to have been recognized even in ancient times. Any careful observer of his fellows must have come to the conclusion that there are marked differences in the general abilities, or in the intelligences, of different individuals; and he must also have a good deal of confidence in his ability to pick out merely from general observation of his acquaintances those who are superior intellectually and those who are inferior. Between these extremes there are large numbers who differ less in amount of general intelligence, though they may show differences in minor traits, and who therefore cannot with much certainty be thus differentiated.

JUDGMENTS OF INTELLIGENCE IMPROVE WITH OPPORTUNITY TO TEST THEM

It is to be conceded, too, that persons who have a great deal of close contact with many individuals can judge differences in ability, other things being equal, better than can

243

those who have more limited contact. One might therefore expect that teachers especially would be able to give a rather accurate rating of children as to mental ability, for they have the advantage not only of close contact with groups of children of nearly equal ages but also of trying the children out constantly on problems about at the limit of their several abilities. This opportunity of checking up their own judgments of the various children in their classes by seeing from day to day what they can do, is a rare advantage on the part of the teacher; and in addition to this the teacher is, as a rule, specially trained to interpret and direct the behavior of children.

Parents, too, have good opportunities to see manifestations of the increasing abilities of children, but their experience is much more limited as to the number of cases coming under their observation, and they are also much more biased and therefore ready to explain noticeable limitations in their offspring in terms more agreeable to themselves than to attribute them to lack of ability.

This advantage of the teacher has been recognized since the beginning of intelligence testing, and numerous investigators, since the example set by Galton, have made use of teachers' judgments as a check on the accuracy of their tests. Teachers' judgments, however, are influenced by many subjective and irrelevant factors and have value only when there is considerable acquaintance with the several children to be rated; but it is obvious that tests whose results would be even as dependable as the estimates of teachers would be extremely valuable both in educational work and in the numerous problems that arise in social and industrial life. It is now a well-known fact that the Binet scale gives a more valid rating of students' mentalities than can be obtained from teachers' estimates.

How do the judgments of intelligence by teachers compare
in reliability with rankings by means of a scale such as that
developed by Binet and Simon? This most interesting
problem was raised by Binet and is discussed rather fully
in his article in the 1911 volume of the *Année*, in which he
presented his revised scale shortly before his untimely death.
A colleague, reproaching him amicably, had told him that
teachers could without difficulty judge the intelligence of
their students. Binet, who frequently met this view, that
the intelligence tests are superfluous, planned to test out the
accuracy of this statement. Through the coöperation of
M. Belot, inspector of the primary schools of Paris, he sent
the following questions to the teachers : "(1) What proportion of errors do you think you have committed in rating the
intelligence of your students? (2) What means do you
employ to obtain an exact rating" (*45*, pages 169, 170)?

Frequency of errors admitted by the teachers. About forty
responses were received. The answers varied from short
ones to some of eight or ten pages, averaging three or four
pages, and they showed great differences of opinion. Some
teachers thought that they made no errors at all, while others
declared that as they came to know their pupils better it
became more and more difficult to rate some of them. The
errors in classification admitted by the teachers varied from
one in a thousand to one in three cases. The average
was one in eight, but, as Binet remarked, this figure cannot
have much meaning in view of the divergence of opinion, a
divergence which was of course to be expected, since there
were no objective standards according to which the different
estimates could be made. "If I say," says Binet, in discussing this fact, "that a plank before me is 3 m. 45 cm. and then

measure it immediately, my error can easily be determined; but if I am content with saying that it is very long, how can my estimate be checked" (*45*, page 170)?   Precision, he continues, is a precondition both of truth and of error.   Some teachers will say of a child that he is "very intelligent," some that he is "above average," and still others may attempt to put him into one of three classes, of superior, median, and inferior intelligence.   Teachers with more accurate habits may even attempt to rate him by a scale of several degrees of value, such as very dull, dull, average, bright, very bright. Obviously comparisons cannot easily be made unless all use the same scale or method.   Moreover, those persons with the most indefinite notions are likely to be most satisfied because they have not attempted to check their judgments by actual tests.   In general, the more definite one's judgments are, the more noticeable becomes their correctness or incorrectness.

Some teachers' conceptions of intelligence.   While the second question did not call for a definition of intelligence, it implied that each teacher had a conception of what it is. Several replies included a definition and others clearly indicated the conception in the mind of the teacher replying. A number of these teachers confounded intelligence with memory, some with the mere ability to take on instruction, and others limited it too narrowly to the power of knowing and comprehending, which Binet says in his comment is only a part of intelligence.   Some of the teachers meant by intelligence a power of developing new ideas, representing thus a reaction against the mere retention view, but again restricting the term too greatly.

Binet's comment on these definitions is interesting.   To find the new, he says, is not the sole function of intelligence; many minds that are original lack ability to balance or weigh the several relevant factors.   The fool who has deliriums wherein one finds new ideas, is certainly not a model of intelligence. "It would be better," says Binet, "to say that intelligence serves to discover truth; but even that conception would be too narrow, and we revert to our favorite theory: intelligence manifests itself in the best possible adaptation of the individual to his environment" (page 172). One teacher reflected this view when she said that intelligence should not be regarded as merely the ability to apprehend; it serves to make one's way in life.

Signs of intelligence. Physiognomy, the form of the head, heredity or ancestry, the eyes, and the expression of the face were all mentioned by some teachers as indicative of intelligence. The expression of the eyes, as active for intelligence and passive for the lack of it, was often the basis of the determination, one teacher regarding a mere glance of the eye as a sufficient indicator of the degree of intelligence. Physiognomy was frequently reverted to: an open, wide-awake, and mobile countenance or a sympathetic expression was associated with intelligence, while an expressionless face signified dullness.   While there is no ground for denying the usefulness in many cases of these characterizations, it is true that serious errors are often made in judgments based on such factors. The reading of intelligence in the features is a superficial and often deceptive method. Moreover, the judgment of intelligence by such signs is largely a subjective procedure. How can it be brought to quantitative standards?

One of the best teachers mentioned as two principal elements serving to reveal the intelligence of a child, his responses in the class and the manner in which he plays. It is true, comments Binet, that intelligence shows itself by initiative and creation, and the lack of it by imitation in such activities, but how can we describe accurately what we see in a child at play? Obviously some sort of standardization is desirable even though the validity of any of these indicators of intelligence is admitted.

Most teachers, however, based their estimates on the class work of the pupils. The teacher was in the school to instruct, and so, perhaps naturally, focused his attention on the instruction, marking as the higher in intelligence those who assimilated it the better and the more easily. Anyway, the pupil was there to learn, and to the degree that he did not learn he failed to play his part, which failure would in most cases be attributed to a lack of intelligence, although numerous factors other than innate general ability may possibly have been influential. Teachers who held this view were too much inclined, unfortunately, to estimate the child by his success in the particular subjects which they taught, these seeming to them of the greatest importance. Thus history, language, or, in particular, mathematics would become the chief means of judging intelligence. Speaking of older students, Binet says: "It is incontestable that knowledge does not measure intelligence. At bottom knowledge represents only the intelligence of others; there is some merit in having assimilated it, a fact that reveals something of memory first of all, then of attention, of comprehension, of work, of method; but on the other hand there is many an intellectual quality that is not comprised in knowledge" (page 176).

It is not just what one has acquired that is significant, as many teachers recognized in their replies, but what one contributes by one's own personality. Mere advance or retardation in school may result from the presence or absence of certain special aptitudes. "Certain children who dislike the ordinary work of the class make their compensation in manual work — sewing, drawing, writing; little girls who are poor in spelling are strong in sewing and in the ability to keep house, and taking everything into consideration these latter

aptitudes are the more important for their future welfare"
(pages 176 f.). Binet held that because of the diversity of
aptitudes it cannot be maintained that students who are good
in mathematics are necessarily intelligent, or the reverse, and
he pointed out that literary men, politicians, and others are
sometimes poor in mathematics even when they are obviously endowed with a high degree of intelligence. Expressive
reading or a good memory of facts, too, may be deceptive
as an indicator of intelligence.

For many teachers, it was found, the best method of determining a child's intelligence is to get his responses to questions
and to make him talk. Thus some teachers would have him
explain what he has just read, pass judgment on an event or
institution, analyze a selection grammatically, cite a rule that
applies to a given case, or point out various applications of a
rule.

Now let us examine the experimental methods reported or
suggested by the teachers. Some of them would determine
intelligence by means of a set of questions and problems
resembling tests, of which they sent samples. Here are a few
of them : Why do you love your parents? If three persons
can do a piece of work in seven hours, can five do it in more
or less than seven hours? Which do you prefer, two pieces
of five francs each or one piece of ten francs? One person
said that to know his pupils better he annually gave them
some simple tests, such as having them estimate a fact of
current life, describe an object placed before them, and learn
ten lines of text in as short a time as possible.

Binet points out that most of the questions asked by the
teachers called to too great an extent for mere information
gained in a certain degree and line of instruction, as in
geography or arithmetic, questions which would embarrass
even a child of good ability who is ignorant because of lack of
opportunity. However, he recognized that the resort to

experimentation and to the objective handling of results was a step toward the right method. It is only under the controlled conditions of experimentation that reliable results can be obtained. All subjects can then be placed under approximately identical circumstances and the responses of one child can be compared with responses of other children of the same age and of somewhat equal training. In this way the responses can become standardized, and definite norms can be set up, according to which the abilities of any child can be evaluated.

An experiment on how three teachers determined intelligence. At Binet's request three of the teachers came to his laboratory to try their methods in his presence on children with whom they were not acquainted. Each teacher spent an afternoon examining the intelligence of five children. Each had full liberty to examine every child according to his own methods. Binet found that they propounded to the children various interesting questions. "Thus, since in the vicinity of the school there was a canal and some locks, one teacher wished to know if the children understood what locks are, what they are used for, and how they work. The problem thus presented appeared curious to me," says Binet, "but the interrogation was laborious. The teacher did not ask each child exactly the same questions, and she aided some children more than others. Moreover, the question thus presented was of a local character, being one that she would not have used in another school; she was wrong in using a particular kind of question which made general comparisons impossible. Another teacher had brought with him some pretty pictures which he had the children observe. He then asked them various questions about the objects which were represented in the pictures; for example, 'Why is this a garret and not an ordinary room?' 'How is a garret to be distinguished from a room?' The idea was excellent, but it was poorly carried out. In the first place the questions appeared to me to be too easy; then they varied from one child to another; and, finally, the examiner lost time teaching a lesson to those children who responded poorly" (page 184). When one examination was being conducted the blow of a hammer resounded from a near-by factory in the course of construction, and the examiner took advantage of the situation to ask whether in a factory it was best to have the walls thick or thin. Some of the questions attempted to ascertain whether the subjects were in the habit of reading the newspapers or understood what they heard others read, while others related to names of streets and other purely particular and local facts, on which all children could not justly be compared. The examinations usually ended in questions about definite school subjects.

The examiners often used questions which merely presented an alternative, and so were answerable in one half of the cases by a pure guess even though the subjects were wholly ignorant of the facts or relations involved. Different methods of scoring or evaluating responses were also noted, the examiners not giving equal weight to identical responses. Moreover, such factors in the response as hesitation, rate of response, and animation of the subject were not uniformly evaluated by the three examiners. In one case two replies to the same question were identical, but one child was given by the same examiner a higher score than the other, because the teacher had already concluded that he was the more intelligent.

The need of standardization of tests made evident. Binet asked the examiners about their methods of scoring the responses. One replied that he took the first child as a standard, comparing the others with him and ranking them higher or lower in intelligence. Another compared all five subjects with a known child of the same age judged to be of about average intelligence. It is obvious that an answer cannot be scored wholly in terms of units on an absolute scale, and also that a child cannot be scored by the same standard as an adult. The method of comparing all subjects with some known child, however, requires for its proper use a wide acquaintance with children on the part of the tester and a similar experience for all the testers. Only under these conditions could their norms be the same. Binet noted a serious defect, in addition to that of the limitations of and differences in the experiences of the testers; this defect is that the known child thought of as a norm was not subjected to the tests himself. It is obvious that nothing but a standardized scale can quite supply the needs of objective measurement, giving each tester like every other one a scale of equal relative units.

The experiments of Binet with these three teachers thus made it very clear that, put into a practical situation with unknown subjects, one is forced to resort more or less directly to the methods of the objective test; that is to say, one is forced, first, to get the reactions of each child to a set of definite questions or problems, and, second, to evaluate the responses according to a set of norms. The more thoroughly these questions have been freed from local circumstances, from dependence as to content upon certain courses of instruction, from a form involving answers of the yes and no type, etc., and the more they are made to stress judgment and other higher mental processes, the better they are; and the more carefully the norms have been derived from a standardization based on numerous responses of large numbers of representative children of the different ages, the less subjective and erroneous will be the evaluation of the reactions of any child to the tests.

Binet asked an alienist, who was a bitter critic of his method, how he would determine a child's degree of intelligence. He replied that he preferred simply to show the child some postal cards and to cause him to talk about them. This, Binet points out, is nothing but the test method poorly used, and he adds this characteristic comment: "Our critic of tests, then, also employs tests, but, let us say to do him justice, he employs them badly" (page 186).

THE USE OF TEACHERS' JUDGMENT OF INTELLIGENCE IN THE CONSTRUCTION OF TESTS

Despite the various shortcomings of teachers' judgments of the intelligence of their students, these judgments were almost indispensable to the pioneer makers of intelligence scales; for in the construction of the tests it was necessary to find out how the responses of children known to be bright and capable differed from those of dull children. Tests that made the most clear differences between these two classes of children were selected as most serviceable in intelligence scales, or as the best tests.

Binet had tried out various individual tests for a period of nearly fifteen years before he and Simon made the now well-known scale. Besides evaluating the several tests by their effects on children of different degrees of intelligence, as explained, these investigators also sought to determine their worth by giving them to groups of children of different ages, assuming that on the whole the older the children, up to a certain limit, the greater their abilities. It was doubtless this use of different age groups to measure the validity of tests that finally led Binet to the idea of mental-age units in an intelligence scale, an idea that proved so useful and simple as greatly to increase the value of the test scale. In standardizing the scale Binet and Simon selected children who were very near to the exact age for which norms were sought and who were also in the right grades for their ages, but they admit that taking all children of each age irrespective of their school classifications would give better norms. This latter method has become in post-Binet testing the one more commonly used.

THE YOUNGEST CHILDREN IN ANY GRADE USUALLY THE MOST INTELLIGENT

With the intelligence scale completed for practical use, Binet found ample evidence for the view, already prevalent among investigators using tests, that old dull children were usually overrated by their teachers as to mental ability because of being compared with younger children with whom they were classed, the teachers not taking note to a sufficient degree of accuracy of the age differences. Applying himself to this problem of agreement between intellectual level as determined by the tests and scholastic standing, Binet found that there was a general agreement between the rankings of children by the tests and their respective degrees of success in school. The very intelligent were never found to be retarded in school if opportunities had been normal, and those of very low rating by the scale were never advanced scholastically; there were, however, dull children who were classed according to age in the schools, this probably being due to the tendency in lower grades to promote on the basis of age. A tendency was noted also for bright children to be somewhat behind the school grade normal to their mental age, or normal to children whose mental level they equaled. This was partly due to a failure of the teachers to recognize their mental superiority and to advance them according to their abilities, and also partly to the lack of opportunity on the part of certain of the children.

It was found in any grade that the oldest children were as a rule retarded mentally, that their mental-age levels determined by the test were below their real ages. On the other hand, the youngest children in any grade were found to be mentally advanced, to receive intelligence levels higher than those normal to their chronological ages (pages 159 ff.). When teachers were asked to compare given children in their classes as to intelligence, they showed a tendency to rate the older children higher and the younger children lower mentally than the scale rated them. In explanation of this fact it was pointed out by Binet that teachers in any given school grade were inclined to compare the children simply on the basis of their work, not taking account of ages; and that they therefore would call, say, a 10-year-old child equal intellectually to a 13-year-old child if their work was of about equal grade, even though the former child had had fewer years of training. The scale showed its superiority in the way of giving a more objective rating and one based more on native ability, and also in comparing the performance of each child directly with that of normal children just his age.

THE PSYCHOLOGIST'S ADVANTAGE IN THE CHARACTERIZATION OF INTELLIGENCE

With the improved means of mental measurement thus afforded by the intelligence scale it was possible for the psychologist to give a better rating of a child's mental ability than the teacher who had known the child for a year or more in close personal contact could give. The psychologist can constantly check his conceptions of intelligence experimentally and can thereby steadily improve them. It is evident that the moment we get a definite scale for the measurement of anything, such as atmospheric pressure, blood pressure, per cent of cream in milk, bodily temperature, or what not, we begin to observe more closely the thing thus measured and the effect of different conditions upon its variations. We are then more likely to make assertions about the conditions which determine the changes and about the thing measured, and, inasmuch as these assertions are erroneous in any way, to have them checked up more definitely as differences of opinion arise; and so improvements in our conceptions come about more rapidly than they do when we have no accurate means of measurement. Without such definite means of check on our views it is not easy to locate differences in them, and unless the matter is of supreme importance the conceptions are perpetuated from generation to generation with little change. Moreover, the lack of means of accurate measurement conduces to vagueness as well as to fixity of view. Compare, for instance, the definiteness and rate of change of conceptions of the electron in physics with those of faith healing in popular life, of survival after death, or of the Trinity![1]

Now, applying this principle, that the more accurately our conceptions are checked, the more rapidly they tend to become correct, to changes in conceptions of intelligence, we are prepared to expect great progress in these conceptions during a period of the construction of intelligence tests, especially as far as the psychologists working on this subject are concerned. If one supposes, as Binet seems to have supposed at one time, that literal memory is an important element of intelligence, it is only a matter of time until the tests, whose ratings are constantly checked with other criteria, will reveal whether or not this view is correct. This is not true, of course, if the giving of the tests is solely for the placement of the children, and not principally for purposes of testing the tests. Since Binet spent most of the time he devoted to testing, and indeed most of his adult lifetime, in determining the accuracy of various tests and in checking their results against other criteria, and since he had unusual

[1] The charge often brought against science, that its conceptions change so often and are therefore evidently not reliable, shows an unfortunate misunderstanding by the popular mind of the facts we have here pointed out. The untrained, mediocre mind seems to sense a profound security in vague, unchanging notions.

opportunities for trying out his tests on children of all grades of intelligence from idiocy to mental superiority, it will be profitable and interesting to examine his views of intelligence.

BINET'S CONCEPTIONS OF INTELLIGENCE

Binet in no place gave a full and systematic definition of intelligence, so we must gather his ideas from his various more or less partial statements from special points of view. In his early writings, as we have seen, he reacted against the views of Galton and the German psychologists, who attempted to measure intelligence, or the intellectual ability of the individual, by means of certain sensory discrimination and reaction tests. He urged that tests of the higher complex processes are more significant, and maintained that they cannot easily be classified as tests of attention, of memory, of imagery, etc., each of these processes being complex and present to an extent in all higher mental operations. He also criticized Gilbert's attempts to find differences between children of different ages and adults, on the ground that the child has not simply less memory, less perception, less reason, less motor ability, etc., than the adult; the child, he held, has a manner of thinking, of reasoning, of willing, and of remembering peculiar to himself as a child; he differs qualitatively from the adult. Binet certainly yielded a good deal in this stand when later he developed the idea of an intelligence scale in which were repeated at higher and higher levels, tests that were largely of the same kind. From the time of his first test series in 1896, however, he insisted rather generally that mental tests should be complex and should measure a variety of processes, especially the higher ones. A notable exception to this insistence is his attempt in the last part of the nineties to measure attention by two-point discrimination methods.

Early stress on memory and imagery. Binet's early tests
and investigations of exceptional persons and of groups of
children dealt considerably with memory and imagery, which
he seemed to regard as of special significance in the constitution of general ability or intelligence. It is significant that
he rejected the associationists' account of memory as revival
by mere association. The process of recall he held to be
directed mainly by attention and the will, the subject being
able voluntarily to direct his efforts to recall toward certain
groups of experience with which he felt that the desired facts
would be found. His interest seems at that time to have
been more in attention, or the power thus to direct one's
mental operations, than in memory as the mere ability to
retain, and with Henri in 1895 he enthusiastically described
their memory-of-sentences method as a veritable "dynamometer of attention." There seems to have been great hope
in his mind at one time for suggestibility tests as indicators
of intellectual ability, the mentally weaker children seeming
to have less self-direction and more suggestibility than the
more intelligent; but Simon probably dampened this hope
somewhat when he found an absence of suggestibility in low-
grade defectives. Dresslar had shown, moreover, that the
more intelligent subjects were influenced by the size-weight
illusion — suggestion of weight by size — more than were
the duller ones.

Attention. The article on attention and adaptation,
published in 1900, reported numerous tests the practical aim
of which was to measure the force of voluntary attention.
The attempt to isolate and measure this "faculty" was not
very successful, though certain tests showed differences
between the more and the less intelligent children used as
subjects, and some of them showed a much quicker adaptation on the part of the former group. It is clear in Binet's
discussion in this article that he regards attention as a very

essential characteristic of general intelligence. The definition of attention which he gives here is indeed so broad as to
suggest very definitely the source of Stern's later definition
of intelligence. "Attention," we are told, "consists in a
mental adaptation to a situation which is new to us." Further studies of two-point discrimination, which Binet had
hoped would measure the degree of voluntary attention,
failed to yield anything of value to him. It is interesting to
note that in this view Binet came close to the idea of Galton
and his disciples, who sought to get a measure of intelligence
in one's sensory discrimination capacity. Indeed, Binet
approximates here the view of the school which he earlier
opposed in the article on individual psychology, but he was
unable to get any high correlations of discrimination with
intelligence, or indeed even to get a reliable measure of a
subject's two-point discrimination (*38*, page *252*). In the
extended experiments on his two daughters, published in
1902 in his book *L'étude expérimentale de l'intelligence*, he
uses the term "intelligence" as the sum total of the higher
mental processes.

Judgment. Throughout his practical work on the intelligence scale, as well as in his several later writings, Binet
plainly regards intelligence as a complexity of mental functions, though the importance of certain general functions
such as attention, self-determination of will, and judgment is
never overlooked; and he thus steers between the two
extreme views of Thorndike and Spearman, later to be considered. At the time of the construction of the first scale,
judgment was regarded as the essential characteristic of
intelligence, but this was for him by no means a simple
process. In his enthusiasm over the intelligence scale he
seems seldom to have lost sight of the diversity of intellectual
aptitudes, which in the report on the 1908 revision he announces (*61*, page *2*) as one of his special objects of study. At

this late period of his life he finds the matter of intelligence more complex than he had ever imagined it to be. "Our minds always simplify nature" (*ibid.*).

His extensive studies of defectives and of disorganized minds gave Binet an opportunity to observe the workings of intelligence at low levels. In 1909 he and Simon published a long article (*62*) on studies in which they attempt by different experiments to throw light on the various cognitive processes of defectives, leaving out of consideration for the time, as they note explicitly, any direct evaluation of the instincts and emotions. They consider especially the intellectual differences between these unfortunate individuals and normal persons. Studies of the thought processes have too frequently become merely investigations of mental images, but Binet's studies had convinced him "that thought is not a passive state, but above all a state of action"; that thinking is not just taking note of things in one's consciousness, but making attempts, groping one's way, and choosing between alternatives (page 128).

Direction, adaptation, and auto-criticism. Thought, in his view as here expressed, is composed of three distinct elements : a direction, an adaptation, and an auto-criticism, and the defective lacks in all three. We can make clear by illustration what is meant by these "elements" or aspects of the thought process. First, effective, thoughtful behavior takes and keeps a definite direction. If you instruct a young child to do something, as to pick out from a heterogeneity of objects of different colors all those that are red, you will find that he easily becomes sidetracked, so to speak, by various distracting conditions. He does not maintain his direction of thought and activity as one of higher mentality would do. In some of our present-day group mental tests the subjects are shown some pictures that are incomplete in certain respects or that lack parts, such as the mouth of a face, an arm of a man, a wheel of a wagon, the shadow of one tree in a group of trees all the others of which have shadows, and so on. As "fore-exercises" in what is to be done the children are directed to complete certain practice pictures. When it is clear that each child understands what he is to do, the children are instructed to turn a page to a number of pictures all of which lack certain parts. These the children, each of whom has a copy, are to study one by one and then supply whatever is lacking, keeping on until time is called. The exercises get harder gradually and so require more and more careful scrutiny for the detection of successive incompletenesses. It is found that very young children as well as persons of low mental development soon get "off the track" and occupy themselves in mere random decoration of the pictures, if indeed they continue working with the pencil at all (*172*, page 37). Effective work here obviously involves keeping in mind what is to be done and continuing to look critically for incomplete parts in the pictures. This illustrates what Binet meant by maintaining a direction in thinking, and he found that differences in ability to do this were significant of intelligence differences. "Thus one of the chief characters that distinguish a superior from an inferior intelligence is the power of direction of thought, and this ability manifests itself in two ways: by its complexity and by its persistence" (page 131). Psychology, he says, has treated sensations, ideas, movement, etc., too much in isolation, whereas he believes that "the prime fact, the most important of the facts of the psychic life, is a coördination which gives to the current of ideas a definite direction" (pages 131 f.).

But mere direction in thought is not enough. There must be adaptation of means to ends. Thinking is choosing constantly between various ideas and means, which become clearer and more definite in successive experiences. The idea is not a disinterested process without reference to the necessities of life. Like nutrition and respiration it is a vital function, and exists only because it serves some end. The child and the person of low ability are influenced unduly by immediate circumstances; they do not calculate and take into consideration remote consequences as do individuals of greater intelligence. The *choice* of ends, however, depends less on intelligence than on emotional, sentimental, and instinctive factors, while the *means* of reaching the ends depend on intelligence.

Yet Binet recognized that intelligent action is, after all, but a more long-range trial-and-error adaptation, not an infallible bolt from the blue sky. "In the case of a new act, adaptation is not made with precision in the first attempt; it is effected only gradually by successive trials" (page 134). In simple perceptual situations that do not involve reflection and in various discrimination and association tests the persons of low-grade intelligence differ but little from those of higher grades, but in adaptive processes involving the choice of means to remote ends the difference becomes more clearly evident. A number of tests requiring this more complex adaptation to remote ends are cited as being troublesome alike to young children and to persons of low mentality.

There is also in effective thought a critical spirit, judgment, an appearance of control of the situation, for which the term "auto-criticism" has been fortunately suggested by certain alienists, we are told. Besides comprehension of the objective aspects of the situation there is a criticism, a reflection, that involves or turns upon and evaluates one's own reactions in reference to the objective situation. The imbecile does not see the inadequacy of his attempts, and so he cannot gradually adapt himself by trying better methods. Thus in the disarranged-sentence test, satisfaction with an order of the words that conveys no adequate thought whatever is frequently shown by persons of low mental age.

Comprehension and invention.   In Binet's book, *Les idées modernes sur les enfants*, published also in 1909, which summarizes in a popular way many of his researches and conclusions, a full chapter of sixty-three pages is devoted to a consideration of "Intelligence, Its Measurement and Education," and a slight change in his view is found.   "Comprehension, invention, direction, and criticism — intelligence is contained in these four words," he says (page 118).   Here comprehension and invention seem to have replaced adaptation, and so indicate to us more precisely Binet's meaning of adaptation.   It is not a mere passive fitting into immediate circumstances, but rather an active organization of responses in relation to a complexity of conditions.   "In our opinion," we read, "intelligence considered independently of the phenomena of sensibility, emotion, and will is above all a faculty of apprehension which is directed toward the external world and which works toward the reconstruction of it as a whole on the basis of the small fragments which we are given of it.   That which we perceive is the element *a*, and all the complicated work of our intelligence consists in welding to this a second element, *b*.   All knowledge is then essentially an addition, a continuation, a synthesis" (pages 117 f.), whether made automatically or deliberately; and in this addition to element *a* a number of mental functions co-operate, — comprehension, memory, imagination, judgment, and above all speech.

Binet makes clear his view that "the mind is unitary, despite the multiplicity of its faculties, that it possesses one essential function to which all the others are subordinated" (page 117).   This function he has elsewhere stated as adjustment to environment for the continuity of the life of the individual.   He says that while there exist between the child and the adult differences in experiences, in knowledge, in ideas, and in vocabulary, and while the two have different ends, interests, preoccupations, and instincts, the main difference from our present standpoint is one of intelligence, and to characterize this difference he recurs to his scheme consisting of *direction, comprehension, invention,* and *criticism.* Compared with the adult as to *direction,* the child is deviating and inconstant; he is seized by fantasies, by caprices, and by passing ideas, wandering in conversation from one subject to another as mere contiguous associations may determine. On his way to school he does not follow a straight course, as does the adult, but zigzags hither and thither, being deviated from his course by every spectacle that interests him and causes him to forget his purpose and change his path. When absorbed in any one thing, he loses other things from view.

THE NORMAL CHILD'S INTELLIGENCE COMPARED TO THAT OF AN ADULT IMBECILE

The child's *comprehension* is superficial. Though perceiving as well as the adult the form, contour, distance, and sounds of exterior objects, and not suffering anything in the acuity of his senses, which is strong, and though readily comparing weights, colors, and lengths with an exactness which astonishes us, he shows a feebleness when it comes to a question of discernment between the merely incidental and the essential, a question of comprehending abstract relations. He has a comprehension only of a sensorial nature, which dwells on the surface of things. His power of *invention,* we are told, is equally limited; he is more randomly imaginative than rational, sensorial than verbal, and he neither evolves anything nor differentiates. Binet brings out these points in the picture test. The young child only enumerates or describes, but does not interpret.

The power of *criticism* is, in the child, as limited as are the other thought characteristics considered. "He judges poorly of the accuracy of what he says and does. He is just as awkward in mind as he is with his hands. He is remarkable for the ease with which mere words satisfy him and does not realize the limitation of his comprehension. The *why's* with which his curiosity harasses us are hardly embarrassing, because he will be naïvely satisfied with the most absurd *because's*. He disentangles very poorly the difference between what he imagines or wishes and what he has really seen, and this confusion explains many of his falsehoods. Finally, everybody knows his extreme suggestibility, which lasts until about the age of 14 years. It is of a complicated nature, for it depends on his character as much as on the imperfection of his intelligence; in any case this suggestibility is another proof of his lack of criticism" (page 122).

The child in these respects resembles in intelligence the adult imbecile, as is shown by the fact that to numerous tests the responses of the two exhibit the same defects of criticism and direction, the same superficial comprehension, and the same random invention. There are, however, important advantages to the child because he is still in the stage of development. Of these Binet mentions in particular the child's prompt and durable memory (which he probably exaggerates), his plasticity, his incessant play and activity, and his constant experimentation. He also mentions tests in the scale which he considers most suitable for measuring each of the four characteristics: e.g., arrangement of weights, for "direction"; indicating the prettier of two pictures, pointing out differences between pairs of familiar objects recalled in memory, and answering comprehension questions, for "comprehension"; definition of familiar objects, description of pictures, and constructing a sentence to include three given words, for both "comprehension" and "invention"; criticizing absurd statements, for "criticism."

It is evidently not well to stress very greatly this matter of different tests for different functions, however, for the tests of the scale were not made with these functions particularly in mind, but were mostly devised long before Binet had analyzed out these four functions — indeed, when his views of intelligence were somewhat different from those here expressed. Furthermore, Binet was an empirical worker to the extent that he would not work directly from mental function to test, as Kraepelin had done. It is also to be noted that distinctions between these four general functions or aspects of intelligence are often hard to make.

BINET WAS VERSATILE AND OPEN-MINDED

His first series of proposed tests, published in 1896, were, to be sure, devised to measure certain preconceived functions, and they were based to a very small extent on experimental work and correlation; but he departed very far from this procedure later, and criticized this method of procedure in the case of Kraepelin's work. Examples can be pointed out, however, to show that Binet was not at any time wholly free from the practice of devising tests to measure some sort of preconceived function supposed to be of major importance in intelligence; this, for instance, was the procedure in the experiments discussed in the article on attention and adaptation. It must be acknowledged that a wholly empirical method of selecting tests would be a waste of time, and that selection according to certain ideas and observations is inevitable. Binet was the type of investigator that will not allow himself to be too greatly biased by his own theory, and he showed considerable willingness to cast aside any view that did not test out well. For instance, his early stress on memory gave way later to an exaltation of attention, and this seemingly later to adaptation, probably as the essence of attention; then at the time of the making of the first scale judgment was supreme; and finally he found intelligence so complex that several chief characters received the emphasis — direction, comprehension, invention, and auto-criticism. If he had lived longer, he would certainly have found difficulties in the way of keeping these functions appreciably distinct, and would doubtless have tried other characterizations of intelligence.

EMOTIONS, INSTINCTS, AND SPECIAL TALENTS

It may be well to mention here again the fact that Binet did not mean to exclude from intelligent behavior the emotions and instincts, but he seems to have regarded them as motivations or drives, as Woodworth regards them. To Binet it was the emotions and instincts that determine our ends, what we work and struggle for; while the "elements of thought," which we have described, determined the means to their attainment. Throughout his productive period, as far as tests are concerned, Binet recognized to a considerable extent certain special talents or aptitudes, and he made detailed studies of certain talented individuals. In his *Idées modernes sur les enfants* he put very great stress on the need of educating each child according to his aptitudes.

EXERCISES

1. Write down a number of mental traits and characteristics on which you think very intelligent and very dull persons differ most.
2. Name the characteristics that a good intelligence test should have, considering especially what Binet's experiment with the teachers revealed.
3. Show how the use of tests may rapidly increase our knowledge of what intelligence really is. If this result does not follow the use of good tests in every case, why does it not?

CHAPTER THIRTEEN

PROBLEMS REGARDING INTELLIGENCE AND USES OF TESTS

THE INTERRELATIONS OF MENTAL FUNCTIONS

THE characterizations of intelligence as given in the foregoing chapter are as far as Binet got, and psychologists have not yet added a great deal to what this pioneer in intelligence testing accomplished in this regard, except that tests and quantitative methods have of late received considerable development. Stern, as we have noted, took up Binet's view of adaptation as the characteristic of attention, as held in the latter's article on this subject published in 1900, and he made this in his own view the essence of intelligence. But Binet's views developed very materially beyond this point. Stern's definition of intelligence, thus arrived at, seems to have been taken up too uncritically by the majority of educators, and even of psychologists, at the present time. In the face of very little evidence many writers are practically identifying intelligence with the "ability to learn," without specifying which ability this is. The correlations among learning rates in different kinds of performance are not encouragingly high (*179, 128, 171*). Learning ability seems now to be no more homogeneous and simple than is the collection of mental operations known as sensory discrimination, attention, imagery, memory, judgment, reasoning, etc., if, indeed, these are not in the main the same things as the processes involved in different learning adjustments, but viewed from another angle as it were.

TWO OPPOSITE EXTREME VIEWS AND THEIR EXPERIMENTAL SUPPORT

The question of the interrelation of the various factors constituting "general ability" or intelligence was early investigated experimentally with the use of the correlation method of Pearson. We have already noted that Wissler obtained evidence of very little or no relationship among the abilities tested in Cattell's early investigations.[1]

Thorndike's multiple-factor view. Data and conclusions published the next year after this report appeared, by Aikins, Thorndike, and Miss Hubbell (2), were in general agreement with Wissler's results. These latter investigators assert that "any consideration of the nervous basis of mental life or of the patent facts of human nature suggests *a priori* that it is more rational to look on the mind as a multitude of particular capacities, all of which may be highly independent of each other" (page 374). Various studies are cited in support of this view, and it is backed by their own experiments, which attempt to measure particular functions that depend on quickness as well as on accuracy in the association of "certain thoughts or acts with certain percepts either directly or indirectly through other ideas which the percepts call up. The associations were in every case such as involved (in the subjects tested) attentive selection of correct and purposive inhibition of incorrect ideas" (*ibid.*).

The tests used were certain cancellation and association tests now well known. The results obtained were interpreted as enforcing Thorndike's view of special abilities as just stated. Quickness of association, as a general ability determining the speed of all one's associations, was declared to be a myth. Speed and accuracy in finding words containing *r* and *e* does not involve anything like equal accuracy in finding misspellings. "Our results," they say, "also suggest the possibility of clearly defining the classes of functions which we may expect to find closely related" (page 375). Thorndike soon after the appearance of this report, published a book on educational psychology (*212*), which is based upon

[1] *Supra*, pages 108 f.

the position here taken and which has had very much influence in this country.

Spearman's view of a general factor. In 1904 Spearman committed himself to a position, based on careful experimentation and statistical determinations, which is extreme in just the opposite direction. "All branches of intellectual activity," he says, "have in common one fundamental function (or group of functions), whereas the remaining or specific elements of the activity seem in every case to be wholly different from that in all the others" (*198*, page 284). This is the famous two-factor theory of intelligence as opposed to the multiple-factor theory of Thorndike, and it maintains that any mental function involves something of the general-intelligence factor and also some specific factor that is discrete so far as other such specific factors are concerned. The extreme view here taken has been of late years somewhat modified.

Spearman points out that former investigators who had found low correlations among the several test scores of their subjects had neglected to measure the reliability of their results; had wholly disregarded the question of the homogeneity of their subjects as to age, training, zeal, endurance, etc.; and had not corrected their coefficients or correlation for errors of observation. He maintains that the neglect of these errors and precautions has tended to lower their coefficients. Choosing for his tests a number of simple and supposedly elementary functions, in whose study the results are least affected by "irregularities, complications, and unknown factors," he carried out a large number of carefully controlled experiments in which the tests were repeated so that a check on their reliability would be possible. Thus from a few sensory discrimination tests which could be controlled best he hoped evidently to get relations that are true of all discrimination when irrelevant factors are removed.

He shows that by correcting his coefficients for "attenuation" with a formula of his own, then but recently developed (*197*), very high coefficients of relationship can be obtained between the sensory discrimination processes tested and general intelligence as determined by the estimates of teachers, of comrades, and of the rector's wife (on the basis of "common sense"), and by school standing, coefficients showing practically a one-to-one relationship.

Spearman points out that his theory may be tested by the possibility of making a hierarchical arrangement of the correlation coefficients, an arrangement of such a nature that the coefficients will decrease successively both in the columns, say, to the right and also in the rows downward. This hierarchical arrangement cannot be expected, however, if the coefficients are not reliable and are complicated by various irrelevant factors and by errors of observation. He claims in this article that the hierarchical arrangement of the corrected coefficients obtained by him is a practical demonstration of the correctness of his theory that intelligence involves a general common factor. He and Krueger again support the general-intelligence-factor theory in a later study (*199*).

Binet's reaction to Spearman's conclusion. This study opened up a controversy that is yet unsettled, but it probably reveals too great a confidence in mathematical refinements of meager and imperfect data. Though Binet, reviewing Spearman's article in the *Année* for 1905, referred to this work as very interesting and original, he was not greatly impressed, and less influenced in his later work, by Spearman's results. With reference to Spearman's findings, that the corrected correlation between sensory discrimination and general intelligence is practically perfect, Binet says: "He regards this conclusion as *profoundly* important. It may possibly be. We ourselves are *profoundly* astonished at the conclusion because of the very defective character both of the sensory experiments of the author and of the manner in which he determined or had others determine general intelligence [as a criterion with which to correlate the tests]. Before committing oneself it is necessary to wait until other investigators obtain similar results" (page 624).

Burt's experiments interpreted as favoring Spearman's view. In 1909 Burt (*82*) carried out a thorough and extensive study of the nature of general intelligence. As subjects he used two groups of boys in Oxford, England. One of these groups was in the superior elementary schools and represented socially the middle class; the other was in a high-class preparatory school and consisted of children of the professional class. The performances of the latter group manifested a superior degree of intelligence, and in this regard agreed with the results of other studies of class differences which we have already considered. Results of various tests of perceptual discrimination, reaction time (simple and discriminative), immediate memory, mirror learning, and range of apprehension were correlated with estimates of intelligence by teachers, head masters, and fellow students. The coefficients of relationship obtained were interpreted to support the general-factor theory of intelligence. "We may agree," the author says, "that so-called 'voluntary' attention is, of all recognized psychological processes, the essential factor in general intelligence" (page 169). This common factor, he supposes, runs through all mental operations, increasing in amount, as it were, from the elementary sensory processes up through the higher processes to reasoning. This factor of general intelligence Burt found also to be hereditary, probably following the Mendelian Law.

Brown's experiments support Thorndike. In the year following this report there appeared an article by William Brown (*77*), of King's College, London, who employed tests in the addition of digits, cancellation, dividing of lines into halves and thirds, illusions in visual perception, speed of uncontrolled association, memory of nonsense syllables and of poetry, and the Ebbinghaus completion test. School marks in drawing, total school marks, and two independent teachers' estimates of ability were also used. Nearly all the tests were given twice, for purposes of studying effects of correction of correlation coefficients for attenuation. Brown's results were interpreted as contradicting the two-factor theory of Spearman, since they failed to form a hierarchical order of coefficients. Brown and Thomson, especially the latter, have continued to combat this theory in numerous studies which run beyond the range of time covered in this book. In this article Brown criticizes the attenuation formula as leading to error unless all the "observational errors" are unrelated, which he finds they are not.

Additional experiments and conclusions. Thorndike and some of his students (217) investigated this problem, using tests on accuracy of estimating the length of lines as determined by attempting to draw lines equal in length to a standard, and accuracy in estimating weight as shown by attempting to reproduce a standard weight by filling a box with the necessary quantity of shot. The intelligence of the subjects, who were high and normal school students, was estimated by teachers and by fellow students. Correlations between the discrimination functions and intelligence were very low, thus contradicting, as did Brown's experiment, the general factor of Spearman. Various later experiments have yielded similar results. It is questionable, however, whether these tests have met the conditions laid down by Spearman to test the theory.

There can be little doubt that a somewhat median position between the extreme early views of Spearman, on the one hand, and of Thorndike, on the other, is nearer the truth.

Neither view seems to be supported by a consideration of the neuromuscular bases of behavior. At any rate, that intelligence is associated with biological structures which are complete in development at a comparatively early age — at about 16 years of age — may now be regarded as established; also that the relative degree of one's general efficiency at any given age is largely determined by heredity.

CAN INTELLIGENCE BE IMPROVED BY TRAINING? BINET'S POSITION

Binet did not discriminate closely between innate intelligence factors and the improvement of these factors by training. There is, of course, a degree of plasticity or training possibility in any mental function, so that with any degree of innate ability the efficiency of the individual can be considerably increased by systematic and well-directed training. This fact was recognized by Binet; and meaning by the term "intelligence" to designate one's abilities in a general way, he included both the elements due more directly to innate organization and those due to training. On this view it was natural for him to take the position — contrary to the one usually taken today by psychologists — that *intelligence* can be improved by training. In *Les idées modernes sur les enfants*, which summarizes much of his life's work and certainly gives some of his ripest views, Binet reacts against what he calls the "brutal pessimism" (page 141) of those who regard intelligence as a fixed quantity that cannot be increased. This pessimism, he says, has led to a lack of interest in backward children and to a consequent danger to society. He admits that if he had been asked five or six years earlier to back up his opinion by arguments, he would have had nothing but theoretical reasons to bring forward. He would have shown, for example, that instruction and education go together and interact upon each other; that certain kinds of instruction impart ideas which regulate, to some extent, one's conduct and so actually influence one's ability. He would have offered particular examples of young men who have returned less naïve and more active and resourceful after a foreign voyage or a year or two in the military service. But he would have taken special advantage of the information furnished by experimental psychology, which, he asserts, has proved that "all that we have of thought and function is susceptible of development. Every time that one has taken the trouble to repeat methodically a work the effect of which can be measured, one has obtained results that can be represented by a characteristic curve which merits the name of a *curve of progress*" (pages 141 ff.).

"Now if one considers that intelligence is not a single, indivisible function with a particular essence of its own," he argues, "but that it is formed by the combination of all the minor functions of discrimination, observation, and retention, all of which have been proved to be plastic and subject to increase, it will seem incontestable that the same law governs the ensemble and its elements, and that consequently the intelligence of any one is susceptible of development. With practice, enthusiasm, and especially with method one can succeed in increasing one's attention, memory, and judgment, and in becoming literally more intelligent than before; and this progress will go on until one reaches one's limit. And . . . what is important in order to act intelligently is not so much the force of the faculties as the manner of using them; that is to say, as the *art* of intelligence, which art is necessarily capable of being refined by practice" (page 143).

In what he considered his justification by facts, Binet cites the remarkable progress made by children in the special classes organized by him and certain schoolmen for retarded children. The children chosen for these classes were retarded three years in their school work despite their having been regular in attendance. After a year's training in these schools they were found to be only two years retarded, having made up an extra year in addition to the normal progress of one year. To the objection that this progress was due only to instruction, that it shows only the possibility of rapidly educating the ignorant when conditions are especially favorable, Binet replies: "They were not merely ignorant persons; all had a mental defect, a weakness of attention, a feebleness of comprehension, or some other limitation. And it was this defect that prevented them from profiting by the instructions given in the ordinary classes by the usual methods. In the special schools the instruction has been assimilated; that is a fact. Habits of work, of attention, and of effort have been acquired; this is another fact, and this second fact is even more important than the first. What is the exact part of instruction in this result and what that of intelligence? That would be extremely difficult to know, and perhaps it would be useless to try to find it out; for the production of an individual, his social utility, his functional value, depends on these two factors together. The mind of such a child is like a field the method of cultivation of which has been changed by a wise farmer, with the result that the ground once a waste land now bears fruit. It is in this practical sense, the only one applicable here, that we say that the intelligence of these children has been augmented. The thing that has been augmented is what constitutes the intelligence of the pupil, the capacity to learn and to assimilate the instruction" (page 146). There is evidently a little confusion of thought in these passages.

BINET'S "MENTAL ORTHOPEDICS"

The process of increasing the practical intelligence of a child Binet called *mental orthopedics*. "Having on our hands children who did not know how to listen, to pay attention, to keep quiet, we pictured our first duty as being not to teach them the facts that we thought would be most useful, but *to teach them how to learn.* We have therefore devised, with the aid of M. Belot and all our other collaborators, what we call exercises of mental orthopedics. The word is expressive and has come into favor. One can guess its meaning. In the same way that physical orthopedics straightens a crooked spine, mental orthopedics strengthens, cultivates, and fortifies attention, memory, perception, judgment, and will" (page 150).

This practice, to which Binet had apparently given a good deal of attention, consisted of such characteristic exercises as keeping oneself absolutely immobile for a period of time, carrying a cup full of water without spilling any out, exerting all one's strength in a prolonged pressure on the dynamometer, and naming groups of objects or of pictures of objects which had been viewed for a short time. Binet's method differs somewhat from that of Seguin (*187*), a famous teacher of defectives, "who," say Binet and Simon (*60*, page 3) "showed experimentally how one may, by dint of much ingenuity and patience, increase the intelligence and improve the character of some of these unfortunate children." In a note on the page cited they say that "Seguin's work must not be examined too closely; those who praise it have certainly not read it. Seguin impresses us as an empiric, endowed with great personal talent, which he has succeeded in embodying clearly in his works. These contain some pages of good sense, with many obscurities, and many absurdities." Yet Binet has clearly drawn somewhat upon Seguin's work.

PHYSICAL BASES OF MENTAL DEFECT : MEDICAL TREATMENT

As to the causes and physical bases of mental deficiency, Binet and Simon summarize as follows what they say is known : "The dominant etiological feature is that mental deficiency and want of balance depend upon hereditary conditions, or conditions acquired in the earliest stages of development. By hereditary conditions must be understood strictly those which result from alterations in the germ cells of the parents. An intoxication alone seems capable of exercising upon the latter a sufficiently general action to reach the germ cells, and by far the most frequent poison is alcohol. By acquired conditions must be understood the results of diseases of the fœtus or of infancy, and especially the cerebral complications of the infectious fevers — e.g., meningitis in the course of an eruptive fever. In all such cases, with rare exceptions to be mentioned immediately, by the time the mental deficiency is discovered, its causes are no longer active, and consequently cannot be affected by medical intervention" (*60*, page 102). The exceptions referred to are (1) the ingestion of thyroid glands from sheep for cases of threatening cretinism, (2) the giving of bromides (in cases of epilepsy) and treatment by hydrotherapy, both of which means "enable the subject to master the emotional reactions which are habitually exaggerated," and (3) the moral influence that the physician can give to assist the educative work of the teacher in the special school, his advice and suggestive effects being intended here and not hypnotism (pages 104–106).

TRANSFER EFFECTS ON INTELLIGENCE PROBABLY TEMPORARY

Even though Binet was less inclined than are present-day psychologists to draw closely the distinction between the effects of a conceivable innate organization determining the possibilities of intelligence, on the one hand, and the effects of training, on the other, and was therefore likely to consider favorably the possibility of increasing one's intelligence by training, the various uses which he suggested or actually made of intelligence tests were practically those recognized today, except that more uses have developed with greater experience. Binet in no place shows any hope of considerably improving one's degree of intelligence, unless it should be in the case of cretinism. That there are transfer effects of training which may temporarily somewhat increase one's efficiency in certain rather general mental functions, no experimental psychologist can now well deny; but it is well not to regard this as an increase in intelligence, as Binet evidently regarded it. There is probably no good evidence that such improvement, even as it might be shown in intelligence tests, is permanent. It seems to fade away with lack of practice.

BINET A PIONEER IN EDUCATIONAL TESTS

Binet distinguished between intelligence tests and educational tests, or what he termed tests of instruction, just as we distinguish between them today; and, with the help of M. Vaney, he and Simon worked out and published age-level scales for testing the instructional status of defectives in reading, arithmetic, and spelling, scales of which they say they made much use (*60*, pages 52 ff.). They established by experimentation the average acquirement of all school children of each age from 6 to 11, 12, or 13 years, the upper limit varying for different tests. The children used for these norms were taken independently of their school classification, this plan being preferred to that of taking the acquirements of only the typical children, those of the proper grade classification for their ages. The method of standardization accepted by them in the establishment of these norms was regarded as being less artificial than the other one and as giving norms that are more nearly true expressions of actual conditions. They found that these norms were lower than those obtained by taking only typical children.

The arithmetic scale was published as early as 1905 by

Vaney [1] (*224*), having apparently been standardized on the reactions of 293 children; and the reading and spelling scales, together with the arithmetic scale containing only a sample problem for each age, appeared in *Les enfants anormaux*, 1907, and also in *Les idées modernes sur les enfants*, 1909. These scales were in age units, so that the educational age of a child could be determined and compared with his chronological age, or with the score normal to his age, due allowance being made for any irregularities in school opportunity. The idea of developing other scholastic tests was explicitly entertained. "It would be possible, and indeed easy, we believe," said Binet in 1909, "to add some typical interrogations on history, on geography, and on the sciences, and to grade exercises in composition" (*42*, page 26). The reading test developed by Binet was administered individually, requiring not more than ten minutes for each child (page 33).

EDUCATIONAL DEFINITIONS OF IDIOTS, IMBECILES, AND MORONS

In the rating of defectives for diagnostic purposes these investigators gave both mental and "instructional" tests, taking note in both cases of the opportunity that the child considered had had, as well as of his age. Thus in what they called knowledge retardation, measured with the instructional scales, they recognize that a 9-year-old child of three years' retardation in knowledge, for instance, was to be regarded differently from a 12-year-old child also of three years' retardation, the former having learned absolutely nothing. As a result of their studies with these three instructional scales, as well as with the intelligence scale, Binet and Simon

---

[1] It appears that Vaney was working under the direction of Binet in this investigation. In one place Binet says: "It is my collaborator, M. Vaney, who has been charged with this work," referring to the article here cited. In another place he and Simon say that the scales were "arranged with the help of M. Vaney" (*41*, page 25, and *60*, page 53).

were able in 1907 (*60*, pages 77 f.) to formulate in educational terms definitions of the three main classes of feeble-mindedness. These definitions of idiocy, imbecility, and moronity are stated in terms of the child's ability to learn, as follows:

Definition of an idiot. "*An idiot is any child who never learns to communicate with his kind by speech — that is to say, one who can neither express his thoughts verbally nor understand the verbally expressed thoughts of others, this inability being due solely to defective intelligence, and not to any disturbance of hearing, nor to any affection of the organs of phonation.*" A normal child of 2 years of age surpasses this limitation in the use of language.

Definition of an imbecile. "*An imbecile is any child who fails to learn how to communicate with his kind by means of writing — that is to say, one who can neither express his thoughts in writing, nor read writing or print, or, more correctly, understand what he reads, this failure being due to defective intelligence, and not to any defect of vision or any paralysis of the arms which would explain his inability.*" A child who does not know his letters after having been at school for two years is likely to become an imbecile, we are informed.

Definition of a moron. "*A moron is one who can communicate with his kind by speech or writing, but who shows a retardation of two or three years (according to the rules already indicated) in his school studies, this retardation not being due to insufficient or irregular attendance.*" Children who are retarded because of the lack of opportunity are, of course, not morons by this definition.

These distinctions are pedagogical, and will easily be made by teachers. It may be added here that the two or three years' deficiency in school work is a very unsatisfactory criterion, since an absolute retardation of this amount is much more serious at an early age than later, when it may not indicate that the person is a moron at all. Binet did not use the intelligence quotient in mental measurement, or he could easily have overcome in a general way this difficulty as far as the tests are concerned. The various legal definitions, to some of which the reader may have access, seek to state the limits of the different degrees of mental debility in terms of the subject's fitness for carrying on a normal social life and for assuming economic and moral responsibility. Binet recognized that all definitions must ultimately be based on criteria of ability to get on in life.

BINET URGED THAT EDUCATION BE ADAPTED TO THE LEARNER'S APTITUDES

Thus Binet carried his work on defectives to the point of a considerable clarification of many problems that had arisen both as to classification of these individuals and as to their general treatment, and in this work he had developed both intelligence tests and educational tests. This was at a time when educational tests were unknown in America.[1] It seems evident that but for Binet's untimely death, at the age of fifty-four, he would have carried his tests fully into the field of normal education in the schools. He not only looked upon tests of children as very useful both to parents and teachers, but he also saw clearly, probably more clearly than most psychologists and educators today see, the need of training each child for a career suitable to his special aptitudes; that is, he recognized that the curricula are too conventional and are based too much on abstractions which a large per cent of the children are incapable of learning, even though they may be able to do very good work of a kind that the majority of men and women must do in the world.

In *Les idées modernes sur les enfants* Binet tells us that in the use of tests which stress literary ability and the handling of general ideas he found high agreement between the school

---

[1] Thorndike's handwriting scale (*215*) was published in 1910.

directors' estimates of intelligence and the intelligence-test scores, but that tests involving manual skill or the discernment of sensation differences often ranked highest those who were dull in school work of the conventional type. "And I understood then what an error was being made in judging these children according to tests that were not made for minds of their nature, and especially in giving them a kind of instruction that was contrary to their intellectual type. . . . As for myself, after an already long experience — I have been making investigations in the schools for twenty-five years — I believe that the determination of children's aptitudes is the matter of greatest importance in instruction and education. It is according to their aptitudes that they should be instructed and that they should be directed toward a profession" (page 11). In this excellent book Binet discusses in an illuminating way the qualifications that a teacher of children should have, and shows the need of a knowledge of what he called "individual psychology." He pointed out that the teacher should not only know the students from talks with them and from close personal contact in general recreation and in games, but should be acquainted with the different kinds of child mentality. Moreover, the teacher should be able to give mental tests and, in emergencies, to attack new problems experimentally.

A very definite suggestion is made by Binet as to the classification of children in school according to their several abilities : "In schools with large enrollments, where the law requires the organization of parallel classes, a method of sectioning the pupils into such classes on the basis of their aptitudes would be possible. In certain classes instruction that is of a predominantly literary character might be given, in others science would have the first place, and in still others the emphasis could be placed on work of a much more immediately practical nature and on shop work" (page 13).

Certainly the use of tests in the normal educational process is to find out each child's capabilities and to determine whether he is doing what he can do with the greatest advantage. To measure the effects on one's abilities of different kinds of training, of differences in environment and in social status, of fatigue, of different motivating conditions, etc., is an important field for intelligence tests to supplement other kinds of measurement.

THE HEREDITY OF INTELLIGENCE

The scientific study of heredity has also afforded a useful field for intelligence tests. This work early attracted Galton, who used not only observational and rating methods but actually made certain tests of specific capacities, as we have already noted. As early as 1869 Galton (*114*) published a study of 977 eminent men, of whom each was the most prominent among about 4000 persons. He found that a high degree of innate ability was essential to the attainment of eminence however favorable the social advantages, that highly gifted individuals are likely to rise to eminence even against unfavorable circumstances and social rank, and that genius follows laws of heredity as do such traits as height, complexion, etc. His study of twins (*115*) is an illustration of his use of certain tests, such as imagery tests, in investigating effects of heredity as related to those of environment. In America, Cattell (*89, 90*) in studies of scientific men and Woods (*236*) in studies of royal families made good use of methods of ranking, while Thorndike (*214*) as early as 1905 applied tests to twins in a study of the relative influences of heredity and environment.

INTELLIGENCE TESTS APPLIED TO THE PROBLEM OF RACE DIFFERENCES

The use of Binet's 1908 scale, as we have already seen, raised in several different countries the question of the effects of differences in social class and in parentage, and in this work it at once became evident that hereditary factors played an important rôle in differences revealed by the tests. From this point there is but a short step to race differences, which had already received attention by Rivers and a number of other investigators (see *237*), who employed chiefly sensory discrimination tests. In 1904 Woodworth and Bruner (*237*) tested various races in the St. Louis Exposition, finding that the keenness of the senses of the races tested was "about on a par." Unfortunately, language difficulties and the unsatisfactory development of suitable tests of intelligence at that time greatly limited these researches.

As early as 1895 Bache (*6*) applied reaction time tests to twelve white, eleven Indian, and ten negro subjects, with equivocal results. In the next two-year period A. T. Smith (*196*) and Stetson (*204*) tested negroes in certain memory functions; the former studied but a single individual, while the latter tested five hundred white and five hundred negro children in Washington, D. C. The negroes were slightly older than the whites, and they also surpassed them in the memory-of-verse tests used. In 1899 McDonald (*161*) applied certain rough sensitivity tests to ninety-one negro children. These various early tests were of very little scientific value, partly because test methods were inadequately developed and largely because the tests used were of a kind that later were shown to be of little significance as to mentality. Numerous other tests [1] have been applied to various race groups since the appearance of the Binet intelligence scale, and the practical problems regarding race differences have been forcefully urged by Brigham (*76*) and by other investigators.

[1] A rather complete summary of quantitative race tests to 1923, and their results, will be found in the author's monograph, "The Comparative Abilities of White and Negro Children," *Comparative Psychology Monograph*, 1923, Vol. I, No. 5.

TESTS IN ANIMAL BEHAVIOR STUDIES

A variety of tests of sensory-motor learning capacity, of sensory discrimination, and even of intelligence were applied to animals in the early part of this century, before the Binet scale appeared to stimulate progress in the testing of humans, some of these tests having also more recently been applied to man. The general progress in this field may be gathered from a few books by such authors as Hobhouse (*132*), Thorndike (*216*), Washburn (*229*), and Watson (*230*). In this field an important problem has been how to develop tests of intelligence that would be fair to animals of different forms and instincts. It is obvious that in animal forms so different as those that have already been studied, intelligence has qualitative variations which cannot be overlooked; that it is not a homogeneous power or faculty in any sense of these terms. The experimental work in this field — a field, it will be recalled, to which Binet gave some attention early in his scientific career but which he influenced only to a small extent — makes up one of the best chapters in modern psychology, and has in a relatively small range of years contributed valuable results on various problems in learning, in cerebral functions, in the relative importance and development of different sensory capacities, and in heredity. Indeed, the psychologist and educator who is ignorant of the progress in this field of psychology is considerably handicapped even in his work with humans.

A SUMMARY OF BINET'S SUGGESTIONS AS TO THE USES OF TESTS

Though Binet everywhere emphasized the practical value of tests for the selection and classification of individuals of inferior ability, he recognized also the extensive use that can be made of a good intelligence scale in the solution of numerous scientific problems relating to our general social life as well as to the work of education in the schools.   Indeed, the scale was for him but a tool for various kinds of research work in psychological problems as well as a means of segregating persons for purely practical purposes, and in the practical applications which he made of the scale he was but following, though by more scientific methods, other investigators or responding to certain needs of his environment. In his numerous writings he made and indicated various uses of the intelligence scale, but failed to summarize these or to gather them together in any one place.   It may be well, therefore, to mention briefly here the various uses that he made of his scale or that he suggested.

Binet held that the most important application of the tests of intelligence was to persons of inferior intelligence (*61*, page 85).   He did not recognize explicitly the great value of testing for superior intelligence and for outlining for supernormal children an education according to their abilities, though this was doubtless in his mind or would have been urged if he had lived to carry out his idea of sectioning classes according to the abilities of the children.   As we have already seen, he formulated a simple rule for the selection of the brightest students in any class, that of choosing the youngest children.   He was aware that the brighter children were usually underrated as to ability by their teachers, because of the unfair comparison of them with the older and more experienced children of their classes independently of considerations of age.   One of the chief post-Binet developments of mental testing has been a more explicit recognition of the problem of selecting and training super-normal children according to their greater possibilities.   At the end of their description of the 1905 scale Binet and Simon say : "We end here the list of tests that we have used.   It would have been easy to continue the scale by adding more complicated tests, if one had wished to make a hierarchy of normal children. The scale could even be extended for adults to the normal, to the intelligent, to the very intelligent, and to the super-intelligent, and used to measure, or at least to try to measure, talent and genius. We defer to another occasion this difficult study" (page 223). This study was apparently never attempted by them.

As to the subnormals, Binet used the intelligence scale in a practical way both as a means to their selection for special education and to their classification for special treatment. In a more scientific and theoretical sense he used it to define and characterize the three degrees of feeble-mindedness which we have already considered. Among children that had been sent to institutions for feeble-minded individuals Binet and Simon found some that were normal in intelligence and two that were at least one year above normal (*61*, page 86), and they seem to have been very much impressed by the injustice of such errors in classification. They point out that certain investigations in medicine, such as the effect of thyroid treatment on mentally defective children, might be greatly facilitated by the application of the intelligence tests both before and after the treatment (*ibid.*, page 89). Another use suggested in the medical field is that of establishing relationships between various pathological conditions determined by autopsies and intelligence as previously measured by the scale.

Binet and his collaborators made extensive studies, as we have already seen, of the relations of various physical and mental traits as determined by anthropometric measurements on the one hand and intelligence tests and teachers' estimates of mental ability on the other. These studies were useful chiefly in making it clear that no very definite relationship exists between intelligence and size and shape of the head or other physical features measured, contrary to theories that have often been propounded by individuals in different fields of science.

It was evident to Binet that any instrument by means of which a trained tester could in less than an hour arrive at a juster estimate of a child's intelligence than that held by his teacher or by his parents is very useful to parents, teachers, and administrators of justice and of education. With the knowledge afforded by such measurements as could be made with the intelligence scale, to supplement their information from other sources, they could have a fair idea of the child's possibilities and therefore adapt instruction to his particular needs.

In the determination of the degree of responsibility of persons charged with criminal acts the scale would be very useful so far as subnormals, as distinct from those suffering from functional disorders, are concerned.

THE TESTING OF SOLDIERS

As early as 1908 Binet became active in urging the desirability of testing young men who are to be taken into the army, so as to eliminate those who are incapacitated for such service. Investigations had been carried out in the German army with a view to devising tests for the detection of defectives, so that they might be saved from the maladjustment and even the suicide that experience showed was so frequent in the lives of these unfortunate persons in the army. In February, 1905, a commission under the leadership of Professor Ziehen had studied this situation in Germany and had developed certain mental examinations designed to eliminate defectives. These consisted of questions to be answered, of the digit span test, of the giving by the subject of the days of the week and the months of the year, of the repetition of a story that had just been told by the examiner, of the Ebbinghaus completion test, and of the construction of a

sentence to include four given words (*4*). Binet seems not
to have been aware of this work, but he knew of a questionnaire prepared by the psychiatrist Dr. Schultze, which
was so designed that a 12-year-old child of average intelligence, even though without culture, could pass it. He
tells us in a footnote (page 94) that he had taken up the question of testing recruits in the French army with the Minister
of War, who replied that he would ask for a report on the
matter by his bureau. Binet hoped to be able to report to
his readers in the near future that tentative experiments on
the testing of recruits were in progress. Subsequent events
showed that he had not counted sufficiently on the selfishness
of human nature; that the psychiatrists on whom rested the
responsibility of eliminating feeble-minded persons from the
army were not ready to let him seemingly encroach upon
their duties, however ill performed they were.

In 1910 Binet and Simon published an article (*63*) in which
they inform us of the progress of the proposed army testing.
Soon after bringing the question to the attention of the Minister of War they had asked for an authorization to make in
a regiment some experimental trials, thus carrying their tests
into a field that was new to them. Dr. Simonin, professor
of legal medicine at Val-de-Grâce, was consulted as to an
opportunity for giving some of the preliminary tests. He
selected from among the convalescents in his hospital service
the subjects to be tested, and was present himself at the tests,
which Binet and Simon call only some preliminary gropings,
only eleven individuals being tested at the time. As a
result of such observations and without direct acquaintance
and experience with the tests, we are told, Simonin made a
report (*195*) to a congress of psychiatrists of the French
language, held at Nantes, on a trial of mental tests in the
army. He apparently presented the matter as if he had
himself carried out the tests. Dr. Roubinovitch, one of the

psychiatrists present at the congress, tells us that Simonin in his criticism of the tests had the full support of all the members present (*46*, page 479).

The opinion of the psychiatrists was against the tests in the army. They held that intelligence tests alone cannot lead to a certain diagnosis of mental retardation, but that, on the contrary, they may lead to veritable errors because of the emotions aroused in the subjects when confronted for the first time with these tests in the strange environment. Simonin concluded that a proper diagnosis required not only mental tests that are adapted to each individual, but also, and especially, a thorough "biological observation" including inquiry into hereditary and personal antecedents, as well as into the general somatic conditions of the several subjects. The psychiatrists considered the tests of Binet and Simon as entirely too mechanical and simple and much too short to give an exact picture of the subject's mental condition, and there is evidence in their discussion that they were in the main ignorant of the development of the intelligence scale and of the scientific requirements of objectivity in any such means of measurement.

Binet and Simon seem to have been stirred up by the hasty and unjust method by which Simonin brought his criticism of their proposed army tests before the important meeting of the psychiatrists and secured their support in his opposition. Referring to their preliminary tests, they say in the summary in the *Année:* "These are the preliminary gropings at which Dr. Simonin was simply present, that he reports in his communication; he adds to them only some errors and rashness of interpretation, which are explained by his ignorance of our views, and which he would have spared himself if he had consulted us" (page 476).

Since Simonin had from these preliminary trials drawn conclusions as to the method in general, Binet and Simon find it advisable to state their ideas themselves, this being the first time they had expressed them. Every year, they say, a number of young soldiers, who had been admitted into the army by a general "good for the service" characterization not based on an examination of their mentality, are discharged for insufficient intelligence. These they propose to eliminate on entrance, not after some time in the army spent in maladjustments and personal distress. The number of those to be eliminated is not large, probably not even 1 per cent of the conscripts; but the difficulties of eliminating them are increased by the necessity of having the tests short and also by the possibilities of simulation on the part of the subjects.

The authors do not propose merely to apply to the soldiers the intelligence scale as worked out in the 1908 revision, but they state explicitly that the process of testing must be adapted to the end which it is to serve. Preliminary tests would be necessary to determine whether the methods adopted would eliminate the individuals actually found in the life of the barracks to be inefficient; that is, degree of efficiency in the army would have to be the criterion on which to evaluate and perfect the tests. Moreover, the authors state that they would find by investigation, and not by any preconceived notion, just what intellectual level is necessary for one to be a successful soldier, a level that is presumably not very high. The absurdity of Simonin's statement to the psychiatrists as to the length of time required for the testing of each subject is evident, they point out, from the fact that they had applied only a few preliminary tests to get an idea of which tests to use and which to drop out.

A third point to establish by preliminary experimentation would be that of deciding upon a method of eliminating rapidly from the examination all the normal men, so that the individual tests would be given only to the relatively few about whom there might be some question. It would be ridiculous, Binet and Simon point out, to test all the recruits in just the same way. In their opinion a first elimination of normal individuals could be made by excluding from the examination all the students and graduates of medical schools and of higher educational institutions, and also the men of certain trades which require a fair degree of intelligence. "In the second place," they add, "group tests are possible" (page 477). After these two siftings for the inefficient they suppose that only four or five doubtful cases in each hundred would remain to be studied by individual tests. Simulation would not complicate the matter, because the tests would be arranged in a hierarchy beginning with tests that an imbecile could pass as well as a normal person; so that those attempting to deceive could not easily be consistent, especially as they would not know what scores would be possible to persons of different degrees of intelligence.

Finally, Binet and Simon point out that the objections by the psychiatrists to the proposed tests are ill founded from another standpoint; for this work of sifting out and locating the persons of mental deficiency is not intended to supplant the medical and biological examinations. On the contrary, it would only serve, as far as these examinations are concerned, to indicate the individuals most in need of them. It was thus obviously the intention of the psychological testers to confine their attention only to cases of mental deficiency, and not to attempt to give psychiatric examinations to the mentally disorganized.

The opposition to the proposed army testing seems to have been great enough to frustrate the plan of Binet. This opposition, together with the death of Binet in 1911, left to the American psychologists (*240*, *241*) in the World War the carrying out for the first time and on a big scale of a plan which in many of its details as to procedure and method was worked out by Binet, but which was also independently developed in America. The American army testing was, however, largely an indirect product of the work on tests by the great French psychologist, whose experiments so greatly influenced testing in this country.

Hardly a field has been entered by the more recent developments in psychology that this great genius did not actually work out in a measure or plan for future work. He recognized that society is organized on a poor basis as to the selection of individuals for the different kinds of work demanded by human welfare, and he pointed out as a more ideal project for future psychological work the development of tests and other scientific procedures for the better organization of social life and for better vocational selection, education, and guidance, so that each individual could work at that for which he is most fit by nature. This program is yet, at the close of the first quarter of the twentieth century, largely a hope of the future; but it is an inviting field of endeavor for those persons who are sincerely devoted to the good of humanity, and already certain notable efforts by psychologists have at least indicated that the plan is not a mere idle dream. These contributions by tests of various kinds will, of course, in no sense take the place of the great work of education, of training each generation and of educating men to use to the greatest advantage the contributions of past generations; they will only help make such training and education more effective than at present.

The contributions of Alfred Binet toward the solution of problems of the sort that we have considered in the foregoing pages — due to his great industry, his keen practical sense, his versatility, his readiness to try in an empirical manner one means after another and to give up cherished opinions when they proved of little value — will stand as landmarks to encourage those who must go farther than he could go in his day, and who must yet continue to push a long way the analyses of the complex response and appreciation possibilities of the biological organizations which we know as personalities.

EXERCISES

1. Make a bibliography of the Thorndike-Spearman controversy to the present time. State the chief developments in the problem in later years and the reason why Spearman holds that Thorndike and his students have really not met the conditions which test the theory. Why is Spearman's theory called a two-factor theory?

2. How do you account for the differences in results obtained by the Spearman school and the Thorndike school?

3. What effects does practice in taking intelligence tests have on one's efficiency in tests which one has not seen (the transfer effects)? Get definite facts from the periodical literature. Do these facts justify the view that intelligence can be increased in an adult by training? Why? Suppose one should contend that intelligence tests afford better material for mental discipline than do the ancient languages; that they give better motivation in the competition for high marks; that they represent better material for stressing judgment and other higher mental functions; and that they train one in more useful and practical functions than do the ancient languages. What can you say for and against this contention? (Remember that the uses of intelligence tests do not include that of training the intellect.)

4. Now write out again the very best definition of intelligence that you can formulate.

A LIST OF MODERN BOOKS ON INTELLIGENCE

On the Binet-Simon Tests

BURT, CYRIL. *Mental and Scholastic Tests*. P. S. King & Son, London; 1922.

HERRING, J. P. *Herring Revision of the Binet-Simon Tests* (Examination Manual: Form A). World Book Company, Yonkers-on-Hudson, New York; 1922.

KUHLMANN, F. *A Handbook of Mental Tests*. Warwick & York, Inc., Baltimore; 1922.

TERMAN, L. M. *The Measurement of Intelligence*. Houghton Mifflin Company, Boston; 1916.

YERKES, R. M., BRIDGES, J. W., and HARDWICK, ROSE. *A Point Scale for Measuring Mental Ability*. Warwick & York, Inc., Baltimore; 1915. (Revised in 1923 by R. M. Yerkes and Josephine Curtis Foster.)

On Group Tests

PINTNER, RUDOLF. *The Mental Survey*. D. Appleton & Co., New York; 1918.

—— and PATTERSON, D. G. *A Scale of Performance Tests*. D. Appleton & Co., New York; 1917.

PYLE, W. H. *The Examination of School Children*. The Macmillan Company, New York; 1913.

WHIPPLE, G. M. *A Manual for Mental and Physical Tests*. Warwick & York, Inc., Baltimore; 1910. (Later enlarged editions in two volumes, 1919 and 1921.)

YERKES, R. M. (Editor). *Memoirs of the National Academy of Sciences*. 1921, 15.

YOAKUM, C. S., and YERKES, R. M. *Army Mental Tests*. Henry Holt & Co., New York; 1920.

On Applications of Tests to Races and Sub-races

BRIGHAM, C. C. *A Study in American Intelligence*. Princeton University Press, Princeton, N. J.; 1923.

FERGUSON, G. O. "The Psychology of the Negro," *Archives of Psychology*, No. 36; 1916.

PETERSON, JOSEPH. "The Comparative Abilities of White and Negro Children," *Comparative Psychology Monographs*, Vol. I, No. 5; 1923. (A summary of all quantitative racial tests to date is given.)

On Intelligence and Intelligence Tests in General

HINES, H. C. *Measuring Intelligence.* Houghton Mifflin Company, Boston; 1923.

PINTNER, RUDOLF. *Intelligence Testing: Methods and Results.* Henry Holt & Co., New York; 1923. (This book gives a list of tests and results to date. Some of the most important group tests available are listed in this book on pages 166 f. As a rule each set of standardized tests is accompanied by a manual of directions. The Otis tests and manuals are especially worthy of mention in this connection, being pioneer and still leading examples of group tests.)

RICHARDSON, C. A. *Methods and Experiments in Mental Tests.* World Book Company, Yonkers-on-Hudson, New York; 1922.

SPEARMAN, C. *The Nature of Intelligence and the Principles of Cognition.* The Macmillan Company, New York; 1923.

STERN, W. *Die Intelligenz der Kinder und Jugendlichen und die Methoden ihrer Untersuchung.* Bart, Leipzig; 1920.

THURSTONE, L. L. *The Nature of Intelligence.* Harcourt, Brace & Co., New York; 1924.

WOODROW, H. *Brightness and Dullness in Children.* J. B. Lippincott Company, Philadelphia; 1919.

REFERENCES

1. ABELSON, A. R. "The Measurement of Mental Ability of 'Backward' Children." *British Journal of Psychology*, Vol. 4 (1911), pages 268–314.
2. AIKINS, H. A., THORNDIKE, E. L., and HUBBELL, ELIZABETH A. "Correlations among Perceptive and Associative Processes." *Psychological Review*, Vol. 9 (1902), pages 374–382.
3. AMES, E. S. *The Psychology of Religious Experience.* 1910.
4. ANONYMOUS. "The Experience of the German Army with the Defectives and the Feeble-minded." (Reprinted from the *Military Surgeon*, Vol. 27, No. 5.) *Journal of Psycho-Asthenics*, Vol. 16 (1911), pages 68–76.
5. AYRES, LEONARD P. "The Binet-Simon Measuring Scale for Intelligence: Some Criticisms and Suggestions." *Psychological Clinic*, Vol. 5 (1911), pages 187–196.
6. BACHE, R. M. "Reaction Time with Reference to Race." *Psychological Review*, Vol. 2 (1895), pages 475–486.
7. BAGLEY, W. C. "On Correlation of Mental and Motor Ability in School Children." *American Journal of Psychology*, Vol. 12 (1901), pages 193–205.
8. BAIN, ALEXANDER. *The Senses and the Intellect.* 1855.
9. BALDWIN, J. M. *History of Psychology, Vol. I.* 1913.
10. BARR, M. W. *Mental Defectives: Their History, Treatment, and Training.* 1904. Revised, 1910.
11. BENEKE, F. E. *Lehrbuch der Psychologie als Naturwissenschaft.* 1833.
12. BERKELEY, GEORGE. *Essay towards a New Theory of Vision.* 1709.
13. —— *A Treatise Concerning the Principles of Human Understanding.* 1710.
14. BINET, ALFRED. *La Psychologie du raisonnement.* 1886.
15. —— *Sur la vie psychique des micro-organismes.* 1887.
16. —— *Les Altérations de la personalité.* 1891. Trans., 1896.
17. —— *Contribution à l'étude du système nerveux sous-intestinal des insectes.* 1894.
18. —— "La mémoire des joueurs d'échecs qui jouent sans voir." *Revue Philosophique*, Vol. 37 (1894), pages 222–240.
19. —— *Psychologie des grands calculateurs et joueurs d'échecs.* 1894.
20. —— *Introduction à la Psychologie expérimentale.* 1894.
21. —— "La mesure des illusions visuelles chez les enfants." *Revue Philosophique*, Vol. 20 (1895), pages 11–25.
22. —— *La création de classes spécials pour les enfants arriérés.* 1896.
23. —— "Description d'un objet." *L'Année Psychologique*, Vol. 3 (1897), pages 296–332.
24. —— A review of (*124*). *L'Année Psychologique*, Vol. 3 (1897), pages 610–613.

299

25. BINET, ALFRED. A review of (*108*). *L'Année Psychologique*, Vol. 3 (1897), pages 532–546.
26. —— A review of (*117*). *L'Année Psychologique*, Vol. 4 (1898), pages 653–659.
27. —— "La mesure en psychologie individuelle." *Revue Philosophique*, Vol. 46, 2d Sem. (1898), pages 113–123.
28. —— "Recherches sur la sensibilité tactile pendant l'état de distraction." *L'Année Psychologique*, Vol. 5 (1899), pages 405–440.
29. —— "Attention et adaptation." *L'Année Psychologique*, Vol. 6 (1900), pages 248–404.
30. —— *La Suggestibilité.* 1900.
31. —— "Un nouvel esthésiomètre." *L'Année Psychologique*, Vol. 7 (1901), pages 231–239.
32. —— "Technique de l'esthésiomètrie." *L'Année Psychologique*, Vol. 7 (1901), pages 240–248.
33. —— Five articles on researches in cephalometry. *L'Année Psychologique*, Vol. 7 (1901), pages 314–429.
34. —— *L'Étude expérimentale de l'Intelligence.* 1902.
35. —— "La mesure de la suggestibilité." *L'Année Psychologique*, Vol. 9 (1903), pages 79–128.
36. —— "Les simplistes : enfants d'école et adultes." *L'Année Psychologique*, Vol. 9 (1903), pages 129–168; "Les distraits," pages 169–198; "Les interpréteurs," pages 199–234.
37. —— "Influence de l'exercice et de la suggestion sur la position du seuil." *L'Année Psychologique*, Vol. 9 (1903), pages 235–245.
38. —— "Le seuil de la sensation double ne peut pas être fixé scientifiquement." *L'Année Psychologique*, Vol. 9 (1903), pages 247–252.
39. —— "La graphologie et ses révélations sur le sexe, l'âge, et l'intelligence." *L'Année Psychologique*, Vol. 10 (1904), pages 179–210.
40. —— *Les révélations de l'écriture d'après un contrôle scientifique.* 1906.
41. —— "Essai de chiromancie expérimentale." *L'Année Psychologique*, Vol. 14 (1908), pages 390–404.
42. —— *Les Idées modernes sur les enfants.* 1909.
43. —— "Les signes physiques de l'intelligence chez les enfants." *L'Année Psychologique*, Vol. 16 (1910), pages 1–30.
44. —— "A proposito delle 'Ricerche di Psicologia individuale nei Dementi' di Baroncini e Sarteschi." *Rivista di psicologia*, Vol. 6 (1910), pages 184–185.
45. —— "Nouvelles recherches sur la mesure du niveau intellectuel chez les enfants d'école." *L'Année Psychologique*, Vol. 17 (1911), pages 145–210.
46. —— A review of (*63*). *L'Année Psychologique*, Vol. 17 (1911), pages 475–480.
47. —— and FÉRÉ, C. *Le Magnétisme animal.* 1886.
48. —— and HENRI, V. "Simulation de la mémoire des chiffres." *Revue Scientifique*, June, 1894.

References 301

49. BINET, ALFRED, and HENRI V. "Le développement de la mémoire visuelle chez les enfants." *Revue Philosophique*, Vol. 37 (1894), pages 348–350. (Also in *Revue générale des Sciences*, 1894.)
50. —— and HENRI, V. "De la suggestibilité naturelle chez les enfants." *Revue Philosophique*, Vol. 38 (1894), pages 337–347.
51. —— and HENRI, V. "La mémoire des mots." *L'Année Psychologique*, Vol. 1 (1895), pages 1–23.
52. —— and HENRI, V. "La mémoire des phrases." *L'Année Psychologique*, Vol. 1 (1895), pages 24–59.
53. —— and HENRI, V. "La psychologie individuelle." *L'Année Psychologique*, Vol. 2 (1896), pages 411–465.
54. —— and HENRI, V. *La Fatigue intellectuelle.* 1898.
55. —— and PASSEY, J. "La psychologie des auteurs dramatiques." *Revue Philosophique*, Vol. 37 (1894), pages 240 ff.
56. —— and PASSEY, J. "Études de psychologie sur les auteurs dramatiques." *L'Année Psychologique*, Vol. 1 (1895), pages 60–118.
57. —— and SIMON, TH. "Sur la nécessité d'établir un diagnostic scientifique des états inférieurs de l'intelligence." *L'Année Psychologique*, Vol. 11 (1905), pages 163–190.
58. —— and SIMON, TH. "Méthodes nouvelles pour le diagnostic du niveau intellectuel des anormaux." *L'Année Psychologique*, Vol. 11 (1905), pages 191–244.
59. —— and SIMON, TH. "Application des méthodes nouvelles au diagnostic du niveau intellectuel chez des enfants normaux et anormaux d'hospice et d'école primaire." *L'Année Psychologique*, Vol. 11 (1905), pages 245–366.
60. —— and SIMON, TH. *Les enfants anormaux*, 1907; *Mentally Defective Children*, tr. by Drummond, 1914. (References in the text refer to the translation.)
61. —— and SIMON, TH. "Le développement de l'intelligence chez les enfants." *L'Année Psychologique*, Vol. 14 (1908), pages 1–94.
62. —— and SIMON, TH. "L'Intelligence des imbéciles." *L'Année Psychologique*, Vol. 15 (1909), pages 1–147.
63. —— and SIMON, TH. "Sur la nécessité d'une méthode applicable au diagnostic des arriérées militaires." *Annales médico-psychologiques*, January–February, 1910.
64. —— and SIMON, TH. "La mesure du développement de l'intelligence chez les jeunes enfants." *Bulletin de la Société libre pour l'Étude psychologique de l'Enfant*, 1911; "A Method of Measuring the Development of the Intelligence of Young Children," tr. by Clara Harrison Town, 1915.
65. —— and VASCHIDE, N. "The Influence of Intellectual Work on the Blood Pressure in Man." *Psychological Review*, Vol. 4 (1897), pages 54–66.
66. —— and VASCHIDE, N. "La psychologie en l'école primaire." *L'Année Psychologique*, Vol. 4 (1898), pages 1–14.

302   *Early Conceptions and Tests of Intelligence*

67. BINET, ALFRED, and VASCHIDE, N. "L'historique des recherches sur la céphalomètrie." *L'Année Psychologique*, Vol. 5 (1899), pages 245-298.
68. BLIN. "Les débilités mentales." *Revue de Psychiatrie*, August, 1902.
69. BOBERTAG, O. "A. Binets Arbeiten über die intellektualle Entwicklung des Schulkindes." *Zeitschrift für angewandte Psychologie*, Vol. 3 (1909), pages 230-259.
70. —— "Über Intelligenzprüfungen nach der Methode von Binet und Simon." *Zeitschrift für angewandte Psychologie*, Vol. 5 (1911), pages 105-203; Vol. 6 (1912), pages 495-538.
71. BOLTON, T. L. "The Growth of Memory in School Children." *American Journal of Psychology*, Vol. 4 (1891-1892), pages 362-380.
72. BONSER, F. G. "The Reasoning Ability of Children." *Columbia University Contributions to Education*, No. 3 (1910).
73. BOURDON, B. "Influence de l'âge sur la mémoire immédiate." *Revue Philosophique*, Vol. 19 (1894), pages 148-167.
74. BRETT, G. S. *A History of Psychology, Ancient and Patristic.* 1912.
75. —— *A History of Psychology*, Vol. 3. 1921.
76. BRIGHAM, C. C. *A Study in American Intelligence.* 1923.
77. BROWN, W. "Some Experimental Results in the Correlation of Mental Abilities." *British Journal of Psychology*, Vol. 3 (1910), pages 296-322.
78. BRUNER, F. G., BARNES, EARL, and DEARBORN, W. F. "Report of Committee on Books and Tests Pertaining to the Study of Exceptional and Mentally Deficient Children." *Proceedings of the National Education Association*, Vol. 47 (1909), pages 901-914.
79. BRYAN, W. L. "On the Development of Voluntary Motor Ability." *American Journal of Psychology*, Vol. 5 (1892), pages 125-204.
80. BRYANT, SOPHIE. "Experiments in Testing the Character of School Children." *Journal of the Anthropological Institute of Great Britain and Ireland*, Vol. 15 (1886), pages 338-349.
81. BURIDAN. In *Encyclopædia Britannica.*
82. BURT, CYRIL. "Experimental Tests of General Intelligence." *British Journal of Psychology*, Vol. 3 (1909), pages 94-177.
83. —— *Mental and Scholastic Tests.* 1922.
84. CALKINS, MARY W. "A Study of Immediate and of Delayed Recall." *Psychological Review*, Vol. 5 (1898), pages 451-456.
85. CANNON, W. B. *Bodily Changes in Pain, Hunger, Fear, and Rage.* 1915.
86. CAROTHERS, F. EDITH. "Psychological Examinations of College Students." *Archives of Psychology*, No. 46; 1921.
87. CATTELL, J. McKEEN. "Mental Tests and Measurements." *Mind*, Vol. 15 (1890), pages 373 ff.
88. —— "A Statistical Study of Eminent Men." *Popular Science Monthly*, Vol. 62 (1903), pages 359-377.
89. —— "Statistics of American Psychologists." *American Journal of Psychology*, Vol. 14 (1903), pages 310-328.

References 303

90. CATTELL, J. McKEEN. "A Statistical Study of American Men of Science. III : The Distribution of American Men of Science." *Science,* New Series, Vol. 24 (1906), pages 732–742.

91. —— and FARRAND, L. "Physical and Mental Measurements of the Students of Columbia University." *Psychological Review,* Vol. 3 (1896), pages 618–648.

92. CHOTZEN, F. " Die Intelligenzprüfungsmethode von Binet-Simon bei Schwachsinnigen Kindern" (Unter Mitwirkung von Dr. M. Nicolauer). *Zeitschrift für angewandte Psychologie,* Vol. 6 (1912), pages 411–494.

93. COOLEY, C. H. "Genius, Fame, and the Comparison of Races." *Annals of the American Academy of Political and Social Science,* Vol. 9 (1897), pages 317 ff.

94. DECROLY, O., and DEGAND, (Mlle.) J. "Les tests de Binet et Simon pour la mesure de l'intelligence: contribution critique." *Archives de Psychologie,* Vol. 6 (1906), pages 27–130.

95. —— "La mesure de l'intelligence chez des enfants normaux d'après les tests de Binet et Simon: nouvelle contribution critique." *Archives de Psychologie,* Vol. 9 (1910), pages 81–108.

96. DEMAYE. *Essai de diagnostic entre les états de débilité.* 1903. (Thesis at Paris.)

97. DEMOOR, J. *Die abnormalen Kinder und ihre erziehliche Behandlung in Haus und Schule.* 1901.

98. DE SANCTIS, SANTE. "Types et degrés d'insuffisance mentale." *L'Année Psychologique,* Vol. 12 (1906), pages 70–83.

99. DESCARTES, RENÉ. *Les passions de l'âme.* 1650.

100. DESCŒUDRES, ALICE. "Les tests de Binet et Simon et leur valeur scolaire." *Archives de Psychologie,* Vol. 11 (1911), pages 331–350.

101. DESSOIR, MAX. *Outlines of the History of Psychology* (tr. by D. Fisher). 1912.

102. DEWEY, J. "Interpretation of the Savage Mind." *Psychological Review,* Vol. 9 (1902), pages 217–230.

103. —— Article on "*Nous.*" *Dictionary of Philosophy and Psychology* (edited by J. M. Baldwin).

104. DOWN, J. R. *Mental Defectives of Childhood and Youth.* 1887.

105. DOWNEY, JUNE E. *Graphology and the Psychology of Handwriting.* 1919.

106. —— *The Will-Temperament and Its Testing.* 1923.

107. DRESSLAR, F. B. "Studies in the Psychology of Touch." *American Journal of Psychology,* Vol. 6 (1894), pages 311–368.

108. DUMAS, G. "Recherches expérimentales sur la joie et la tristesse." *Revue Philosophique,* Vol. 41 (1896), pages 577–601; Vol. 42, pages 24–45 and 113–138.

109. DUNCAN, P. M., and MILLARD, W. *A Manual for the Classification, Training, and Education of the Feeble-minded, Imbecile, and Idiotic.* 1866.

304 *Early Conceptions and Tests of Intelligence*

110. EBBINGHAUS, H. *Über das Gedächtniss.* 1885.
111. —— "Über eine neue Methode zur Prüfung geistiger Fähigkeiten und ihre Anwendung bei Schulkindern." *Zeitschrift für angewandte Psychologie,* Vol. 13 (1897), pages 401–459.
112. ESQUIROL. "Observations pour servir à l'histoire de l'idiotie." *Les maladies mentales.* 1828.
113. FERRARI, G. C. "Come si mesura lo sviluppo dell' intelligenza nei bambini normali." *Rivista de psicologia,* Vol. 4 (1908), pages 465–471.
114. GALTON, F. *Hereditary Genius: An Inquiry into Its Laws and Consequences.* 1869.
115. —— *An Inquiry into Human Faculty.* 1883.
116. GILBERT, J. A. "Researches on the Mental and Physical Development of School Children." *Studies of Yale Psychological Laboratory,* Vol. 2 (1894), pages 40–100.
117. —— "Researches upon School Children and College Students." *University of Iowa Studies in Psychology,* Vol. 1 (1897), pages 1–39.
118. GODDARD, H. H. "The Binet and Simon Tests of Intellectual Capacity." *The Training School,* Vol. 5 (1908), pages 3–9.
119. —— "A Measuring Scale for Intelligence." *The Training School,* Vol. 6 (1910), pages 146–155.
120. —— "Four Hundred Feeble-minded Children Classified by the Binet Method." *Pedagogical Seminary,* Vol. 17 (1910), pages 387–397.
121. —— "Two Thousand Normal Children Measured by the Binet Measuring Scale of Intelligence." *Pedagogical Seminary,* Vol. 18 (1911), pages 232–259.
122. —— *Feeble-mindedness: Its Causes and Consequences.* 1913.
123. —— *The Kallikak Family.* 1914.
124. GUICCARDI, G., and FERRARI, G. C. "I testi mentali per l'esame degli alienati." *Rivista sperimentale di freniatria,* Vol. 22 (1896), pages 297–314.
125. HALL, B. F. "The Trial of William Freeman." *American Journal of Insanity,* Vol. 5 (1848), pages 34–60.
126. HART, B. *The Psychology of Insanity.* 1912.
127. HARTLEY, D. *Observations on Man: His Frame, His Destiny, and His Expectations.* 1749.
128. HAUGHT, B. F. "The Interrelation of Some Higher Learning Processes." *Psychological Monographs,* Vol. 30, No. 6; 1922.
129. HENRI, V. A review of (*170*). *L'Année Psychologique,* Vol. 2 (1896), pages 795–797.
130. HOBBES, THOMAS. *Leviathan.* 1651.
131. —— *Human Nature, or the Fundamental Elements of Policie.* 1651.
132. HOBHOUSE, L. T. *Mind in Evolution.* 1901. Revised Edition, 1915.
133. HOFFDING, H. *A Brief History of Modern Philosophy* (tr. by B. E. Meyer). 1900.
134. HUEY, E. B. "Retardation and the Mental Examination of Retarded Children." *Journal of Psycho-Asthenics,* Vol. 15 (1910), pages 31–43.

135. HUEY, E. B. "The Binet Scale for Measuring Intelligence and Retardation." *Journal of Educational Psychology*, Vol. 1 (1910), pages 435–444.
136. HUME, D. *A Treatise of Human Nature.* 1739–1740.
137. —— *An Enquiry Concerning the Human Understanding.* 1748.
138. JACOBS, J. "Experiments on 'Prehension.'" *Mind*, Vol. 12 (1887), pages 75–79.
139. JAMES, W. "Great Thoughts, Great Men, and the Environment." *Atlantic Monthly*, Vol. 46 (1880), pages 441–459.
140. —— *The Varieties of Religious Experience.* 1902.
141. JASTROW, J. "Some Anthropological and Psychologic Tests on College Students — A Preliminary Survey." *American Journal of Psychology*, Vol. 4 (1891–1892), pages 420–427.
142. JENNINGS, H. S. "Heredity and Personality." *Science*, New Series, Vol. 34 (1911), pages 902–910.
143. JOHNSTON, KATHERINE L. "An English Version of Binet's Tests for the Measurement of Intelligence." *Report of the British Association for the Advancement of Science*, Vol. 80 (1910), pages 806–808.
144. —— "M. Binet's Method for the Measurement of Intelligence: Some Results." *Journal of Experimental Pedagogy*, Vol. 1 (1911), pages 24–31.
145. KELLEY, T. L. *Statistical Method.* 1923.
146. KIRKPATRICK, E. A. "An Experimental Study of Memory." *Psychological Review*, Vol. 1 (1894), pages 602–609.
147. KLEMM, OTTO. *History of Psychology* (tr. by Wilson and Pintner). 1914.
148. KRAEPELIN, EMIL. "Der Psychologische Versuch in der Psychiatrie," *Psychologische Arbeiten*, Vol. 1 (1895), pages 1–91.
149. KRAMER, F. "Die Intelligenzprüfung bei kriminellen und psychopathischen Kindern." *Arbeiten des Bundes für Schulreform.* Vol. 5; 1911.
150. KUHLMANN, F. "Experimental Studies in Mental Deficiency: Three Cases of Imbecility (Mongolian) and Six Cases of Feeble-mindedness." *American Journal of Psychology*, Vol. 15 (1904), pages 390–446.
151. —— "Binet and Simon's System for Measuring the Intelligence of Children." *Journal of Psycho-Asthenics*, Vol. 15 (1911), pages 76–92.
152. —— "Dr. Ayres' Criticism of the Binet and Simon System of Measuring the Intelligence of Children — A Reply." *Journal of Psycho-Asthenics*, Vol. 16 (1911), pages 58–67.
153. —— "A Revision of the Binet-Simon System for Measuring the Intelligence of Children." *Journal of Psycho-Asthenics, Monograph Supplement;* 1912.
154. LAWRENCE, ISABEL. "A Study of the Binet Definition Test." *Psychological Clinic*, Vol. 5 (1911), pages 207–216.
155. LEY, AUG. *L'Arriération mentale.* 1904.

306   *Early Conceptions and Tests of Intelligence*

156. LECLÈRE, A. "Description d'un objet." *L'Année Psychologique,* Vol. 4 (1898), pages 379–389.
157. LINDLEY, E. H. "A Study of Puzzles with Special Reference to the Psychology of Mental Adaptation." *American Journal of Psychology,* Vol. 8 (1897), pages 431–493.
158. LOCKE, JOHN. *An Essay Concerning Human Understanding.* 1690.
159. —— *Some Thoughts Concerning Education.* 1693.
160. MAETERLINCK, MAURICE. *The Unknown Guest.* 1914.
161. McDONALD, A. "Colored Children — A Psycho-Physical Study." *Journal of the American Medical Association,* Vol. 32 (1899), pages 1140–1144.
162. McDOUGALL, W. *Body and Mind.* 1911.
163. MEUMANN, E. "Intelligenzprüfung an der Kinder der Volkschule." *Experimentelle Pädagogik,* Vol. 1 (1905), pages 35–100.
164. MILL, JAMES. *Analysis of the Phenomena of the Human Mind.* 1829.
165. MÜLLER, G., and SCHUMANN, F. "Experimentelle Beiträge zur Untersuchung des Gedächtnisses." *Zeitschrift für angewandte Psychologie,* Vol. 6 (1894), pages 81–190, 257–339.
166. MÜNSTERBERG, H. "Zur Individualpsychologie." *Centralblatt für Nervenheilkunde und Psychiatrie,* Vol. 14 (1891), pages 196 ff.
167. —— and BIGHAM, J. "Memory." *Psychological Review,* Vol. 1 (1894), pages 34–38, and (by Bigham alone) pages 453–461.
168. MYERS, C. S. "The Pitfalls of 'Mental Tests.'" *Report of the British Association for the Advancement of Science* (1910), pages 808–809. (Also in *British Medical Journal,* Vol. 1 (1911), pages 195–197.)
169. NORSWORTHY, NAOMI. *The Psychology of Mentally Deficient Children.* 1906. (Columbia University thesis.)
170. OEHRN, A. *Experimentelle Studien zur Individualpsychologie.* 1889. (Dorpater dissertation.) (Also published in *Psychologischen Arbeiten,* Vol. 1 (1895), pages 92–152.)
171. PETERSON, JOSEPH. "Intelligence and Learning." *Psychological Review,* Vol. 29 (1922), pages 366–389.
172. —— "The Comparative Abilities of White and Negro Children." *Comparative Psychology Monographs,* Vol. 1, No. 5; 1923.
173. PHILIPPE, J. "Jastrow. — Exposition d'anthropologie de Chicago. — Tests Psychologique," etc. *L'Année Psychologique,* Vol. 1 (1894), pages 522–526.
174. PINTNER, R. *Intelligence Testing: Methods and Results.* 1923.
175. PLATO. *Phædo* (Jowett's Translation, 3d edition). 1892.
176. POHLMANN, A. *Experimentelle Beiträge zur Lehre vom Gedächtniss.* 1906.
177. PORTER, W. T. "The Growth of St. Louis Children." *Transactions of the Academy of Sciences,* Vol. 6 (1894), pages 263–426.
178. PYLE, W. H. "A Suggestion for the Improvement and Extension of Mental Tests." *Journal of Educational Psychology,* Vol. 13 (1912), pages 95–96.

179. PYLE, W. H. *The Psychology of Learning.* 1921.
180. RAND, B. *Modern Classical Philosophers.* 1908.
181. —— *The Classical Psychologists.* 1912.
182. ROSSOLIMO, G. *Die psychologischen Profile: Die Methodik.* Moscow; 1910.
183. SAFFIOTTI, F. U. "L'échelle métrique de l'intelligence modifiée selon la méthode Treves-Saffiotti." *L'Année Psychologique,* Vol. 18 (1912), pages 327–340.
184. —— *La misura dell' intelligenza nei fanciulli.* Rome; 1916.
185. SEASHORE, C. E. "Suggestions for Tests on School Children." *Educational Review,* Vol. 22 (1901), pages 69–82.
186. SEEBECK, H. *Geschichte der Psychologie, II.* 1880–1884.
187. SEGUIN, E. *Traitement moral, hygiène et éducation des idiots et des autres enfants arriérés.* 1846.
188. SHARP, STELLA E. "Individual Psychology: A Study in Psychological Method." *American Journal of Psychology,* Vol. 10 (1898–1899), pages 329–391.
189. SHAW, J. C. "A Test of Memory in School Children." *Pedagogical Seminary,* Vol. 4 (1896), pages 311–361.
190. SHRUBSALL, F. C. "The Examination of Mentally Defective Children." *School Hygiene* (1911), pages 613 ff.
191. SIMON, TH. "Recherches anthropométriques sur 223 garçons anormaux agés de 8 à 23 ans." *L'Année Psychologique,* Vol. 6 (1900), pages 191–247.
192. —— "Expériences de suggestion sur des débiles." *L'Année Psychologique,* Vol. 6 (1900), pages 441–484.
193. —— *Documents relatifs à la corrélation entre le développement physique et le développement intellectuel.* Paris; 1900.
194. —— "Recherches céphalométriques sur les enfants arriérés de la colonie de Vaucluse." *L'Année Psychologique,* Vol. 7 (1901), pages 430–489.
195. SIMONIN. "Essai des tests psychiques scolaires pour apprécier l'aptitude intellectuelle au service militaire." *Revue Neurologique,* August 30, 1909.
196. SMITH, A. T. "A Study of Race Psychology." *Popular Science Monthly,* Vol. 1 (1896), pages 354–360.
197. SPEARMAN, C. "The Proof and Measurement of Association between Two Things." *American Journal of Psychology,* Vol. 15 (1904), pages 72–101.
198. —— "'General Intelligence' Objectively Determined and Measured." *American Journal of Psychology,* Vol. 15 (1904), pages 201–293.
199. —— and KRUEGER, F. "Die Korrelation zwischen verschiedenen geistigen Leistungsfähigkeiten." *Zeitschrift für Psychologie und Physiologie der Sinnesorgane,* Vol. 44 (1907), pages 50–114.

200. STERN, W. *Über Psychologie der individuellen Differenzen.* 1900.

201. —— *Die Differentielle Psychologie.* 1911.

202. —— *The Psychological Methods of Testing Intelligence* (tr. by Whipple). 1914.

203. —— *Die Intelligenz der Kinder und Jugendlichen,* 3. Auflage. 1920.

204. STETSON, G. R. "Some Memory Tests on Whites and Blacks." *Popular Science Monthly,* Vol. 4 (1897), pages 285–289.

205. STRATTON, G. M. *Experimental Psychology and Culture.* 1903.

206. TERMAN, L. M. "Genius and Stupidity: A Study of Some of the Intellectual Processes of Seven 'Bright' and Seven 'Stupid' Boys." *Pedagogical Seminary,* Vol. 13 (1906), pages 307–373.

207. —— "The Binet-Simon Scale for Measuring Intelligence; Impressions Gained by Its Application." *Psychological Clinic,* Vol. 5 (1911), pages 199–206.

208. —— "The Mental Test as a Psychological Method." *Psychological Review,* Vol. 31 (1924), pages 93–117.

209. —— and CHILDS, H. G. "Tentative Revision and Extension of the Binet-Simon Measuring Scale of Intelligence." *Journal of Educational Psychology,* Vol. 3 (1912), pages 61 ff., 133 ff., 198 ff., 277 ff.

210. THOMPSON, HELEN B. *The Mental Traits of Sex.* 1903.

211. THORNDIKE, E. L. "Mental Fatigue." *Psychological Review,* Vol. 7 (1900), pages 466–489, 547–579.

212. —— *Educational Psychology.* 1903.

213. —— *An Introduction to the Theory of Mental and Social Measurements.* 1904.

214. —— "Measurements of Twins." *Archives of Philosophy, Psychology, and Scientific Methods,* No. 1; 1905.

215. —— "Handwriting." *Teachers College Record,* Vol. 11, No. 2 (1910).

216. —— *Animal Intelligence.* 1911.

217. ——, LAY, W., and DEAN, P. R. "The Relation of Accuracy in Sensory Discrimination to General Intelligence." *American Journal of Psychology,* Vol. 20 (1909), pages 364–369.

218. —— and WOODWORTH, R. S. "The Influence of Improvement in One Mental Function upon the Efficiency of Other Functions." *Psychological Review,* Vol. 8 (1901), pages 247–261, 384–395, 553–564.

219. TITCHENER, E. B. *Text-Book of Psychology.* 1910.

220. TOWN, CLARA HARRISON. "The Binet-Simon Scale and the Psychologist." *Psychological Clinic,* Vol. 5 (1912), pages 239–244.

221. TREDGOLD, A. F. *Mental Deficiency.* 1908. Revised Edition, 1914. (Revised Edition referred to in text.)

222. TREVES, Z., and SAFFIOTTI, F. U. *La "Scala metrica dell' intelligenza" di Binet et Simon.* Milan; 1910–1911.

223. TRÜPER, J. *Die Anfänge der Abnormen Erscheinungen im kindlichen Seelenleben.* Altenberg; 1902.

224. VANEY, V. "Nouvelles méthodes de mesure applicables au degré d'instruction des élèves." *L'Année Psychologique*, Vol. 11 (1905), pages 146–162.

225. VASCHIDE, N. "Sur la localization des souvenirs." *L'Année Psychologique*, Vol. 3 (1897), pages 199–224.

226. WALLIN, J. E. W. "A Practical Guide for the Administration of the Binet-Simon Scale for Measuring Intelligence." *Psychological Clinic*, Vol. 5 (1911), pages 217–238.

227. WARD, JAMES. *Psychological Principles.* 2d edition, 1920.

228. WARREN, H. C. *A History of the Association Psychology.* 1921.

229. WASHBURN, M. F. *The Animal Mind.* 2d edition, 1917.

230. WATSON, J. B. *Animal Behavior: An Introduction to Comparative Psychology.* 1914.

231. WHIPPLE, G. M. *Manual of Mental and Physical Tests.* 1910.

232. WINDELBAND, W. *A History of Philosophy.* Revised (tr. by J. H. Tufts), 1905.

233. WISSLER, C. "The Correlation of Mental and Physical Tests." *Psychological Review, Monograph Supplement*, Vol. 3, No. 6 (1901).

234. —— A review of (*233*). *Psychological Review*, Vol. 8 (1901), pages 539 and 540.

235. WOODROW, H. *Brightness and Dullness in Children.* 1919.

236. WOODS, F. A. *Mental and Moral Heredity in Royalty.* 1906.

237. WOODWORTH, R. S. "Race Differences in Mental Traits." *Science*, New Series, Vol. 31 (1910), pages 171–186.

238. —— *Psychology: A Study of Mental Life.* 1921.

239. WUNDT, W. *Elements of Folk Psychology* (tr. by E. L. Schaub). 1916.

240. YERKES, R. M. (Editor). *Memoirs of the National Academy of Sciences*, Vol. 15; 1921.

241. YOAKUM, C. S., and YERKES, R. M. *Army Mental Tests.* 1920.

242. YOUNG, KIMBALL. "The History of Mental Tests." *Pedagogical Seminary*, Vol. 31 (1924), pages 1–48.

INDEX

Abelson, A. R., 221
Abnormal psychology, 117
Achilles, 18
Adaptation, and attention, 142-146;
an element of thought, 260, 261,
262; mental, 259
Affections, the, 37
Age, and test scores, 120, 175, 219,
220, 240; levels, scholastic and
mental, 181-184, 214, 253, 279;
norms, two kinds, 115; scores,
used to evaluate tests, 54
Aiken's school, tests in, 126
Aikins, H. A., 114, 269
Alhacen, 44
Alienists, 25
Ames, E. S., 27
Anaxagoras, 11
Animal intelligence, tests of, 286
Animal spirits, 38, 42
Année Psychologique, origin and
purpose of, 100
Anthropological measurements, 74,
75, 83, 152-158; laboratory for, 75
Aptitudes, 230, 249, 259, 267, 282;
sectioning children according to,
283
Arabian psychologists, 44
Aristotle, 11, 37, 38, 39, 40, 54
Association, a gentle force, 63; and
sensory psychology, 71; as basis
of beliefs, passions, and will, 47;
compared with attraction in
physics, 64; general speed factor
in, a myth, 269; laws and classes
of, 58, 59, 63, 67, 69; recognized
by the Greeks, 52, 53, 57
Associationism, 52-71; beginnings
of, 56; defects in, 14, 67, 70, 71,
72, 73; effects of, on views of
intelligence, 52-71; later developments in, 69-71; neglected individual differences, 70

Associationists, 13, 64-73
Asylums for the insane, 22
Atomists, 38
Attention, and adaptation, 142-156,
259; as mental adaptation, 259;
distraction effects on, 146; "dynamometer" of, 124, 258; force
of voluntary, 122, 272; habits of,
acquired, 276; two-point discrimination as measure of, 259;
voluntary, as essential of intelligence, 259
Attenuation effects on correlation,
271; correction of, 271; formula
criticized, 273
Augustine, St., 40
Auto-criticism, 260, 261, 262, 267
Automatic activities, 42; distinguished from voluntary acts, 68
Ayres, Leonard P., 225, 228, 229, 232

Bache, R. M., 285
Bacon, Francis, 15
Bagley, W. C., 224
Bain, A., 15, 70, 72 f., 100
Baldwin, J. M., 37, 40, 41, 44, 93
Barnes, Earl, 227
Baroncini, 222
Barr, M. W., 165
Beaunis, H., 117
Behavior, animal, 73, 285; human,
complex, 4-9; naturalistic view of,
6, 10, 30, 34, 65-70; two deter-
mining conditions of, 68
Belot, 245, 277
Beneke, F. E., 50
Berkeley, George, 59
Bigham, J., 119, 123
Binet, Alfred, 79, 80, 82, 84, 85,
86-93, 96, 97, 100, 101, 102, 103,
106, 107, 108, 109, 110, 111, 113,
114, 115, 117, 118, 121-161, 162-
185, 186, 189, 190-213, 215-224,

311

Vaschide, N., 117, 123, 133 f., 150 ff.
Vibration, molecular, as basis of association, 65
Voisin, 164
Voluntary action puzzling, 6
Voluntas, 40

Wallin, J. E. W., 227
Ward, James, 12
Warren, H. C., 53, 57, 63, 69
Washburn, 286
Watson, J. B., 286
Weber, 71
Weber's law, 75
Whipple, G. M., 124, 172, 174, 190, 191, 227 f.
Will, as a force, 5, 6, 14, 51, 56; freedom of, 9; balanced between equal motives, 55; mechanistic basis of, 61 f.; not an original force, 48, 55, 62
William of Occam, 55
Windelband, W., 11, 13

Wisconsin, University of, early tests in, 82
Wissler, Clark, 108, 109, 116, 154, 269
Witmer, L., 93
Wolff, C. von, 49, 50
Woodrow, H., 184
Woods, F. A., 30, 284
Woodworth, R. S., 113, 233, 267, 285
Wundt, W., 2, 71, 98, 146; unfavorable to individual psychology, 78
Wundtian experimental psychology, 110

Yerkes, R. M., 293
Yoakum, C. S., 293
Young, Kimball, 226, 227
Yule, G. U., 224

Zeno, 54
Zero-point, no absolute, in test scales, 142
Ziehen, 289